To Brian and Marina Jarman – for
making everything possible

To our wives, Elizabeth Stubbs and
Hilary Rowell, and our children – for
being able to see right through us and
know us for who we are

The muck and dirt, the king with fleas. For theft, mutilation; for the wrong thoughts, death. An infant mortality rate as astronomical as the life-expectancy was minute, and the whole grisly, working package wrapped in a skein of wealth and advantage designed to maintain the dark dominion of the knowing over the ignorant (and the worst of it was the pattern; the repetition; the twisted variations of the same depraved theme in so many different places).
Iain M Banks – *Use of Weapons*

Contents

About the authors   vii
Acknowledgements   ix
Foreword by Beth Simone Noveck   xii

Introduction   1

Section A   Theory   **7**

Part One   Background   **8**
1   History and methods   9
2   Critiques of transparency   31

Part Two   Definitions and models   **53**
3   Definitions of transparency   55
4   Fair allocation systems   73
5   Population-level transparency   85
6   Equality of narrative power   99
7   Transparency in an age of big data   113

Section B   Practice   **129**

Part One   Transparency 1.0   **130**
8   Every day is a fight for information   131
9   Access to information laws (ATI)   151
10   Social audit and public reporting   173
11   International initiatives   187
12   Open data and forced disclosure   195
13   Editorial control   209
14   Regulation and transparency   225

Part Two   **Transparency 2.0**   **247**
15   Ceding control of the data   249
16   Independent narratives   265
17   Getting my own data   281
18   Surveillance, transparency and privacy   297

Part Three **Transparency 3.0**   **319**
19   Artificial intelligence and allocation systems   321
20   What happens next?   337

Index   351

TRANSPARENCY AND THE OPEN SOCIETY

Practical lessons for effective policy

Roger Taylor and Tim Kelsey

First published in Great Britain in 2016 by

Policy Press
University of Bristol
1-9 Old Park Hill
Bristol BS2 8BB
UK
+44 (0)117 954 5940
pp-info@bristol.ac.uk
www.policypress.co.uk

North America office:
Policy Press
c/o The University of Chicago Press
1427 East 60th Street
Chicago, IL 60637, USA
t: +1 773 702 7700
f: +1 773 702 9756
sales@press.uchicago.edu
www.press.uchicago.edu

© Policy Press 2016

British Library Cataloguing in Publication Data
A catalogue record for this book is available from the British Library.

Library of Congress Cataloging-in-Publication Data
A catalog record for this book has been requested.

ISBN 978-1-4473-2536-9 paperback
ISBN 978-1-4473-2538-3 ePub
ISBN 978-1-4473-2539-0 Mobi

The right of Roger Taylor and Tim Kelsey to be identified as authors of this work has been asserted by them in accordance with the Copyright, Designs and Patents Act 1988.

The statements and opinions contained within this publication are solely those of the authors and not of the University of Bristol or Policy Press. The University of Bristol and Policy Press disclaim responsibility for any injury to persons or property resulting from any material published in this publication.

Policy Press works to counter discrimination on grounds of gender, race, disability, age and sexuality.

Cover design by Andrew Corbett
Front cover: image kindly supplied by Yastremska / Bigstock
Printed and bound in Great Britain by CMP, Poole
Policy Press uses environmentally responsible print partners

About the authors

Roger Taylor is an entrepreneur and writer. He is co-founder and chair of the Open Public Services Network at the Royal Society of Arts. His first book *God Bless the NHS* was published by Faber and Faber and was a Guardian best-seller. He co-founded Dr Foster, the healthcare information business that has pioneered transparency in healthcare and was one of the UK's fastest growing start-ups.

He is a board member of Ofqual, the exam regulator in the UK and a trustee of SafeLives, the domestic abuse charity. He has worked with governments, NGOs and leading media organisations globally on the use of open data and public reporting. He is a strong advocate for the role of greater transparency as a mechanism for improved public services and consumer protection. He is currently working with the Careers and Enterprise Company in the UK, a social enterprise working to help young people move successfully from education into work.

Roger began his career as a journalist working as a correspondent for the Financial Times in the UK and the US and, before that, as a researcher for the Consumers' Association.

Follow Roger on twitter @RTaylorOpenData

Tim Kelsey was the British government's first director of transparency and open data. In 2012 he was appointed national director for patients and information in the National Health Service (NHS) – the world's largest unitary health system - a role which combined the functions of chief technology and information officer with responsibility for patient and public participation. At that time, he was also chair of the National Information Board and, in that capacity, led design of a new strategy for technology and transparency in English healthcare to 2020 which has been adopted by the British government as formal policy. In 2014 Tim was named one of the 500 most influential people in the UK by the Sunday Times.

In 2000, Tim was co-founder of Dr Foster, a company which pioneered publication of patient outcomes in healthcare. Before Dr Foster, Tim was a national newspaper journalist and a television reporter. He worked for the Independent and the Sunday Times, as well as Channel 4 and the BBC. He is author of *Dervish: Travels in Modern Turkey*, published by Hamish Hamilton and Penguin Books.

Tim Kelsey is now a director of Telstra Health, and lives in Melbourne, Australia. He is also a visiting professor in the Institute of Global Health Innovation, Imperial College, London.

Follow Tim on twitter @tkelsey1

Acknowledgements

For giving us their time and wisdom in writing this book: Joel Adler, Prof. David Anderson, Paul Arnott, Prof. Ian Ayres, Ranajit Battacharyya, Sir Tim Berners-Lee, Godfrey Boniventura, Ania Calderon, Risha Chande, Ana Christina Ruelas, Eduardo Clark, Martyn Day, Sam Eastwood, Prof. Paul Elliott, Nancy Fletcher, Prof. John Fox, Paul Freeman, Alex Gordy, Helena Hofbauer, Ellen Klaus, Tariq Khokar, Warren Krafchik, Prof. Julian LeGrand, Tim Leunig, Kati Lopez, Adriana Lukas, January Makamba, Fina Mango, Anthony Maskell, Caroline Mauldin, Nick Maxwell, Cassie McGoldrick, Jonas Moberg, Karin Mochan, Prof. Beth Simone Noveck, Juan Pardinas, Haydee Perez Garrido, Ashley Petrons, Rakesh Rajani, Marko Rakar, Anthony Richter, Joel Salas, Eric Schadt, Florian Schweitzer, Chad Smolinski, Amanda Spielman, Glenys Stacey, Martin Tisne, Alexandra Zapata Hojel, Enrique Zapata

Thanks

To colleagues and friends with whom we have debated these topics over many years – and especially Baron Adebowale of Thornes, Charlotte Alldritt, Prof Ross Anderson, John Appleby, Jake Arnold-Forster, David Ashby, Prof. Paul Aylin, Neil Bacon, Tania Baker, Duncan Baldwin, Jane Barnacle, Paul Bate, Zoe Bedford, Don Berwick, Maureen Bisognano, Dame Carol Black, Prof David Blumenthal, Jeremy Bolt, Alex Bottle, Mark Britnell, Beverley Bryant, Dame Fiona Caldicott, Alessandro Campana, Duncan Campbell, Jonathon Carr-Brown, Baron Carter of Coles, Harry Cayton, Jocelyn Cornwell, Will Cavendish, Paul Charman, Sir John Chisholm, Robert Cleary, Stephen Colegrave, Naaz Coker, Paul Corrigan, Baroness Cumberlege of Newick, Lisa Darnell, Baron Darzi of Denham, Penny Dash,

Dame Sally Davies, Rhidian Wynn Davies, Sir Ciaran Devane, Anna Dixon, Jennifer Dixon, Michael Dixon, Ian Dodge, Sir Liam Donaldson, Tim Donohoe, Rt Hon. Stephen Dorrell, Emma Doyle, Prof Stephen Dunn, Helena Earl, Nigel Edwards, Deborah El-Sayed, Simon Enright, Omar Faiz, Marc Farr, Mike Farrar, Katie Farrington, Paul Farmer, Prof Steve Field, Brian Fisher, Hugo Ford, Claire Fox, Susannah Fox, Lisa Franklin, George Freeman MP, Simon Gallacher, Tony Gallagher, Pam Garside, Bridget Gill, Ben Goldacre, Malcolm Gooderham, Noel Gordon, Prof Sir Muir Gray, Sir Malcolm Grant, Tim Hailstone, Andrew Haldenby, Dame Barbara Hakin, Baroness Hayter of Kentish Town, Nicolaus Henke, Rt Hon Patricia Hewitt, Jamie Heywood, Sir Jeremy Heywood, Prof Howard Hiatt, Dame Deirdre Hine, Frank Hollendoner, John Holman, Matthew Holt, Phil Hope, John Horner, Rt Hon Jeremy Hunt MP, Baron Hunt of Kings Heath, Baron Hutton of Furness, Jen Hyatt, Sir Donald Irvine, Tom Jackiewicz, Julian Jarman, Katherine Jarman, Sian Jarvis, Hilly Janes, Ed Jones, Gareth Jones, Prof. Simon Jones, Alex Kafetz, Prof Cor Kalmann, Prof Sir Bruce Keogh, Vinod Khosla, Roger Killen, Andrew Kliman, Baron Knight of Weymouth, Peter Lawrence, Simon Lebus, Prof Tom Lee, Charles Lewington, Geraint Lewis, Jenny Lewis, Will Lewis, Roy Lilley, Sam Lister, Ben Lucas, Jonathan Luff, Steve Macauley, Craig Manson, Baron Maude of Horsham, Liam Maxwell, Professor Alan Maynard, Barry McCormick, Alan McDermott, John McLaren, Alastair McLellan, Andy McKeon, Gita Mendis, Steve Middleton, Rt Hon Alan Milburn, Chaand Nagpaul, Sir Robert Naylor, Sir David Nicholson, Dame Una O'Brien, Ronan O'Connor, Christine Outram, Todd Park, Sir Nick Partridge, Alan Plunkett, Bernie Porter, Prof Michael Porter, Katie Potts, Sir Chris Powell, Ambassador Samantha Power, Phil Reid, Prof Walter Ricciardi, Sir Mike Richards, Samantha Riley, Dame Jane Roberts, Eve Roodhouse, Rosamond Roughton, Helen Rowntree, William Salomon, Heather Savory, Helen Scott, Nick Seddon, Prof Martin Severs, Prof Sir Nigel Shadbolt, Joanne Shaw, Rohan Silva, Jenny Simpson, Peter Sinden, Bryan Sivak, Clive Smee, Richard Smith, Shane Solomon, Patrick Soon-Shiong, Emma Stanton, Simon Stevens, Geraldine Strathdee, John Stewart, Holly Sutton,

Matthew Swindells, Sir Hugh Taylor, Jeremy Taylor, Matt Tee, Sir Richard Thompson, Dave Thomson, Mike Treadaway, Andrew Vallance-Owen, Chris Vein, Sir Mark Walport, Tom Whitwell, Peter Wienand, Patricia Wilkie, Andy Williams, Prof Sir Norman Williams, John Witherow.

Foreword

Beth Simone Noveck

While clean water from the City of Zanesville, Ohio's water pipes reached white residents throughout Muskingum County during the last fifty years, residents of Coal Run, the predominantly African-American area of Zanesville, were only able to use contaminated rainwater or drive to the nearest water tower to truck water back to their homes. A resident could spend the whole morning trying to get water, meanwhile he could see his white neighbor sprinkling his lawn. "It became clear if you were white and living outside Zanesville you would get water," said a lawyer representing the black residents, "but if you were black, you wouldn't."[1]

After years of legal battles, the residents won an $11 million dollar verdict against the city. A key piece of evidence used in *Kennedy v The City of Zanesville* was a map derived from open government data from the water company. The map showed which houses were connected to the water line and who lived in them. It revealed significant correlation between the houses occupied by the white residents of Zanesville and the houses hooked up to the city water line.

Making the city's data available for public scrutiny laid bare the inequitable treatment of which the government of Zanesville was

---

[1] The Governance Lab Open Data Impact Case Studies (2016), available at http://odimpact.org

guilty and enabled this important public discrimination lawsuit to be brought to court. Seeing the gross injustice and unfairness in the city's decision making with regard to the allocation of water resources created the potential for change.

Zanesville is emblematic of the path-breaking theory of transparency laid out in *Transparency and the open society*. Transparency does not matter because of some theoretical notion that the legal right to information in and of itself will produce better government. What Roger and Tim powerfully prove is that access to data *and* the algorithms used by governments and corporations to make decisions about us reveals the rationale (or absence thereof) underlying important societal choices, such as who does and who does not get water or a liver transplant or a bus route in front of their house.

This is the first book to put forward a new and convincing explanation of transparency in the era of open and big data when more information about the workings of institutions is available than ever before along with the technologies to make sense of it. As more and more data from government, corporations and individuals become available thanks to the internet, the long held but deeply magical thinking that the legal right to, and availability of, information under freedom of information legislation will de facto produce greater government accountability has not borne itself out in practice.

We are no longer fighting for basic transparency. Since 2009, a global movement to open up the data government holds about the economy, society and its own workings has taken off. In the United Kingdom, there are already almost thirty thousand datasets freely available in raw and computable formats and in the United States ten times that number. Sixty-nine countries have committed under the Open Government Partnership to move toward greater transparency and many of those same countries, cities and regions have endorsed a new Charter on Open Data. The Open Contracting Partnership promotes the practice of governments publishing their procurement data online.

But we are still far from a world in which government reveals all the information it collects. From public spending to the annual inventory of sheep and goats in the United Kingdom, government still over-zealously protects and classifies too much information. Scandals involving the United States military and diplomatic corps disclosed via Wikileaks, international money laundering and tax avoidance practices revealed in the Panama Papers, and corrupt activities from FIFA to Petrobras are among the almost daily revelations in the news. Each leak of private information provides an insight into what goes on when people act under a cloak of secrecy.

Yet more information by itself has not resulted in significantly more legitimate or more effective government. Rates of trust in government globally are at an all-time low. The more the practice of open data takes off, the more incongruous and out of step with technological developments our old good government theories of transparency are revealed to be, and the greater the need for them to be updated.

The strength of this important book comes from the fact that neither Tim nor Roger is a professor of law or philosophy. They did not start out seeking a career as a transparency advocate. Hence they are not content with an abstract notion of transparency. Rather, through their work as journalists, public officials and entrepreneurs fighting for more open data about the UK's health care system, they have been at the forefront of witnessing and championing the use of public data to save lives and reduce real suffering in practice. They have come to understand first hand what so many of us have missed, namely that the power of transparency to remedy injustice in practice comes when transparency lays bare the whys and wherefores of public action.

They are also familiar with the mechanics of a world increasingly driven by big-data – with the trade-offs that society must make between our conflicting desires to protect privacy while at the same time protecting people from unfair treatment or abusive institutions.

For transparency to result in improving government, empowering citizens, creating economic opportunity, and solving public problems, what is vital, they tell us, is access to the data used by governments and corporations to make decisions about us in sufficient detail to be able to question those decisions and independently assess their impact. It is not enough to publish economic performance data without the models used to create the budget. We need the data about how people fared in hospital together with the logic used to determine who received which test and why. Often managers do not know themselves why they made a decision. Discrimination is often subtle. But we can use data science techniques to allow us to spot patterns in data that will reveal our own biases back to us.

If the ultimate goal is to redesign the workings of ineffective institutions, shining a light on their misdeeds can no longer be the only goal. Naturally, having the raw information about where the bus stops are located is a first step. But transparency cannot stop there. When we focus on the *transparency of decision making* then institutions can invest resources in disclosing that information that enables the public to make sense of and critique the rationale (or absence thereof) underlying important societal decisions.

Cognizant of the fact that we now have the tools to do so, *Transparency and the open society* demands that we re-center our theory of transparency on understanding decision making. It offers a theory of transparency consistent with the advent of big data technologies for making sense of large quantities of data, the practical conclusion of which is that true transparency demands that we also focus on the tools and talent to enable us to make sense of why the bus stops are only in wealthy neighborhoods and bypassing those of lesser means.

These two transparency pioneers have given us a profound new understanding of transparency as it comes of age in the era of big data, challenged all of us to think about the principles, platforms, and policies needed to reveal and, above all, to rectify the inequality and unfairness perpetuated by even our most democratic institutions.

Beth Simone Noveck
Jerry M. Hultin Global Network Professor,
New York University
Former head of The White House
Open Government Initiative

Introduction

Increasing transparency – by which we mean reducing the monopolistic control over information by government and private organisations – is becoming a central concern for the information age. The combination of big data and increasingly intelligent computer algorithms is creating a world in which the rules around the control of information will be as important to a fair society as freedom of speech is to democracy. However, as more and more data is generated with all the information technologies at our collective disposal, we risk having less and less transparency.

The immediate impetus for writing this book has been an awareness that transparency policy is not keeping up with changes in the power of technology and data. Access to information legislation may have some relevance to understanding how decisions are made by bureaucrats and committees. It has less to offer when decisions are driven by big data, machine learning systems and artificial intelligence.

This book sets out a personal view regarding the most useful direction in which transparency policies could be developed. It comes from two entrepreneurs who have spent the past 15 years working in transparency and promoting it as a practical enabler in the improvement of public services.

We come from a background in the media, working both in the UK and abroad as correspondents for national newspapers and consumer advocacy groups. In 2000 we founded a transparency business in the UK which created a precedent. Dr Foster was set up as an organisation which worked with a university research department at Imperial College London. The research department was allowed access by the government to the identifiable data set covering all hospital treatment throughout the National Health Service in England under strict terms of confidentiality but with freedom to publish anonymised analysis. The only constraint was that it had to be in the public interest, a constraint overseen by an independent ethical oversight framework.

It was a unique and brave experiment. Over the 15 years that followed, Dr Foster published independent assessments of standards of care, supplied data monitoring systems to hospitals and put quality of care at the centre of the political debate about the NHS. The Dr Foster publications identified significant failings in healthcare that were leading to high excess death rates and poor standards of treatment for patients – information that, up until then, patients had been unaware of.

One of us, Tim Kelsey, went on to be the UK's first director of transparency and then to work with the NHS on improving transparency and use of information. The other, Roger Taylor, has been working to bring greater transparency to education, health and other public services through the Open Public Services Network.

We are not academics but practitioners. The value we bring to the discussion on transparency is our experience of trying to make it work. That brings with it predispositions and biases born of the particular triumphs and defeats we have experienced. We have attempted to present the evidence to support our position as clearly and objectively as possible.

We argue that new technologies require a new approach to transparency – one built on control of data that is more evenly shared with citizens and civil society. Our point of view can be boiled down to two simple propositions:

1. That transparency does not increase with the volume of information provided to the individual. It increases only to the degree I have information that can evidence whether I am being treated fairly.
2. That transparency, by this definition, requires shared access to underlying raw granular data.

The second proposition rests on the belief that the institutions and rules of society cannot be judged adequately by making only the process of their implementation transparent. It is necessary to

2

also make public the results of such systems across society. This is a necessary requirement for establishing whether governments and corporations are acting fairly as opposed to squandering resources or discriminating against certain groups.

This problem has historically been addressed by requiring the relevant organisations – whether regulators, government departments or companies - to publish information about their activity and its impact. This, we will argue, is an inadequate mechanism. It is too crude to deal with the complexity of the decision-making systems that currently determine the allocation of public goods across society. It leaves too much control in the hands of those in authority to construct the narrative they wish to present.

This is an issue in many current areas of public concern. But the dangers increase hugely as we adopt computerised decision-making systems driven by big data and machine learning. The scale of the data now available to us means that there is no realistic means to understand the information in our hands without using these technologies. Without transparency we have no way to know if they are proving beneficial or harmful. We will have no way to know whether we live in a fair society. The only way to use information technology without impairing democracy is to share control over the necessary data with individuals and across a plurality of organisations with different interests and perspectives.

Shared access to raw data presents a number of obstacles which mean it is one of the least used methods of increasing transparency. We argue that there are a growing number of areas where it is essential to fairness.

The first section of the book examines the history of transparency and related ideas. It sets out the rationale for our initial proposition and defines transparency in terms of fairness.

The second section looks at the world today and describes the range of transparency initiatives designed to combat corruption, inefficiency or poor quality outcomes in public authorities or to make markets fairer. We highlight strengths and weaknesses, successes and failures, while always driving towards the second of our two propositions.

We look at the degree to which transparency based on data sharing currently exists and the two principal difficulties it faces:

1. How to adequately protect the privacy of individuals and the commercial secrets of companies in a world of data sharing.
2. Identifying the necessary institutional arrangements to ensure that access to data serves the public interest.

We end by describing what the world might look like with a more complete model of data sharing in place and wider use of computer-driven decision making.

We argue that transparency as 'publishing' of accounts and aggregated information might have been sufficient in an age when publishing and documentation were primary systems for disseminating information. In a digital age it is no longer adequate. It is too costly and too ineffective. Instead, transparency needs to be built on foundations of data shared in its rawest verifiable format, in electronic machine-readable formats. It means allowing independent checking of the reliability of that data. It means creating a world in which the content of that data is determined not only by government and corporate organisations but by citizens as well. It means ensuring that the legal control over this data is shared between the government or corporate entities that created it and independent judicial authorities that have a remit to promote the public good.

This change allows transparency to stop being simply about organisations and start to be about individuals. It is not enough for transparency to ensure judges are honest and drugs are safe. It needs to be a mechanism that enables me to know that I have received a just verdict or that the medicine I take is the one that is best for me. It needs to be more than a bulwark against the grossest failings in government but instead provide me with the same ability to assess the behaviour of the organisations that determine the quality of my day-to-day life as those organisations have to assess my day-to-day behaviour.

Transparency, in this sense, is not simply about shining light on the integrity of government and commerce. It is a powerful driver not just of a fairer society but of better, more efficient and higher quality public services and a more productive growing economy. We spend some time in the book studying the impact of data sharing in healthcare – in this case, transparency of clinical outcomes reduces harm to patients and the costs of many of the services they receive. Giving patients access to their own data is also beginning to support them to take more control of their health and wellbeing and to enable new, digitally supported and more personalised modes of treatment. We aim to demonstrate that transparency, done correctly, is an instrument of social justice and improvement.

In *The Open Society and its Enemies*, Karl Popper[1] described how democracy can be undermined by claims that political philosophies are objectively true. He showed how this attitude is used to promote closed 'tribal' forms of society in which authority cannot be questioned.

Today, the Open Society faces another threat – the threat of authority that cannot be questioned because it has privileged access to information. We live in an age when 'evidence based policy' is in vogue and statistics are front and centre in most political debates. We are rapidly moving into an age when data-driven calculations will dictate how you are treated by governments and companies. However, control over the underlying information sources is becoming concentrated, making it harder to question the authority of ever more powerful institutions.

There is widespread recognition of the problem and no shortage of commitments to increase transparency. However, we believe that most efforts at solving this problem are inadequate to the task. We have outlined aspects of the approach that we think has greater potential. In part, we do this tentatively, recognising that there is much to be publicly debated in terms of the details of how society fixes this particular problem. On the other hand, we do this with a deep sense of urgency, having some familiarity with the enormous gulf between the rhetoric around transparency and the reality. Our background in health information gives us an awareness of the tragic consequences when decision systems are driven by information that is misused but cannot be questioned.

The building blocks of true transparency are simple to grasp. Government and public services need to make information about

---

[1]   K R Popper, *The Open Society and Its Enemies*, George Routledge & Sons, London, 1947.

citizens available to those citizens in standard machine-readable formats and allow them to do with it whatever they choose, including pooling it through data organisations to support research and other purposes. Commercial organisations need to make individual-level information available to customers in the same way. Both need to be open to mechanisms that allow the querying of data across whole populations in order to assure the fairness of their operations.

But while the principles may be straightforward, implementation is complex and difficult. In many cases legal rights and powers to make these changes already exist but are either not enforced or not used.

We have attempted to set out as clearly as possible why we think that a system of transparency built on data sharing transforms the social and economic effectiveness of government and business. But, perhaps more importantly, we want to persuade you that it is the *only* approach which can provide public assurance of a fair society if the potential benefits of the next generation of information technologies and their machine-driven decision-making capabilities are to be realised.

SECTION A | THEORY

This section of the book sets out in Part One the historical background to thinking about transparency and, in Part Two, the models and definitions of transparency that we will use.

Part One
Background

This part reviews historical and current theoretical perspectives on transparency. The first chapter identifies the three historical traditions behind transparency, which have defined its key benefits and the mechanisms by which each operates.

The second chapter lists the costs involved and the unintended harms that have been attributed to increased transparency. We identify the principal costs that are an inevitable result of particular forms of transparency and the main negative consequences of increased transparency.

1

History and methods

Hanslope Park is a large Regency house a few miles outside Milton Keynes in England. Surrounded by a complex of office buildings and a high-security perimeter fence, it does not invite scrutiny. This is a place where secrets are kept.

Together with its better known neighbour, Bletchley Park, this former stately home was taken over by the British government during the Second World War. Bletchley Park was the centre of Britain's efforts to learn the secrets of our enemies and became famous as the place where Alan Turing cracked the Enigma code. Hanslope Park was given the opposite job. It was, and remains, home to Her Majesty's Government Communication Centre – the organisation tasked with keeping our codes and communications out of enemy hands.

In 2012, Hanslope Park found itself in the headlines when we learnt just how good it was at keeping secrets. A vast archive was uncovered within the complex, containing over one and half miles of shelving stacked with files and boxes.

To conceal so much material, the archive had been hidden in plain sight. Employees at Hanslope Park were misinformed about the nature of what was on the shelves. Some had been told the files were administrative records of no interest; others that they belonged to another organisation. The shelves were labelled 'Hayes', the name of a company that had once briefly stored them while in transit. There was a good reason for dissuading staff from investigating these files.

The archive contained many of the most sensitive and incriminating documents from Britain's history. It held documents going back over a century, relating to the administration of more than 30 colonies including Cyprus, Palestine, Malaya and Kenya.[1]

The Public Records Act in the UK requires that government documents of historical interest are published after 20 years. An exceptional extension can be applied to documents where there are ongoing national security considerations. This had not been applied to the Hanslope archive, however, and the legal status of these files remained undetermined. When the new governments of independent former colonies requested them, they were told firmly that they were the property of the British government. But the logical conclusion that they were therefore British government documents was never established. They remained in a legal limbo – the property of no longer extant administrations of former colonies – a twilight world that was deemed beyond the reach of the Public Records Act.

The Freedom of Information Act (FOIA) gives the public the right to access British government records subject to limitations such as national security and personal privacy. In 2005 and 2006, a number of freedom of information (FOI) requests were received in relation to documents held in the archive, including requests from Leigh Day, lawyers representing four Kenyans who were claiming compensation for torture at the hands of the British in the 1950s. The British government had rejected their claims as unfounded. The FOI requests were rejected on the grounds that the records did not exist.

The staff at Hanslope Park responded in good faith. They had no idea that the archive contained a great deal of information relevant to the Kenyans' case - ministerial letters, cables from the Foreign Office to colonial governors and minutes of meetings between cabinet ministers.[2] Among the documents of interest that came to light in 2012 were exchanges between the colonial administrators and government ministers which made clear that

---

[1] David M. Anderson, 'Mau Mau in the High Court and the "lost" British Empire archives: colonial conspiracy or bureaucratic bungle?', *Journal of Imperial and Commonwealth History* Vol 39, No 5 (2011), 699-716. DOI: 10.1080/03086534.2011.629082

[2] Anthony Cary, 'The migrated archives: what went wrong and what lessons should we draw?', 24 February 2011, www.gov.uk/government/uploads/system/uploads/attachment_data/file/255562/migrated-archives.pdf

politicians at the highest level had been aware of and sanctioned policies that involved Kenyans being burnt, beaten, raped and mutilated by British forces.

For over half a century, one of the most violent acts of political repression in British history had been largely removed from the history books and replaced with a false account. The treatment of the Kenyans had been a cause of considerable debate at the time. An independent inquiry into the beating to death of 11 men at Hola camp had caused outrage and had helped speed the closure of the detention centres. But the government had maintained that the problems were due to 'bad apples' – rogue individuals acting beyond their authority. While many might have been sceptical of the official explanation, the full scale of what had occurred was successfully obscured.

It is extremely difficult to completely eradicate the truth. It was there in the memories of the Kenyans who had been through the camps. It was there in the box files quietly sitting on the shelves at Hanslope Park. And faint traces of it were to be found in the archives in Kenya.

US historian Caroline Elkins[3] was one of the first to pick up the trail when she found documents in Nairobi referring to a detention centre she had never heard of and which did not seem to be referred to elsewhere. She was shown similar passing references to other camps. While official records existed describing most of the activities of the police and army during the 1950s, there was a gap when it came to these camps.

The records had been destroyed. Those authorising the camps understood the need to keep what they were doing secret. In 1957 Eric Griffiths-Jones, attorney general for the Kenyan colonial administration, said: 'If we must sin, we must sin quietly.' In the period immediately prior to Britain ceding control of Kenya to the newly independent country in 1963, a huge programme was undertaken to destroy the records of what had taken place.

The officers in charge of administering the mistreatment of prisoners understood the gravity of what they had been asked

---

[3] Caroline Elkins, *Imperial Reckoning: The Untold Story of Britain's Gulag in Kenya*, Henry Holt, 2005.

to do. They had been careful to seek written confirmation of their orders. They were happy to cover up their actions, but they did not want to destroy the evidence that it was sanctioned from above.

The historian David Anderson is the man primarily responsible for revealing the existence of the archive. It was he who discovered in Kenya one crucial document that had been overlooked and left behind by the British. It was the bill of lading showing that on the day before independence a large consignment of documents had been flown out of Kenya. He followed the trail and found further evidence that the plane had come to London. He could show that the documents had been unloaded and driven away. But after that the trail went cold.

The court hearing the case against the British government was provided with a report setting out why Anderson believed that the truth was still being concealed. The court indicated that if the British government was hiding any information relevant to the case they would be in contempt. It was only when a civil servant in the Foreign Office, frustrated at the impasse and concerned at the gravity of what was being alleged, phoned up Hanslope Park and threatened to come down and search through the building himself that someone thought to check the shelves marked Hayes.

The documents that were uncovered showed beyond any doubt that the government had approved the rounding up of hundreds of thousands of Kenyans, to be placed in camps where the most brutal mistreatments were known to be common practice. Days later, after decades of maintaining a fiction about British actions in Kenya, lawyers for the government stood up in court and accepted what had happened. In an out-of-court settlement, claimants were awarded compensation of £3500 each.

From the fall of Berlin to the overthrow of Gaddafi, the last days of tyrants have been marked by bonfires of files and the shredding of documents as those involved attempt to cover up their actions. Secrecy was an enabler of the British actions in Kenya in the 1950s. It prevented those who would have raised political opposition from knowing the truth. It was essential to efforts to deny compensation to the victims of torture. And it left posterity with a false record of British rule.

This book is about transparency and power – and the view that stopping powerful people keeping their actions secret will stop them from doing bad things. As Joseph Pulitzer put it: 'There is not a crime, there is not a dodge, there is not a trick, there is not a swindle, there is not a vice which does not live by secrecy.' Lack of transparency – or the ability of those in power to control access to information – has been blamed for many ills from the First World War to the 2008 financial crash. The first of Woodrow Wilson's 14 points to ensure future peace stated that there should 'be no private international understandings of any kind but diplomacy shall proceed always frankly and in the public view'.[4]

Today it is a lack of transparency in international financial markets that gets more attention. The IMF, the World Bank and the G20 all regard transparency as an essential element in global financial stability as well as a significant contributor to the grip of corruption on developing countries. The same line of thinking informs the idea that public sector institutions in developed economies are also at fault, in a more subtle way, by placing the interests of the institutions that provide services over the interests of those that receive them. The hope that transparency could tip the balance in favour of the service user has informed many policies in this area.

Corporate financial collapses almost always involve a degree of financial dissembling. The Sarbannes-Oxley Act and the Dodd-Frank Act both used transparency to respond to financial disasters. Scandals from product safety cases to concern about medical errors to the way the Catholic Church handled allegations into child abuse have all prompted calls for greater transparency.

Many people have concluded if you can stop people keeping secrets you can stop bad things from happening. Indeed it seems so obvious that transparency has become, at times, unquestioned as an appropriate policy response to a vast range of failures in

---

[4]   Woodrow Wilson, Address to a joint session of congress on the conditions of peace, January 8, 1918 http://www.presidency.ucsb.edu/ws/?pid=65405

government, international relations, public services, companies and consumer markets. However, the record of demonstrable success from such efforts is at best thin and in many cases absent. The aim of this book is to explore why this is and to suggest approaches that might prove more effective.

Despite this, there are reasons for optimism. In the 1950s in Kenya, the colonial administration was the only organisation that had evidence of the scale of the repression taking place across the country. That was because it was the only organisation capable of operating an information system that could capture the necessary data. When Caroline Elkins tried to collect her own data, it took her five years of interviews to piece together even a moderately complete picture of what had happened.

In 2008, Kenya again experienced an upsurge in political violence following a contested general election. The sitting president claimed victory and was hurriedly sworn in at night, despite claims that the ballots had been rigged. The next day supporters of the losing candidates began a series of violent protests. In one incident, 50 women and children were burnt to death in a church. The scale and speed with which the violence spread made it difficult for the media to know what was happening.

One group of activists turned to the internet. They created a website – Ushahidi – which allowed people to report by phone, text or email any acts of violence they witnessed. These were then displayed on a map and published, providing immediate and verifiable reports of where violence was occurring. Subsequent analysis has confirmed that the reporting was accurate.[5] It had an immediate impact on the political process by making it impossible to play down or dismiss the violence. What had taken Caroline Elkins five years to piece together 50 years after it happened, Ushahidi achieved almost instantaneously.

The two stories – the successful suppression of information for over half a century by the British colonial administration

---

[5] Meier, Patrick and Kate Brodock (2008) *Crisis Mapping Kenya's Election Violence: Comparing Mainstream News, Citizen Journalism and Ushahidi*, (Harvard Humanitarian Initiative, HHI, Harvard University: Boston). URL: http://irevolution.net/2008/10/23/mapping-kenyas-election-violence

of Kenya and the almost instantaneous creation of information by Ushahidi – highlight both the challenge and the promise of transparency. On the one hand, the careful suppression of information can thwart attempts to know the truth even when laws require information to be public and the truth has been witnessed by hundreds of thousands. On the other hand, making information visible can have a dramatic effect on events – stripped of the cover of darkness, injustice can be put on the back foot.

The case we will put forward argues that transparency policy is often ineffective because it fails to cede sufficient control over information flows. Instead, the organisations being subjected to transparency retain enough control over the information of interest that, while they are forced to increase the total amount of information released, their ability to determine what is released and how it is presented has meant that the informational advantage of those in power is to a large extent undented.

But before we go any further into these issues, we first want to take a step back into the history of thinking about transparency and review the various reasons why it was ever thought to be a good idea in the first place and to then review the objections that have been put forward. Our starting point is to look at three quite different traditions that have led people to argue for transparency – politics, economics and science.

These three traditions have led to three quite different policies – legal rights of access to records; forced disclosure of standardised information; and data sharing – each of which has been adopted in transparency policy today and which are summarised in Table 1.1. The first of these traditions is that of political and ethical philosophy. Eric Griffiths-Jones' words about the need to 'sin quietly' remind us of Kant's formulation: *All actions relating to the right of other human beings are wrong if their maxim is incompatible with publicity.*[6] Or put more simply, if you have to keep what you are doing secret, then what you are doing is wrong.

The key word here is 'maxim'. Kant is not arguing that all secret actions are wrong. Staking out criminal gangs in secret can be morally justified. Kant's claim is that if it is moral to do

---

[6] Immanuel Kant, *Zum ewigen Frieden* (Perpetual Peace), 1795, 381.

this, it must be possible to make a public defence of said policy. If you can't publicly state and defend your policy – or if your actions are not in line with your publicly stated maxims (for example, a commitment to due legal process or a rejection of torture) then your actions are immoral.

Christopher Hood, Gladstone Professor of Government at All Souls, Oxford,[7] identifies two contrasting political theories that are today associated with ideas of transparency. One sees transparency as an issue of rights and accountability, something that is enacted through laws and institutions. This tradition remains dominant today in government policy. The other is a line of thinking about the value of honesty and openness as a virtue, something that is enacted through the behaviour of individuals.

Both of these traditions have adopted the word transparency, which causes, at times, some degree of confusion. Below we outline these two traditions in more detail to try to separate them and narrow down the concepts we want to discuss later in the book. We start with the idea of transparency as personal openness.

Politics: Rousseau, openness and trust

Jean-Jacques Rousseau believed in the importance of politicians being open but was sceptical that a lack of honesty in a public official could be rectified through inspections, audits and external rights to information. As he put it: 'prudence is never so ready to conceive new precautions as knavery is to elude them'.[8]

The public, he argued, should seek to appoint men of integrity. Audit and accountability – ideas we now associate with transparency – were, he reckoned, largely powerless against fraud and could even make such activity easier by providing false reassurance.

Modern use of 'transparency' to describe a personal virtue of the sort Rousseau conceived is perhaps most often encountered

---

[7]   Christopher Hood, 'Transparency in history perspective', in *Transparency: The Key to Better Governance?*, ed Christopher Hood and David Heald, The British Academy, 2006.

[8]   J J Roussaeu, 'A dissertation on political economy' in *Miscellaneous Works of Mr JJ Roussea T. Becket and P. A. De Hondt*, London 1767, Vol II, p 39.

today in the language of executive coaching. Transparency, along with integrity and authenticity, is used to describe values of personal openness – the idea that your personal effectiveness as a manager will be enhanced by accepting yourself for who you are and being unafraid to speak your mind. It is language that shares much with ideas used in counselling and therapy – that suppressing your thoughts and emotions might help to avoid immediate pressures but will undo you in the long run.

These are powerful ideas with a clear logic when applied to relationships between people who share a common purpose, be they partners in a marriage or business. There is also sense in trying to impose duties of candour on professionals such as lawyers and doctors who, in theory, share the same objectives as their client or patient. However, this idea does not translate well to relationships which are more contested, such as that between buyers and sellers or people in direct competition with each other.

Rousseau applied this model to politics because he believed it was possible for politics to be an uncontested relationship through the identification of our common purpose as a society. He believed in the 'general will' – the idea that all men, if they were to reflect with an honest heart, would come to the same conclusion.

But if politics consists of contested relationships, this view becomes less relevant. If one side of a negotiation opts to be more transparent than the other then they put themselves at an unfair disadvantage. In a society of individuals who have different values, different risk appetites and different desires, the role of politicians is to negotiate a compromise. In these scenarios, it is untrue to suggest that an individual will perform their role more effectively if they are more open and candid than the person they are negotiating with.

Despite the difficulty of applying Rousseau's view of transparency to pluralistic democratic politics, it continues to appeal to politicians. When the UK government introduced a freedom of information law, some of the rhetoric around it was in this vein. Tony Blair, the then prime minister, said that FOIA would lead to a 'fundamental and vital change in the relationship between the government and the governed' by ending 'the traditional culture of secrecy' within government. Lord Falconer, the attorney general at the time, said: 'FOI can mean that the relationship between the government and the people, and between the media and the people, can be different. Can be better. Can be more open. More transparent. More honest.'[9]

Falconer seems to have drifted from the language of politics to the language of personal relationships. Professor Alasdair Roberts of Syracuse University describes the way in which governments have at times tried to persuade themselves that transparency could cause people in public office to stop being defensive and cause the public to trust them more if they are able to recognise just how hard it is to govern. His essay, 'Dashed Expectations: Governmental Adaptation to Transparency Rules',[10] rightly observes that ideas of 'fundamental change in the predisposition of officials regarding the release of government information' or a 'restoration of trust in government' were hopelessly wide of the mark and never likely to come true.

Politics: Locke, Bentham and information as a right

The more prevalent political tradition today has its roots in the seventeenth century reformation; resistance to claims of absolute authority by the pope and rejection of the divine right of kings. In 1644, John Milton published *Areopagitica*, an essay calling for an end to government censorship and state control of publishing. In making his case, he did not question the premise for censorship – that people needed to be protected from false ideas about religion and authority. He argued instead, perhaps counterintuitively, that the best protection from this harm was to allow such ideas to be published so that their failings could be exposed and their arguments defeated in open debate. It

---

[9] Speech of Lord Falconer of Thoroton, Secretary of State for Constitutional Affairs and Lord Chancellor, to the Law for Journalists Conference, at the RSA, London, 26 November 2004 http://www.dca.gov.uk/ speeches/2004/lc261104.htm – See more at: http://www.ariadne.ac.uk/ issue42/bailey#sthash.Et8sbmMc.dpuf

[10] In *Transparency: The Key to Better Governance?*, ed Christopher Hood and David Heald, The British Academy, 2006.

was, he argued, both a more efficient and more reliable way to protect people.

Fear that access to information might lead people into error is as alive today as it was in Milton's day. Medical regulators have cited this argument for preventing release of drug trial data (see Chapter 18). And doctors have argued on the same grounds that the public should not have access to their genetic information. In February 2015, partially lifting a ban on this, the US Federal Drug Administration said: 'in many circumstances it is not necessary for consumers to go through a licensed practitioner to have direct access to their personal genetic information'.[11] Milton's argument that public debate can better protect us than restricting access to information is as relevant today as it was then.

John Locke's *Two Treatises on Government* argued that the social contract between citizens and ruler was based on the ongoing consent of citizens. To provide such consent meaningfully, citizens must be free to speak their mind, share opinions and inform themselves about their government. Locke was instrumental in ending crown censorship and establishing a free press in England.

The first political writings to explicitly address the benefits of access to information as distinct from free speech come with Jeremy Bentham's defence of publicity. In a number of political essays published in 1822,[12] Bentham enumerates the benefits to be gained from 'publicity', by which he means making public the speeches of politicians, the voting records of legislators, and the processes and decisions of executive government. The three key benefits we can derive from his writings are:

1. Government: will act more honestly as a result of scrutiny.
2. Citizens/voters: will be better informed in using their vote and in expressing their views through other means.

---

[11] FDA News Release: FDA permits marketing of first direct-to-consumer genetic carrier test for Bloom syndrome, February 19, 2015, http://www.fda.gov/NewsEvents/Newsroom/PressAnnouncements/UCM435003
[12] *First Principles Preparatory to Constitutional Code*, ed Philip Schofield, Clarendon Press, Oxford, 1989.

3. Experts outside of government: will develop greater understanding and knowledge allowing better policy development.

Bentham's third group of actors is worth further comment. When Bentham refers to expertise developing outside government he is not talking about increasing knowledge among the general public – he has covered that in his previous comments. He is talking about the development of deep expertise within society outside of government – expertise that by definition will not be found in the public at large but will rather be held by particular individuals or organisations.

At the time Bentham was writing, expertise in many areas of government policy existed almost exclusively within government. Today, civil society organisations are regarded as an important part of a healthy democracy. In recent decades there has been a growing recognition of the central role that such organisations play in making transparency effective.

Bentham's writings and those of fellow utilitarian John Stuart Mill are perhaps the high point in the development of what we might call the 'political/judicial' tradition in thinking about transparency. The main policy instrument that has grown from this tradition is legislation granting rights to government information. In its oldest form this consists of public rights to view government in action. In the UK this includes the right to sit in the public gallery and watch parliamentary debates, rights to observe the count at elections and the holding of trials in public. It encompasses public rights to know the law and to be punished only after due process. More recently these rights have been extended by laws – variously referred to as 'freedom of information' (FOI), 'right to information' (RTI) or 'access to information' (ATI) – that grant the right to see the documentary records of government decision making. We will use ATI to refer to all such legislation including access to public documents and individual access to data about themselves. There are three issues to highlight at this point.

i. Access to information as a human right

Writers in this tradition most often identify the right to information as a human right akin to the right to free speech – that is, it does not need to be, and should not be, defended on the grounds of whether or not it can be shown to be beneficial.

ii. Rights relate to government information

The idea of ATI as a right relates to information held by government or other public institutions. These ideas are rarely if ever applied to information in other contexts – for example, rights to information held by corporations or charitable foundations – except in the context of individual rights to view personal data held about them. This produces some curious results in that in one country, where the government runs the health system, it would imply a human right to information about health systems, while in a country where healthcare is provided by private institutions – even one where it is paid for out of tax funding or compulsory insurance - citizens might have no right to the same information.

iii. Rights are broad but non-specific

Rights to information are defined very broadly. ATI legislation in most countries starts from the position that all government information is available to citizens and then defines exceptions to that rule. The default position is that citizens are entitled to information and that right is limited by specific exceptions relating to privacy, national security, crime prevention and economic stability. However, importantly, it says much less about what information should exist. Under ATI laws, if the information you seek has not been recorded you have no right to it.

Economics

The political tradition of thinking about transparency stands in stark contrast to the second lineage we can trace for transparency policies – the regulation of markets and economic theory. The economic tradition gives limited but specific rights to information and imposes a requirement that information be created in standard comparable formats.

Economic thinking is concerned with the relationship between buyers and sellers. From a radical free-market perspective, it has been argued that people entering into contracts are free to determine the level of information they require and no one else need be involved. The problems with this approach have been recognised from the very dawn of history. The earliest known legal code (the Code of Ur-Nammu), written more than four millennia ago, boasts in its prologue that the ruler had 'fashioned the bronze-sila measure, standardized the one-mina weight'.[13] The Magna Carta, just before stating that no one shall be punished without a fair trial, requires that: 'There shall be standard measures of wine, ale, and corn (the London quarter), throughout the kingdom'.[14] Fair trials and standard measures are both needed in a fair society.

The legal imposition of standard weights and measures lowers the information cost to buyers of establishing the value of products on offer and enables the policing of false measures. From the medieval assizes to the nineteenth century introduction of accounting standards for company accounts through to modern safety labelling for consumer products, there has been a consistent recognition of the need to standardise information to make markets fairer and more efficient.

In recent decades, economists have begun to understand how profoundly unequal access to information can undermine markets. In 2013 Joseph Stiglitz, George Akerlof and Michael Spence won the Nobel prize for the development of information economics – the theoretical frameworks used to analyse the problem of information in markets. Their work builds on earlier theorists such as Hayek who conceived of markets as information systems in which buyers and sellers signal their wishes. This

---

[13] http://realhistoryww.com/world_history/ancient/Misc/Sumer/ur_nammu_law.htm

[14] British Library, English translation of Magna Carta, www.bl.uk/magna-carta/articles/magna-carta-english-translation#sthash.cJN65rAm.dpuf

theory offered an explanation of why centralised economic systems fail – they were simply unable to process information about needs as efficiently as hundreds of thousands of people engaging in daily transactions.

If markets are information processing systems, 'asymmetrical information' (where one side of a transaction knows information inaccessible to the other) can be catastrophic to the functioning of markets.

Akerlof illustrated the point with his market for 'lemons' – a lemon in this instance being a poor quality second-hand car.[15] To the consternation of market economists, he demonstrated the apparent impossibility of there ever being a market for second-hand cars since the owner of a used car will always know more about the quality of his vehicle than any potential buyer. At any given price, only people who know their car is worth that amount or less would offer it for sale. Buyers should therefore expect second-hand cars to be worth less than the asking price due to defects they will not be able to spot. If that is correct, only a fool would ever buy a second-hand car.

The way to fix this is an external injection of information. Regulatory requirements for vehicle inspection tests (such as the MOT in Britain) can provide additional externally validated information that guarantees a minimum quality for second-hand cars. This allows a minimum price to be established and a market to develop. Vehicles failing to meet these quality requirements are scrapped.

Joseph Stiglitz explored the same problem in employment markets where people selling their labour are necessarily better informed about their abilities than the employer attempting to assess them. As with cars, we would expect this to result in a market in which the average worker willing to accept any given wage will not be worth the wage. In this example, qualifications can act as an additional externally regulated piece of information to signal a minimum value for any given worker. One prediction of this model is that labour markets, left to themselves, will create

---

[15] George A. Akerlof, 'The market for "lemons": quality uncertainty and the market mechanism', *Quarterly Journal of Economics* Vol 84, No 3 , 488–500. doi:10.2307/1879431

pools of unqualified unemployable workers who end up on the employment scrap heap – which may explain why even in the most open market economies we see persistent unemployment among less skilled groups.

These analyses knocked on the head any idea that markets can be relied on to create the information they need to function. Sometimes, the information has to be created for the market to work. This has led to policies of 'forced disclosure' in which sellers of goods and services are required to provide standardised forms of information.

Within financial services, where sellers usually know far more about the risks and benefits of their products than the buyers, there are strong requirements with regard to disclosure. Perhaps the most familiar and widespread instance of forced disclosure has been the requirement on public companies to issue audited accounts – a process that is now a feature of all developed stock markets. In consumer markets there has been a major focus on product risks, with programmes to identify and publish information on the safety of medicines, allergens, ingredients in foods and cosmetics, car safety and financial risks.

More recently, forced disclosure has been adopted as a policy instrument to address broader social issues such as environmental impact, with consumer products required to carry information about energy use or carbon dioxide output.

There are some key differences between the economic tradition and the political tradition.

i. Right to information is justified on instrumental not fundamental grounds

In economics, transparency has no intrinsic moral value and information is not a human right. Transparency has an instrumental value inasmuch as it prevents individuals from being ripped off and misled by those they are dealing with. It is valuable to the degree that it improves the efficiency of markets. The economic tradition starts from a position of caveat emptor and requires a justification for imposing transparency based on evidence that it is necessary to prevent fraudulent trading or malfunctioning markets.

ii. Transparency is structured as a specific obligation on the provider of information rather than a right for the recipient

The primary policy instruments arising from economics are very different to those that come from political theory. Where political theory resulted in laws granting broad rights, economic theory has resulted in rules that put specific duties on defined people and organisations to reveal certain facts. Data standards (for example, weights and measures) and forced disclosures (such as food labelling) are the primary policy instrument of economic transparency. Although it is a different tradition, there are market aspects to democratic politics which have resulted in forced disclosure policies for politicians, most notably in requirements that they reveal sources of financial income, gifts and political donations.

Science

The third tradition in transparency has its roots in the scientific revolution and can be traced back to the birth of the Royal Society in the seventeenth century and Robert Boyle. A lifelong friend of John Locke and his tutor at Oxford University, Boyle was a founder of the Royal Society, an associate of Sir Isaac Newton and the leading chemist of his generation.

Both Newton and Boyle were interested in the longest standing question in chemistry – alchemy, the search for a reaction that produced gold. The accepted practice in alchemy was that the more valuable information was, the more it should be kept secret.[16]

Newton subscribed to that view. Boyle set himself in opposition. In 1661 he published *The Sceptical Chymist*, seeking to disprove some of the more traditional ideas of alchemy and, at the same time, call into question their attitude to secrecy. He chose to provide enormous detail about how his experiments were conducted in order to force the hand of others: 'to give an

---

[16] Lawrence M. Principe, 'Alchemies of Boyle and Newton', in Margaret J. Osler (ed.), *Rethinking the Scientific Revolution*, Cambridge University Press, 2008.

occasion and a kind of necessity to the more knowing Artists to lay aside a little of their over-great Reservedness'.[17] He wanted chemists to 'either explicate or prove' their theories which should be 'brought it into the open light' so that people could 'be allowed calmly and after due information to disbelieve it'. He predicted that a more open scientific process would achieve far more than his fellow chemists could imagine.

Newton objected, warning on one occasion that Boyle should 'preserve a high silence' on certain matters and, on another, saying he avoided talking to him because of his 'conversing with all sorts of people and being in my opinion too open and too desirous of fame'.[18]

Boyle won the argument. The scientific method is now defined in terms of the reproducibility of findings, which in turn implies providing both a description of the experimental methods used in sufficient detail to allow reproduction and publication in full of the findings.

The growth of big data repositories has changed what reproducibility means. Data sharing has become central to scientific credibility. In many areas it is no longer enough to provide details of methodology and results. Instead, the underlying data used to evidence particular conclusions must be shared, in a form as close as possible to its original unedited format in order to allow it to be reanalysed. There is a growing recognition that each experiment is not a thing in itself but part of a collective enterprise and that by pooling not just the results of succeeding experiments but the underlying data we learn more much faster.

The editorial guidelines for *Nature*, the leading scientific journal, state:

> An inherent principle of publication is that others should be able to replicate and build upon the authors' published claims. A condition of publication

---

[17] Robert Boyle, *The Sceptical* Chymist: *or Chymico-Physical Doubts & Paradoxes,* J Cadwell, London, 1661

[18] As quoted by Lawrence J Principe p 208 *ibid.* and referenced by him to H.W. Turnbull (ed.), *The correspondence of Isaac Newton,* Cambridge University Press 1960

in a *Nature* journal is that authors are required to make materials, data, code and associated protocols promptly available to readers without undue qualifications.

It advocates the use of public data repositories into which all data used to support particular findings should be placed.

Data sharing is also needed to prevent fraud. Studies have identified that massaging of data by academic researchers is much more widespread than has been appreciated and that fraudulent reporting is commonplace. While most occurrences have limited impact, some are much more concerning and can mislead the public or direct academic efforts in fruitless directions. Recently, fraudulent scientists have started to face criminal sanctions. Former Iowa State University scientist Dong-Pyou Han was sentenced in June 2015 to four years and nine months in federal prison after he faked results in AIDS (Acquired Immune Deficiency Syndrome) vaccine experiments.

The idea of data sharing is now widely accepted as both a necessary pillar of academic credibility and as a mechanism to enhance the speed with which science can progress. While this can be straightforward in most sciences, it presents a problem in medicine and social sciences because the data relates to people and sharing data raises privacy concerns (see Chapter 13).

Medicine also has difficulties with large amounts of research being funded by pharmaceutical companies which regard the data produced as commercial property. Pressure from campaign groups and regulators have forced pharmaceutical companies to publish more and more information, but most of this requires them to publish their own findings from their trials. While this is undoubtedly useful, the only way in which their conclusions can be properly checked is by sharing the underlying data. Johnson and Johnson has set up the YODA (Yale University Open Data Access) project, which allows researchers to access the participant-level data from clinical trials.

Table 1.1: Three methods of transparency

Method	Description	Structure	Aim
ATI	Requirement to hold courts, legislative assemblies and committee meetings in public. ATI legislation giving rights to documents and records used in government processes.	Broad legal rights granted to citizens and, ideally, overseen by independent executive agency. No rights to have particular information as part of proceedings or record.	To make the processes of government institutions and public bodies visible to the public to make it harder to behave corruptly.
Disclosure	Requirement or decision to use standard weights and measures, publish audited accounts, label products, report financial donations. Most disclosure is forced by law but in some instances is voluntary.	Legal duty on specified people or institutions to collect and publish specified information or voluntary decision to release standardised information.	To inform individuals' agency in purchasing products, investing, voting or any other activity. To enable and support effective regulation.
Data sharing	Requirement or decision to share underlying data and methods used to support a factual conclusion. Data and methods must be shared with sufficient detail and granularity to allow the conclusion to be tested independently.	A cultural practice in science, also used to a limited degree in regulation.	To enable peers or regulators to validate the truth of statements.

i. Scientific transparency is based on the sharing of data and methods

The scientific tradition can be distinguished from the political and economic traditions by its focus on data sharing and peer review as the primary mechanisms by which transparency operates. What matters is the level of detail and the granularity of the information and data shared; it needs to meet the threshold of reproducibility. Transparency, in the scientific tradition, is an open process in which anyone can engage. But it is not designed to engage the general public – it is designed to support peer review within expert communities.

ii. Scientific transparency is more concerned with discovering truth than revealing secrets

Although it is important as a mechanism to prevent fraud and dishonesty, scientific transparency's primary purpose is to establish truth. Most of the time, people reproduce someone else's experiments not because they think the person is lying but because they believe they may have missed something; they may have made an assumption without realising it or failed to rule out an alternative explanation. Whereas economic and political transparency are in the main designed to alter who has access to a particular piece of existing information, scientific transparency is primarily about opening up control of information with the aim of increasing the total sum of human knowledge.

Summary of the benefits of transparency

US author Alvin Toffler has described power as coming in three basic forms – violence, wealth and knowledge.[19] At base, our ability to influence the actions of others is grounded in one of these three. Violence incorporates all forms of power that are ultimately rooted in threat of force, such as the criminal and civil legal systems, the regulatory and policing functions of the state, and efforts – both legal and illegal – to resist or combat these forces.

Wealth refers to any material benefit that I can freely bestow on another, whether through money or labour, or, by extension, through other favours under my control. Increasingly, one of the most valuable things I can offer in the marketplace is information about my own preferences. This information can be so valuable as to be the foundation of very large internet businesses and it has become of increasing interest to transparency activists on the grounds that it may be unclear what the terms of the exchange are. Knowledge refers to my ability to influence the actions

---

[19] Alvin Toffler, *Powershift: Knowledge, Wealth, and Violence at the Edge of the 21st Century*, Mass Market Paperback, 1991.

of others by informing them of things they did not know or persuading them to defer to my expertise.

The economic tradition has emphasised the use of individual discretionary power within market systems. The key leverage here is the power of individual choice to buy one product over another, to favour one service provider over another. But there are aspects of electoral politics that also depend on agency – with my decisions as a voter being likened to the spending of tokens in a political 'marketplace' for power. The scientific tradition is interested in the potential for new knowledge and discovery to identify alternative and better ways of doing things.

Using this model, we can see a rough relationship between different methods of transparency and the three ways in which changes in control over information affects power – changed ability to use enforcement and power, changes to individual agency (wealth) and discovery of new knowledge (see Figure 1.1).

Figure 1.1: Types of transparency and forms of power

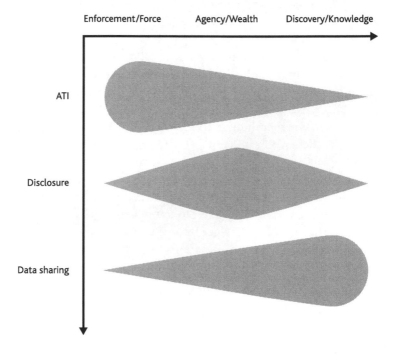

2

Critiques of transparency

Critical theory about transparency has developed rapidly in recent years in response to the strong and sometimes unquestioning support for transparency across widespread areas of government. Below we outline the key lines of such criticism, from the costs to harmful outcomes and the question of efficacy.

The financial cost of transparency

Access to information rights are sometimes described as if they are relatively cost free – as if it is nothing more than making existing information publicly available. In reality there are substantial associated costs. There is the cost of checking that exclusions such as privacy do not apply and redacting information as appropriate. There is the cost of collating information in a format intelligible to someone outside the organisation.

Publishing data brings its own set of costs. All data sets have problems of incomplete or inconsistent recording. Organisations use work-arounds and local knowledge to deal with these internally. It can be a significant piece of work to format data into the most consistent, complete and intelligible format for outside consumption, including production of jargon-free data descriptions and data labelling.

Furthermore calls for transparency in areas such as food labelling can require the compiling of whole new datasets and analyses.

Then there are the costs that follow publication of information that result from the need to respond to issues raised. With regard to access to information (ATI) this primarily involves media handling activities and developing answers to likely follow-on questions.

The handling costs rise to very high levels when we consider transparency around regulatory performance management in public services. Considerable efforts are made to manage internal and external communications around this information, as well as efforts to improve the performance of organisations. The latter activity may be the intended result of the information being public. However these activities also include 'gaming' to improve appearances and defensive efforts to argue against the implications of poor performance.

To the extent that access to information is a right, the cost argument is irrelevant. To the degree that it is instrumental, it is sensible to ask the question of how the benefits and costs compare. Research conducted at University College London (UCL) indicates that ATI legislation has had fewer beneficial effect on politics than hoped for (see Chapter 5), raising the question of whether the cost is worth paying. The same research found that claims about costs and imposition on government are overplayed.

Recognition of the cost of ATI legislation (along with views that many requests are trivial or vexatious) have led to some countries imposing or increasing fees for processing ATI requests or lowering the cost threshold above which organisations are not obliged to provide information.

As well as considering the costs on those required to disclose information, we also need to consider the cost it creates for those who are either obliged or feel compelled to factor the information into their decision making. The publication of more information about products presents consumers with a more complex task in deciding what to buy, even if they do no more than decide to ignore all this additional information.[1]

---

[1]   The potential negative impact of too much information is evidenced by for example Iyengar, S.S., Jiang, W., Huberman G, *How much choice is too much? Contributions to 401(k) Retirement Plans*, Wharton School Pensions Research Council Working Paper. This shows that providing a wider range of investments to choose from reduced participation in pensions. In a similar vein Gourville, J.T., Soman, D. Overchoice and assortment type: When and why variety backfires, *Marketing science*, 24(3), 382-395 (2005) found consumers were turned off by additional choices if they were unable to make comparisons.

The belief that more information about the performance of public services will lead to better decisions by citizens and managers of services, and ensure a more equitable and efficient delivery of such services, hangs entirely on the degree to which people can interpret and act on such information appropriately. Adding more information to the decision-making process can greatly increase the time spent in deliberation without necessarily producing any improvement in decision making.

Even if information improves the quality of decisions, it may decrease the cost-effectiveness of decision making. Medical diagnostics is an area where a great increase in more accurate data – often highly precise data – has also greatly increased the time and cost of reaching a diagnosis because doctors spend more time collecting information and considering it. The degree to which this is beneficial is open to question.

Medical screening programmes are one area where the costs, benefits and harms of adding more information into a decision-making process can be studied. The results show that our assumptions may be wrong. Take, for example, screening women for breast cancer. Breast cancer is a leading cause of death among women. We know that early detection greatly increases the chances of survival. Checking everybody for symptoms sounds like common sense.

In 2012 the Cochrane Review of the evidence on breast screening[2] concluded that to save one person's life it was necessary to screen 2000 people for 10 years. Out of those 2000 people, 200 would receive an incorrect positive test result, causing considerable anxiety. Furthermore, 10 would undergo unnecessary treatment as a result of unfounded concerns. Their conclusion, which remains controversial, was that the programme did more harm than good.

Calculations of this sort will shift as technology alters the accuracy and cost of information collection, but screening is notable as one of the few areas where serious efforts are made to assess the negative consequences that imprecise information can

---

[2] P.C. Gøtzsche and K. Jørgensen, 'Screening for breast cancer with mammography', *Cochrane Database of Systematic Reviews* 2013, No 6. Art No: CD001877. DOI: 10.1002/14651858.CD001877

have on decisions and consequent actions. And the conclusion is that we should be cautious about our assumptions.

The damaging and negative effects of transparency

The following arguments highlight ways in which providing greater access to information is harmful. Some relate only to specific forms of transparency. However they all point to some of the key underlying tensions in transparency.

i. Access to Information laws are hindering executive decision making

Freedom of information legislation has been in retreat in many countries in recent decades because of concerns that it hinders effective government. The main concern about transparency is the damage it does to the deliberative process.

Countries such as Denmark and Canada have taken steps to strengthen rights of 'deliberative privacy' or 'deliberative privilege', while in other areas, such as the US, the existing rights have been much more widely deployed. The number of documents classified as secret by US government organisations has increased from around 10 million at the start of the century to over 75 million.[3] Deliberative privilege is the idea that those in government must be allowed a private space in which to develop ideas or to put forward new proposals for debate. Otherwise, fear of being publicly criticised for suggesting an idea will stifle discussion.

Robert Hazell, professor of government and the constitution at UCL, has researched this area in depth and was asked to give evidence to the parliament on the extent to which government documents such as cabinet minutes should be exempted from the UK Freedom of Information Act (FOIA). He argued that even though 'there is very little hard, first hand evidence of a chilling effect caused by FOI', there is still a problem because 'the belief persists, particularly among ministers and their close

---

[3] The volume of derivative classification activity reported by the Information Security Oversight Office in its 2014 Report to the President.

advisers, that FOI has eroded the safe space which they need to argue and deliberate with each other in private'.[4]

He quoted a cabinet minister saying that if he thought cabinet minutes would be subject to FOI he would simply not create the minutes. Hazell therefore recommended that cabinet minutes should be excluded from FOI, on the grounds that fear of FOI, if not the reality, was damaging.

Tony Blair, the UK prime minister who introduced the Freedom of Information Act 2000, came to the view that it was extremely damaging to internal government debate.[5] In his political memoir he castigated himself for having introduced the law: 'You idiot. You naive, foolish, irresponsible nincompoop. There is really no description of stupidity, no matter how vivid, that is adequate. I quake at the imbecility of it.' (p 516).

More recently in the UK, the cabinet office fought the information commissioner over the publication of the risk registers required as part of the management of major projects. Ministers were concerned not only at the ammunition such documents provided to political opponents but also feared publication would discourage people from talking frankly about risks and that this would significantly increase the risk of such projects failing.[6]

The 2014 review of transparency policy at the Bank of England by Kevin Warsh[7] (prompted by a question from parliament as to why the Monetary Policy Committee did not publish verbatim minutes) led Warsh to recommend an interesting solution to the tensions. He proposed that the evidence going into the deliberative part of the meeting should be published but the

[4] Supplementary submission to the Commons Justice Committee by Professor Robert Hazell, the Constitution Unit, School of Public Policy, UCL, June 2012, www.publications.parliament.uk/pa/cm201213/cmselect/cmjust/96/96we26.htm

[5] Tony Blair, *A Journey*, Random House, 2010.

[6] *Ministerial Veto on Disclosure of the Department of Health's Transition Risk Register*, Information Commissioner's Report to Parliament, TSO 2012, https://ico.org.uk/media/about-the-ico/documents/1042385/ico-report-to-parliament-doh-transition-risk-register-hc77.pdf

[7] Kevin Warsh, 'Transparency and the Bank of England's Monetary Policy Committee Review', Bank of England, December 2014, www.bankofengland.co.uk/publications/Documents/news/2014/warsh.pdf

deliberative part of the meeting (day 1) should have no minutes recorded at all. He argued that 'creating a safe space for true deliberations is among the most critical indicia of organisations that make good decisions'. The second part of the meeting at which decisions were made could then be minuted and published without fear of impinging on the need for deliberative freedom.

His views were partly influenced by his own experience as head of the New York Federal Reserve and partly by the work of Professor Cheryl Schonhardt-Bailey.[8] Schonhardt-Bailey used automated textual analysis to interrogate minutes of monetary policy meetings from 1976 to 2008 and found that as transparency was increased, the contributions from participants were increasingly reduced to formulaic repetitions of established positions rather than open discussions.

Evidence from business research supports the view that transparency can have a damaging effect on free thinking. It builds on psychological research which shows that being observed can increase the reliability of people involved in straightforward tasks but reduces the productivity of those asked to perform creative tasks. Reducing transparency can allow creativity to bloom in even the most mundane areas. Ethan Bernstein in the *Harvard Business Review* catalogues examples of phone production lines in China where output increased by up to 15% when the lines normally open to constant surveillance were curtained off.[9]

Creating this private space allowed employees to cooperate without requiring the sanction of management. Such dynamics can create a powerful sense of what it is to be in a team and strong accountability within teams.

Bernstein emphasises the importance of giving people time in which they are not monitored and clear 'decision rights'. These ideas are similar to those of David Heald, professor of public accounting at the University of Glasgow, in his distinction

---

[8]   Cheryl Schonhardt-Bailey, *Deliberating American Monetary Policy: A Textual Analysis*, MIT Press, 2013.

[9]   Ethan Bernstein, 'The transparency trap', *Harvard Business Review*, October 2014.

between real-time and retrospective transparency.[10] In the former you are continually open to view; in the latter you are expected to account for your actions after the event. The latter unambiguously acknowledges that those being held accountable have decision-making rights between periods of accountability, whereas real-time observation and commentary of an executive can undermine that person's authority to decide.

We can also trace a connection between retrospective transparency and outcome transparency (transparency of the results of decisions) since outcome can only be assessed after the event. In contrast, real-time transparency tends, for the same reason, to be process transparency (transparency surrounding the making of decisions as they are being made). After the event, outcome transparency has only limited impact on deliberative freedom. The ideas of outcome and process transparency are explored in more detail in the next chapter.

ii. Transparency causes unintended harmful shifts in power

A second argument has been advanced to justify rolling back ATI laws. This is the argument that rights to information have not served the public interest but have been used instead to further private interests. In the US, the most prolific users of FOIA are businesses seeking information on competitors. This may be a public benefit, but it was not the intended benefit when the legislation was passed. In the UK, it has been a mix of media and citizens that account for over 60% of requests, which might seem more in line with what was hoped. However, media use of the UK's Freedom of information law has been criticised as being less desirable than direct use by the public.

In October 2015, to the astonishment of the media, a senior minister in the UK Conservative government came out and said exactly what many in politics felt. In his statement to parliament, announcing a review of the workings of FOIA, Chris Grayling said:

---

[10]   David Heald, 'Varieties of transparency', in *Transparency: The Key to Better Governance?*, ed Christopher Hood and David Heald, The British Academy, 2006.

This Government are committed to the Act, but we want to ensure that it works well and fairly, and cannot be abused or misused. It is, on occasion, misused by those who use it as, effectively, a research tool to generate stories for the media, and that is not acceptable. It is a legitimate and important tool for those who want to understand why and how Governments make decisions, and this Government do not intend to change that.

Many people had thought that this type of media activity was precisely what FOI was supposed to achieve. However, Grayling's unease with the media use of FOI reflects a widespread sense that there is a problem with the types of stories that are produced through freedom of information requests. These issues related to the context and salience of information and the difficulty that traditional media companies have working with data-driven stories. Journalists can get an easy story by identifying pieces of information that play on public concerns and will trigger an emotional response – such as the number of children arrested for violence or the amount spent on biscuits by a publicly funded organisation. These are quickly turned into a news item without requiring any analysis of what a good or a bad number might be, since they play on the unspoken and unsupported assumption that the number should always be lower than it is and someone is therefore to blame. This can result in a situation in which ATI can be used to support any story that plays to existing prejudice but is less effective at yielding information that challenges public opinion (see Chapter 7).

To this criticism of ATI we would add a number of other observations that might be called unintended shifts in power that transparency can cause. For example, the publication of outcomes across public services has sometimes been promoted as increasing the power of service users. However evidence of this is thin (see Chapter 10). The more significant shift in power has been away from professions with more control given to managers, budget holders and politically accountable organisations. Whether this is positive or negative depends on your point of view. But it is different from the intended shift in power expressed in support of these policies.

Executive pay disclosure in the UK may also have had negative effects. In recent decades, the UK has introduced requirements that companies disclose the remuneration of company directors and give shareholders stronger rights to approve pay. The intention was to ensure a clearer connection between remuneration and performance. Since then pay has continued to grow and academic research finds little or no relationship with performance. Furthermore, the publication may have contributed to a ratchet effect in which executives bargain for above average pay, playing on the desire of boards to believe they are hiring above average talent.[11]

This outcome should perhaps not come as a surprise. The disclosure of pay quite likely did more to increase the knowledge of executives about the pay of their peers, thereby enhancing their bargaining power more than it increased the information available to shareholders.

Cognitive bias is another source of potentially perverse incentives. The work of psychologists Amos Tversky and Daniel Kahneman has identified a number of ways in which people react irrationally to information. For example, the relative availability of information has an enormous impact on political discussions, and transparency policy can be used to increase the salience of particular issues and decrease that of others by selection of the information made available. Chris Grayling's concern about FOI is the worry that this power has not gone to citizens but to private companies and media organisations with their own agendas.

Another important bias identified by Tversky and Kahneman is human inability to cope rationally with low probabilities and to overestimate the precision of uncertain information. The presentation of league tables in the media has been criticised for presenting insignificant differences between organisations as if they are statistically important. Competition for audiences can

---

[11] Improved Transparency of Executive Remuneration, Policy Impact Assessment for the Department of Business Innovation and Skills, www.gov. uk/government/uploads/system/uploads/attachment_data/file/31360/12-889-improved-transparency-executive-remuneration-impact.pdf

incentivise media organisations to over-interpret information and sensationalise.

The banning of opinion polls in the period immediately before an election is common in a number of countries and is driven, in part, by concerns that uncertain information may have a disproportionate effect on voters' thinking.

iii. Transparency encourages dishonest and perverse behaviours

Economic theory has begun from a position of regarding transparency as necessarily a good thing on the grounds that the more information in a market, the more efficient it will be. More recently, however, economic models have begun cataloguing the conditions under which the assumption breaks down – when does more information result in people behaving badly rather than better; when does it cause people to make worse decisions?

This idea is usually framed in terms of somebody (the principal) hiring someone else (the agent) to do a job. The question is whether it is a good idea to allow the principal to observe and gather information on the agent. The basic insight is that being watched sometimes encourages greater honesty, sometimes greater dishonesty.

People will be more honest if they think dishonesty will be observable. But they may be less honest if they think their true views or behaviours are unacceptable. In this case they may dissemble and say what people want to hear. If forced to be transparent, the agent is incentivised to lie about the best course of action to conform with the principal's beliefs.[12]

Imagine a government representative entering into international negotiations with multiple countries on behalf of a diverse group of citizens who have conflicting interests – and many of whom do not trust said representative. If the representative was required to reveal their bargaining position to the electorate, they would be unlikely to get them the best deal. In order to maintain electoral support and outflank opposition claims, they might instead have

---

[12] Andrea Pratt, 'The more closely we are watched the better we behave?', in *Transparency: The Key to Better Governance?*, ed Christopher Hood and David Heald, The British Academy, 2006.

to pander to the view that the best achievable deal is not good enough. As a result, the best deal available might not be done.

For this reason, the votes by country representatives on the board of the European Central Bank are confidential. It is recognised that all members will need to compromise to reach consensus but that such a compromise may be unachievable if negotiations are conducted transparently.

In a review of reporting requirements for public companies, John Kay, visiting professor of economics at the London School of Economics (LSE), argued that quarterly reporting, as is currently practised in the US, rather than half-yearly reporting (the UK requirement) would encourage more short-term decision making by executives at the expense of longer-term growth strategies.[13] Even if executives feel certain that a longer-term strategy is in the best interests of shareholders overall, they also know that they will be unlikely to survive the ire of short-term investors complaining about weaker interim reporting numbers. To protect their position, they are incentivised to conform to whatever will play best with their audience and focus therefore on short-term performance.

The model of compliance by economist Bengt Holmstrom introduces the issue of the honesty or cynicism of those subject to transparency and monitoring. He constructs a principal-agent model in which a principal asks the agent to perform a task, gets to see the performance of an agent at the end of a certain time period and then has to recommission them or not according to their performance. The information about the agent's performance will lead the principal to make the wrong decision if there are some agents who are honest, hard-working and perform averagely and others who are lazy and dishonest but are able to deliver better results on the measured aspects of performance in the requisite time period.[14]

---

[13] Final Report: The Kay Review of UK Equity Markets and Long Term Decision Making, July 2012, www.gov.uk/government/uploads/system/uploads/attachment_data/file/253454/bis-12-917-kay-review-of-equity-markets-final-report.pdf

[14] B. Homstrom, 'Managerial incentive problems: a dynamic perspective', *Review of Economic Studies* Vol 66 (1999), 169–182.

If monitoring does not wholly capture the benefit the principal is seeking, it will result in a distorted view of performance. Furthermore, if the benefit at stake in the unmonitored portion of activity is as great or greater than that in the monitored portion, transparency could result in a net loss to the principal. Such scenarios are seen most often when target-driven organisations hit their key performance indicators but only by reducing the true quality of their work.

This issue has proved to be central to problems encountered in using transparency to improve the performance of complex public services in which the principal (that is, the government acting on behalf of the public) attempts to gather information about the performance of the agent (for example, a school, hospital or police force) to judge the quality of the service it provides. However the gap between the true quality and the measured quality is at times so great as to run the risk that transparency only rewards those who are both cynical and good at playing the system. One response to this has been to aim to have greater transparency around outcomes rather than processes in the belief that outcome information will more closely capture the benefits that principals want their agents to deliver.

It should be noted that these problems are responses to monitoring by an authority of some sort and are as much a problem for a boss trying to oversee workers or report to a board within a private company as they are for more transparent forms of accountability.

A more important distinction to draw is between monitoring systems that are so susceptible to gaming that they cease to function if made transparent. The main category here is risk assessment in any area of policing – such as national security, child protection or tax fraud – but it is equally true of certain methods of rating, products and services. The precise details of how Google's page rank algorithm works is not transparent because of the speed with which it would then be gamed and computed.

The one thing we would point out at this stage is that the problems of compliance and conformity are increased to the degree that people are measured against a single dominant set of criteria. The more pluralistic the society, the more varied the ways to measure the worth of an individual, and the less pressure there is to conform or comply.

iv. Transparency undermines privacy

A recent critique has identified the conflict between the privacy of citizens and the requirements for transparency. One of the most effective uses of FOIA in recent years was a pan-European effort by journalists (the International Consortium of Investigative Journalists) to force release of data about who was in receipt of farm subsidies from the European Union.[15] The Common Agricultural Policy was under attack for being expensive, damaging to the environment and unfair to farmers in developing countries. One rationale put forward by politicians for maintaining the policy was that it protected smaller farmers from market volatility and ensured their survival. When the numbers were published, it turned out that the vast majority of payments went to large corporations and extremely wealthy landowners. It was of course possible in theory to identify from the rules of the system and the distribution of land ownership that this was likely to be the case. But seeing the detailed numbers showing multimillion pound annual transfers from European taxpayers into the coffers of billionaires such as the Duke of Westminster or multinationals such as Tate and Lyle made front-page news and added to the pressure to reform the Common Agricultural Policy in the EU.

A central challenge to this effort was the claim by some farmers that this was an invasion of their privacy – that this was personal financial information and should not be made public. In some subsequent court cases this view was upheld and the EU has since changed the way it has released information, to exclude details of individuals receiving grants below a certain threshold and thereby respect the privacy of small landowners.

FOI legislation usually contains provisions protecting personal information from public release. Under UK law, personal information is deemed to include personal financial information.

---

[15] See http://farmsubsidy.openspending.org/ and http://datajournalism handbook.org/1.0/en/getting_data_2.html

Such information cannot be released where it would be 'unfair' on the individual because they had no expectation that it might be released.

This system, while manageable in relation to government documents, creates a fundamental issue with transparency in relation to data. Most data about the activities of government or public services – information about, say, arrests or taxes or benefits paid – is also information about citizens. If the information about citizens is considered private it places a fundamental limitation on how transparent government can be. Is the payment of money by the EU to a farmer a private fact about that farmer or a public fact about the EU?

This issue has become more important in recent years as it has become clear that it is not possible to anonymise rich data sets and that people can be re-identified in data with only a handful of data points.[16]

v. Transparency undermines commercial confidentiality

Corporations have been some of the strongest voices against transparency in the form of disclosure requirements on business. The arguments are grounded first on the basis of cost (see above). The specifics of disclosure are always a fierce area of contention

---

[16]   L. Sweeney. k-anonymity: a model for protecting privacy. *International Journal on Uncertainty, Fuzziness and Knowledge-based Systems*, 10 (5), 2002; 557-570. This includes a description of how Latanya Sweeney famously identified William Weld the government of Massachussetts in supposedly anonymised medical records

Arvind Narayanan and Vitaly Shmatikov *Robust De-anonymization of Large Sparse Datasets (How To Break Anonymity of the Netflix Prize Dataset)* Proc. of 29th IEEE Symposium on Security and Privacy, Oakland, CA, May 2008, pp. 111-125. This recounts how the authors were able to identify people in a supposedly anonymous data set from the Neflix database of movie rentals.

De Montjoye, Yves-Alexandre et al, *Unique in the Crowd: The privacy bounds of human mobility* Scientific Reports 3, 1376 (2013) shows that four pieces of location data are usually enough to identify an individual.

Ohm Paul, *Broken Promises of Privacy: Responding to the Surprising Failure of Anonymization* (August 13, 2009). UCLA Law Review, Vol. 57, p. 1701, 2010; U of Colorado Law Legal Studies Research Paper No. 9-12. Available at SSRN: http://ssrn.com/abstract=1450006

with corporations and public sector organisations arguing that any specific form of disclosure is unfair. This is necessarily true since it is impossible to design any measure or presentation of information that wholly captures the issue of interest to the public. The concern is that the public will misinterpret any information made sufficiently simple to be intelligible. So, for example, the argument against labelling genetically modified foods is that people will assume the label is there because genetically modified organisms (GMOs) present some health risk and respond accordingly when, in reality, there is no evidence that GMOs are more risky. In this regard, the issue of labelling is another instance of potential perverse behaviours – whether that is compliance by the company or unintended behaviour by the consumer.

However, there is one other way in which transparency affects business that is becoming increasingly important and this is the degree to which it infringes upon commercial confidentiality. This has come to the fore in debates about opening up access to data on pharmaceutical trials (where companies have argued that this is commercially confidential); opening up information in relation to government contracting; and revealing the ways in which online businesses use information to determine the propensity of consumers to buy particular products. This last issue is, we will argue, one that will be of increasing importance as the use of big data by business grows and will be addressed in greater depth in the final chapters of the book.

The ineffectiveness of transparency

The final set of critiques are those that analyse the reasons why transparency is sometimes ineffective. Attempts to demonstrate that transparency has had a positive effect are highly variable in their results. ATI advocates have argued that ATI is not as effective as it should be and blame laws that are too limited in scope and bureaucracies that put obstacles in the way of those seeking information. Others have argued that the problems go deeper than that.

In the UK, David Heald has distinguished between 'nominal' and 'effective' transparency where nominal transparency is the provision of information without effect.[17] According to Heald, 'Even when transparency appears to be increasing as measured by some index, the reality may be quite different' –something which he terms 'transparency illusion'.

The philosopher Onora O'Neill makes a similar point, saying: 'Huge quantities of information are now made public in order to meet transparency requirements, but a great deal of it is not actually communicated to anyone.'[18]

She describes a tendency to think about transparency as being achieved by the release of information 'detachable from communication' and the failure to recognise that 'information can be disclosed without being seen, read or understood by any, let alone many, others'.

O'Neill argues persuasively that this misuse of transparency may account for the lack of any apparent link between increases in transparency and increases in public trust, saying: 'The thought that transparency has increased trustworthiness without increasing trust overlooks that fact that transparency is supposed to work by making the very evidence needed to place or refuse trust intelligently more available and more public.'

Bentham believed that transparency would increase trust. But across the world, over the decades that ATI laws have become common, trust in government has fallen. Many commentators (for example, UCL's Robert Hazell and Ben Worthy in the UK context; Chapter 9) point out that trust had been falling steadily in the decades prior to the introduction of ATI, so it is hard to say with any certainty whether transparency has contributed to the reduction in trust or whether transparency has been increased in response to falling trust.

The question we want to ask is what sort of transparency would give a reasonable person grounds for trusting particular institutional arrangements? If I am given an account by a government institution of their activity but neither I nor anyone else outside that institution is in a position to challenge that

---

[17] Heald, 'Varieties of transparency', p 34.

[18] Onora O'Neill, 'Transparency and the ethics of communication', in *Transparency: The Key to Better Governance?*, ed Christopher Hood and David Heald, The British Academy, 2006, p 81.

account, should I feel more trusting towards that organisation? If I am given more information about products but am unable to interpret or make use of that information in decision making should feel safer?

We will argue that efforts to increase transparency have rarely achieved the threshold at which they could be said to provide the individual with a good reason to be trusting. If this analysis is correct it should be no great surprise if increased transparency has not improved trust.

A number of US academics have examined in more detail the reasons why particular forms of transparency fail to have the desired effect.

Omri Ben-Shahar, of the University of Chicago Law School, and Carl Schneider, from the University of Michigan, have put together a convincing case that requiring disclosure is, in the main, a waste of time.[19] Their *More Than You Wanted to Know: The Failure of Mandated Disclosure* argues that not only are mandatory disclosures of risk warnings and terms and conditions ineffective, they can be harmful by creating the appearance of having addressed a problem when, in reality, nothing has happened.

Archon Fung and colleagues have developed a more complex model looking at a range of different examples of forced disclosure, some of which work but many of which do not. Their analysis highlights the degree to which disclosers and recipients are likely to respond to new information based on criteria that are likely to 'embed' such information in their decision making.[20]

Lawrence Lessig, professor of law and director of the Edmond J. Safra Center for Ethics at Harvard Law School, has argued that 'naked transparency' – simply putting information into the public domain – can have serious negative consequences because the majority of people do not have time to properly assess the evidence and are instead strongly swayed by salience and simplistic analyses.[21] He claims it is disingenuous of transparency advocates to argue that this is somehow not their concern. Beth

---

[19] Omri Ben-Shahar and Carl Schneider, *More Than You Wanted to Know: The Failure of Mandated Disclosure,* Princeton University Press, 2014.

[20] Archon Fung, Mary Graham and David Weill, *Full Disclosure, The Perils and Promise of Transparency*, Cambridge University Pressm 2007.

[21] Lawrence Lessig, 'Against transparency', *New Republic*, 9 October 2009.

Noveck at New York University has pointed out the inability of information to exert much influence on events without civil society organisations able to interpret and respond to the information for people.

Rosemary McGee and John Gaventa, in a report for the UK government,[22] point out that much transparency policy rests on unreliable assumptions – for example that greater transparency will lead to greater accountability even though 'growing evidence exists that transparency alone is insufficient'.

They continue: 'Very few initiatives articulate a theory of change, making it very difficult to trace or ascertain the changes that are likely to occur.' Theories of change 'do need to offer plausible explanations for how the sought changes are likely to occur'.

This book is in this tradition of criticism. It comes from the viewpoint that the fundamental arguments for the potential good of transparency are sound and supported by persuasive instances of success. The lack of consistent evidence that transparency works is due to the highly variable implementation of such policies. To use an analogy, the benefits of an independent judiciary are clear to most people – but that benefit takes more than simply appointing nine people to a bench and declaring them independent. All political institutions are complex and sensitive to the details of design. They take time to establish themselves culturally. Transparency is no different. It is a fine idea, but designing laws and institutions that deliver it effectively is a difficult and nuanced area.

These criticisms of transparency present us with a situation in which one of the most widely advocated and accepted political policy goals – greater transparency – is an area where the understanding of effective execution is underdeveloped. It is also an area where, if poorly executed, there is the potential to corrode trust, infringe privacy, incentivise dishonest behaviour, undermine the ability of institutions to function and waste public resource. In the face of this, it is no longer good enough to justify transparency on the grounds that it is self-evidently a good idea.

---

[22] R. McGee and J. Gaventa, *Review of Impact and Effectiveness of Transparency and Accountability Initiatives*, DfID Institute of Development Studies, 2010, p 6.

Summary of the downsides to transparency

Table 2.1 lists the key problems that the critiques of transparency described in this chapter have identified. Some of them are things that are necessarily incurred by certain forms of transparency; others are the potential unintended consequences that may occur in some circumstances. So, for example, allowing lots of people to observe and comment on executive decision making will necessarily increase the cost of making decisions because of the increased need to communicate with stakeholders and handle the PR aspects of decision making. There is then a quite separate question as to whether in some circumstances this process will produce a better decision or, in others, will have no effect or even produce worse decision making.

We have not included the impact of transparency on trust in Table 2.1, because the relationship between transparency and trust is too complex to put definitively on either the negative or positive side of the equation. The table is an attempt to provide a simple categorisation of harms and costs that have been clearly demonstrated to be caused by changing control over information at least in some circumstances.

We have related these various disbenefits to the three types of transparency outlined in the previous chapter. For each, we have identified the level of risk in relation to the costs and harms as either high (H), medium (M) or low (L). These are our own personal judgements and the subsequent chapters will set out in more detail how we have reached this assessment.

To explain in a little more detail, however, while all forms of transparency impose costs we believe that data sharing imposes lower costs than ATI and disclosure because the level of work in manipulating data for release is lower (although still not negligible). In contrast, ATI and disclosure pose limited risks with regard to privacy and almost all instances of such policies include specific limitations on personally identifiable data. In contrast, data sharing necessarily creates risks in this area.

Table 2.1: Summary of costs and harms of transparency

Harm	Description	Example	Risk		
			ATI	Disclosure	Data sharing
Financial burden	Responding to ATI request, complying with disclosure requirements or compiling data to be shared. Responding to information	In the UK it is estimated every FOI request costs in the region of £600 to answer	H	H	M
Reduced privacy	Risks to privacy from sharing of information about individuals	Providing information about who receives farm subsidies invades privacy of farmers	L	L	H
Threat to commercial confidentiality	Risks to proprietary data sets and data algorithms from wider access to data	Pharmaceutical companies have argued wider transparency around their research would harm their commercial interests	L	L	H
Loss of deliberative freedom	People unwilling to speak their mind while being watched	Monetary policy committees becoming formulaic when subject to transparency.	H	L	L
Compliance and gaming	Responding to external monitoring by creating a false appearance	Gaming of exam result in schools or by the education system	M	H	L
Conformity to public expectation	Practical or emotional need to conform to public expectation: whether a politician needing to retain confidence of voters or citizens fearful of disapproval of their community	Impact of quarterly reporting on investment strategies of business managers	H	H	L
Unintended redistribution of power	Changes to the bargaining power, influence or behaviour of groups in unintended ways	Complaints of use of FOI by the media; use of information on executive pay to negotiate higher pay	Unknown		

The most important observation we would make at this stage is that ATI and disclosure are expensive but have very limited implications for privacy and commercial confidentiality. ATI poses the greatest threat to deliberative freedom and increased conformity, although as we shall see there are ways for organisations to adapt and thereby restore their freedoms either in law or through practice, both of which undermine the impact of ATI. Disclosure poses the greatest risk of encouraging gaming and compliance.

We have indicated that data sharing poses lower risks of these harms. This assessment, however, depends very much on how data sharing is implemented, and is the topic of later chapters.

Finally, in terms of the broad risks of unintended consequences, this is very hard to quantify. However, our principal observation here would be to reiterate the problem that, all too often, release of information has had relatively little impact either in the intended manner or in any other manner.

Part Two
Definitions and models

This section sets out the theoretical framework within which we discuss transparency and the scientific model of data sharing that lies behind it. We will present the case for making data sharing the foundational mechanism for transparency. The argument is as follows:

1. The aim of transparency is fairness. The definition of transparency is the degree to which I can tell whether the systems that affect me are fair or not (Chapter 3).
2. It is not possible to assess whether systems that affect me are fair without being able to see the outcomes of such systems across whole populations (Chapters 4 and 5).
3. Transparency of population outcomes must be based on data sharing rather than more traditional models of publishing. Transparency driven by data sharing requires new institutional structures (Chapters 6 and 7).

3

Definitions of transparency

In 2009, Gary Reinbach died in University College Hospital, London, aged 22. The cause of death was liver failure, brought on by 10 years of drinking up to three bottles of vodka a day. When Gary was 11, he was a happy child with a passion for tae kwon do. Then his parents split up, he moved with his mum to a run-down estate and the tae kwon do classes stopped. Life became miserable. At 13 he began drinking.

In the 10 weeks before he died, Gary was in hospital waiting to hear whether or not he could have a liver transplant. At any one time in the UK, there are up to 50 people waiting for every liver that becomes available. There are rules to determine who gets preference. One of those rules is that a patient should only get a liver if there is good reason to believe that they will be able to live an abstinent life after the operation.

The usual way to test whether someone is likely to be able to stop drinking – and therefore qualify for a donor organ - is to send them home for some months and test them periodically to see if they are managing not to drink. But Gary's first encounter with the doctors was when he was already at such a critically ill stage he could not be discharged from hospital and consequently was unable to demonstrate whether or not he could live without alcohol.[1] Under the rules, Gary did not qualify for a liver. The National Health Service (NHS) observed that doctors 'have to make tough decisions about who is going to get the most benefit and who is going to take best care of this precious gift'.

---

[1] www.theguardian.com/theguardian/2009/jul/25/gary-reinbach-alcoholic-madeline-hanshaw

Some felt the decision was fair. Liz Hunt writing in the *Telegraph* said it was right that Gary Reinbach did not receive a liver transplant:

> Donated organs are the most precious of gifts, and a hugely limited resource. For every person lucky enough to get a new liver, 20 others with liver disease will die. A liver wasted – and I use that word deliberately – on a chronic alcoholic, whatever his or her age, is a chance of life denied to a more deserving recipient.[2]

Gary's mother felt this was unfair. She said: 'Gary didn't know what he was doing when he was 13. He didn't know it would come to this when he was 22. He didn't know he was going to die. All his friends who were drinking with him are still at home, they are fine.'

One of Reinbach's doctors, Professor Rajiv Jalan, a consultant hepatologist at University College Hospital (UCH), agreed: 'This is a young man who has never known any better. ... We feel this boy deserves a transplant because it is the first time he has come to the hospital with an alcohol-related problem.'[3]

Gary did not qualify for a liver under the existing rules. But the rules had not been drafted with this situation in mind. It is highly unusual. Typically, patients seeking liver transplant are older men who have been drinking too much for most of their lives, despite the advice of doctors to quit.

In general, organs are not given on the basis of how 'deserving' the patient is. It is seen as fairer to allocate organs to patients in on a wholly 'non-judgemental' basis. The degree of personal responsibility for the condition has no bearing on the decision. It is determined purely on the basis of the expected health benefit from the operation. Someone who drinks will get less benefit from a new liver than someone who is abstinent.

---

2   *The Telegraph*, 21 July 2009, www.telegraph.co.uk/comment/columnists/lizhunt/5881334/A-face-that-should-haunt-a-generation.html

3   www.foxnews.com/story/2009/07/20/22-year-old-alcoholic-denied-liver-transplant-faces-death.html

Gary's case presents an argument for a different approach. While being wholly non-judgemental may seem right most of the time, when presented with someone who seems to be so much *less* responsible for his situation than others, it is right to question whether there are exceptions to this rule. Maybe someone who succumbed to alcohol addiction at such a young age should be treated differently. Even if they are only going to get five years from a liver and another person would have 10, perhaps they should nonetheless get preference.

The decision over Gary's liver is an example of what economists call an allocation decision – a decision about how a scarce resource will be allocated to competing claims. In Gary's case it was a matter of life and death. Most allocation decisions are rather less dramatic. But your life is ruled by a series of such allocations, each of which involves putting people and things – but mainly people - into different categories.

Some of these processes intuitively strike us as categorisations - for example, the process by which you are awarded exam grades or the process by which you are offered a job in the civil service. The process by which your tax bill is determined puts your income, expenses and wealth into a series of categories and determines how much you owe the state. Your entitlement to benefits or tax rebates works in the same way.

Whether or not you are promoted or disciplined at work or a court finds you guilty – in each instance there are processes that apply a series of tests to put you into one category or another. In every case the process is determined by a set of explicit rules and defined areas of discretion left to the judgement of an individual or organisation with legal authority.

Each one of these decisions might in one context be completely trivial and in another result in a fundamental change in the direction of someone's life. In every such instance it is right to ask whether or not decisions are fair. A sense of fairness in the operation of social institutions is the foundation of social cohesion.

Fairness creates a dilemma. On the one hand, fairness requires rules. The most fundamental rule of fairness is that like should be treated alike. If decisions are to be made in a fair way, the same principles should be applied to me as are applied to you under the same circumstances. For that to work, those making decisions must have rules to follow. So, for example, university admissions tutors have rules about how places are awarded just as much as judges have rules about what sentences can be given to convicted criminals. There are laws that set out how banks can make loan decisions which outlaw, for example, the refusal of credit on the basis of the race or gender of the applicant. So rules are an essential part of making sure these allocation decisions are fair.

However, we also know that sticking to the rules will result in unfairness because no set of rules can adequately capture in advance the full range of circumstances that the decision makers will encounter. My circumstance is never *exactly* the same as yours. The world is infinitely more variable than any legislator, however wise, can envision. The blind application of rules will most certainly result in things being done that people will regard as unfair. Gary's story is an example.

We are going to define a fair decision as the correct application of fair rules. If the rules are not adhered to, then the basic requirement that fairness must follow rules is broken. But the rules themselves must also be tested against a more fundamental notion of fairness – one that can ultimately only be answered through discourse and dispute resolution, through courts, through formal political processes or, as Bentham would put it, by appeal to the 'tribunal of the public'.

That is what Gary Reinbach's mother was doing when she spoke out about his situation. She was appealing to the wider public and asking them whether or not they agreed with the rules around liver transplants.

Cases like Gary's have led to a decision to review and revise the rules. In the ensuing debate there is a wealth of different evidence to consider. A freedom of information request by the *Sunday Times* in 2014 highlighted that Gary's case was not as exceptional as might have been thought. Four hospitals provided data revealing that there was at that moment across four hospitals, one teenager and two people in their 20s waiting for a liver. Data on the rapidly rising prevalence of severe alcoholism amongst young children added to the concern (at the same time as average alcohol consumption by the young was falling). Stories emerged saying that some people in this position had taken to drink as a result of being abused as children, increasing the sense that their lack of responsibility for their situation should be a consideration.

The issue of childhood alcoholism is only one of a number of issues that have been raised about the fairness of the organ transplant system. A further investigation by the *Sunday Times* found that people who had agreed to donate organs while being treated in a NHS hospital were then having their organs given to patients being treated privately – patients who would not have had to wait as long for treatment, some of whom were coming from abroad. In the UK context, this was regarded as unacceptable. The rules did not specify that UK citizens and NHS patients had priority – neither is relevant clinically. But the public felt that such considerations were relevant in the context where patients donating an organ in an NHS environment might have assumed it went to another NHS patient. The government intervened.

Research in the US has identified another entirely different issue when the impact of competition between transplant centres was examined.

Whether or not you get a transplant depends on whether your doctor decides to list you for transplant. The way the system works in the US, doctors enter the patient onto a computer register with details of their lab tests and other information. This data is used to generate a model for end-stage liver disease (MELD) score which rates the patient according to how sick they are. Organs are then distributed to patients according to whether there is a match and then prioritised according to how sick the patients are and how long they have been waiting.

By analysing the data about patient referrals, the researchers have shown that in areas where there was more competition between hospitals, doctors listed more patients for transplantation. Furthermore, more of their patients had high MELD scores and patients were listed with a higher risk of graft failure and death. The researchers concluded that 'significant variation in patient selection for transplantation is associated with market variables'.[4] The same issue has been identified in

---

[4]   J.B., H.J. Paarsch, J.L. Dodge, A.M. Segre, J. Lai and J.P. Roberts, 'Center competition and outcomes following liver transplantation', *Liver Transplantation* Vol 19, No 1 (2013), 96-104.

kidney transplantation where competition between hospitals is again associated with more patients being listed at higher risk of death or graft failure.[5]

In being more aggressive in treating their patients, it is not immediately obvious whether doctors in areas with more competition are acting for or against their patients' interests. But the one thing that is clear is that a fair system of organ allocation would not be one in which your likelihood of transplantation depends on how many hospitals there are in the region.

A longstanding concern in kidney transplantation has been the significantly lower rates of transplantation to African-Americans. This occurred in part because the rules gave significant weight to matching organ to recipient (human leukocyte antigen or HLA matching). This was due to evidence that a better match would mean the organ achieved a greater increase in lifespan. However, it also had the unintended effect of meaning that in general African-Americans were less likely to find an organ that matched.

There is no definitively wrong or right answer to this issue. Should the rule for transplantation be colour blind and require that the individual who will benefit most from the organ should receive it, even if that means a racial disparity? Or should the rules be adapted to ensure the maximum benefit within limited acceptable levels of racial inequality?

In the end, the development of immunosuppressants has meant that the need to match organs closely has declined. In 2012, the rules were adjusted such that the weight put on HLA matching was reduced, with the result that an increased proportion of organs now go to African-Americans, although significant disparities remain.

These different points all relate to the fairness of the system for allocating donated organs. They come from different perspectives. An individual decision can be criticised as unfair because the rules were not followed or because the rules are not fair – i.e. that the outcome of the correct application of the rules

---

5   Joel T. Adler, Rosh K.V. Sethi, Heidi Yeh, James F. Markmann and Louis Nguyen, 'Market competition influences renal transplantation risk and outcomes', *Annals of Surgery* Vol 260, No 3 (September 2014), 550-557.

offends against natural justice. This was what Gary Reinhart's mother argued.

It is also possible to criticise the system as a whole as unfair without identifying particular decisions. This can be done by raising issues of principle with the rules – for example, questioning whether within a state-funded health system, giving the same priority to overseas or privately funded patients as to state-funded patients. It can also be done by showing that the results of the system are not what we would want. The evidence that African-Americans were less likely to receive a donated organ under the rules was a legitimate complaint about fairness.

Transparency as fairness

We have begun with a story about fairness because calls for transparency are driven by a belief or a concern that somebody is getting away with the opposite. A random week's UK news has included calls for transparency from people concerned that athletes are managing to cheat in competitions and claims that the anti-doping authorities were concealing evidence of their failure to properly police the sport. The prime minister, David Cameron, called for greater transparency of ownership of property in London due to concerns that shell companies were used to avoid tax and to conceal the purchase of property with 'plundered or laundered cash'. Farmers called for transparency over British farming produce, which they wanted to be clearly labelled in shops. It was unfair on UK farmers that UK consumers were prevented from having the information they needed to enable them to buy British, they said. A House of Lords committee called for greater transparency over the plans for the forthcoming referendum on EU membership because of fears that the government would otherwise present them with a fait accompli and prevent parliament from having a fair chance to amend the legislation.

In every case, the worry is that somebody is getting away with something by stopping other people from knowing things they are entitled to know. We want to put the idea of fairness at the heart of our definition of transparency. When people call for transparency they are, in the main, claiming that someone is getting away with something they should not and someone else is being treated unfairly or is at risk of being treated unfairly.

Transparency policy often focuses on the person or organisations alleged to be behaving badly and defines transparency in terms of the degree to which their freedom to do this is limited by having to reveal what they are doing. We want, instead, to turn it around and focus our definition on those who lose out as a result of lack of transparency since, in the main, they are the people motivated to use transparency to change things.

In this view, transparency is the degree to which I am able to evidence whether your treatment of me is fair. The use of the word evidence here is important. People who are calling for transparency may be certain – or may suspect – that somebody is doing them wrong. Either way, what they are seeking is the information to evidence their beliefs or suspicions. The role of transparency is to enable competing claims to be tested and evidenced.

People want this evidence in order to be able to do something. The information has no power in and of itself. It only brings about change to the degree that better evidence enables more effective use of the various mechanisms through which information can be turned into pressure for change – through political pressure, market pressures or through discovery and learning. Transparency is there to improve the effectiveness of accountability systems, market systems and systems for discovery and verification. It needs to be defined in terms of the needs of people using these systems.

This view of transparency is consistent with existing definitions of transparency, but it is broader than most. Christopher Hood has defined transparency as: 'government according to fixed and published rules, on the basis of information and procedures that are accessible to the public'.[6] The Asian Development Bank has

---

[6] Hood C, *Transparency in Encyclopaedia of Democratic Thought* (ed P B Clarke and J Foweraker Routledge (2001) p 700. This is quoted from 'Transparency in a historical perspective', in *Transparency: The Key to Better Governance?*, ed Christopher Hood and David Heald, British Academy, 2006

used: 'the availability of information to the general public and clarity about government, rules, regulations and decisions'.[7]

Any arrangement that failed to meet these definitions would certainly fail our definition of transparency. If rules and processes are secret I cannot assess whether my treatment was in line with those rules or if I regard the rules as fair. However, the fairness definition has broader implications than this. For example, information needs to be timely. It is not transparent to publish the rules of a debate two minutes before the debate starts if one side has known them for months beforehand.

Hood's definition might be read as suggesting that there is a level of disclosure that makes a process 'transparent'. In our definition, there are potentially infinite amounts of information disclosure that people could argue is necessary for identifying whether or not a process is fair. The best that can be aimed for is a reasonable or 'fair' level of transparency.

Both definitions above refer primarily to transparency about processes. We will argue that the growth of systems for data recording and analysis mean that definitions of transparency need to put as much emphasis on transparency around the outcomes of decision processes as around the process itself. Indeed, we will argue that as technology develops, the latter form of transparency will become the more important.

The *Oxford Dictionary of Economics* defines transparent policy measures as: 'policy measures whose operation is open to scrutiny. Transparency includes making it clear who is taking the decisions, what the measures are, who is gaining from them and who is paying for them'.[8] This differs from the earlier definitions by referring explicitly to information not just about rules and roles but also about the outcome of such policies – who gains and who pays. Both are essential to assessing the fairness of such policies.

---

[7]   Asian Development Bank, *Governance: Sound Development Management*, August 1995 p 11, http://www.adb.org/sites/default/files/institutional-document/32027/govpolicy.pdf

[8]   Hood C, *Transparency in Encyclopaedia of Democratic Thought* (eds P B Clarke and J Foweraker Routledge, 2001) p 700. This is quoted from 'Transparency in a historical perspective', in *Transparency: The Key to Better Governance?*, ed Christopher Hood and David Heald, British Academy, 2006.

Also, this definition refers to how the information is used: it must enable 'scrutiny'. Scrutiny and accountability are key concepts in transparency policy. Transparency is sometimes used in contexts that imply it is equivalent to accountability, where accountability is defined as the obligation on organisations or people to give an account of themselves to others. Accountability is also used to refer to systems by which people can act on such information and reward or punish organisations on the basis of the acceptability of their actions.

For our purposes we want to be able to be able to distinguish between failures that occur as a result of inadequate information and failures that occur as a result of weak accountability systems with limited consequences. Our definition of transparency then refers only to the degree that relevant information is available. We use the term 'accountability' to refer to political systems through which individuals and organisations can punish or reward on the basis of such information – including both formal and informal systems from social ostracism and media condemnation, through choosing alternatives or actively boycotting particular organisations or services, through voting in elections and challenging in the courts, all the way through to public protest and insurrection. These are all ways in which people are held to account.

We also want a definition that is relevant not just to public administration but to all areas of public policy, including market regulation and professional regulation. We want a definition that can apply to any area of contested claims where one side can benefit by withholding information from the other: government and electorate; police and detainee; seller and buyer; professional and client; researchers and grant-making organisations, and so on. The list is very long. There are specific circumstances that influence how transparency can operate in these varied circumstances. But there are also some important common features.

When one person accuses another of a lack of transparency they are complaining of a situation in which one person or organisation has control over information to such a degree that they can prevent others from assessing the fairness of their behaviour towards that individual. Our definition of transparency then is:

> The transparency of any organisation, authority or decision-making process is the degree to which someone affected by it can evidence whether or not it is treating them fairly.

As described above, being able to evidence fairness is being able to evidence whether you were handled according to the rules and, also, the degree to which the rules produce outcomes that are fair. Historically, transparency has been primarily about the first question – was your case handled according to the rules. Assessing the fairness of rules was something to which transparency had relatively little to offer. But the growth of big data and surveillance systems has changed that and allowed us to start understanding in great detail the impact that the rules we adopt have on our lives.

We are interested in transparency in all circumstances where people are concerned at possible unfairness. In most cases, somebody suspects that the unfairness is deliberate and information is being withheld to allow the unfairness to go on unchecked. Equally, as the Gary Reinhart story shows, unfairness can occur as a result of people simply being unaware of the impact of their actions or the systems they work within. This is important. We want a concept of transparency that is indifferent to whether or not unfairness is deliberate.

If I suspect that I am being unfairly deprived of an opportunity to live because of how I have been treated by health services, there could be many explanations. It may have occurred because of rules that limit my access to treatment which I think are unfair. But, equally, it may happen because an avoidable human error resulted in an incorrect diagnosis. If it is cheap and easy to prevent such errors, I might argue that it was unfair on me not to have done so.

Similarly, I may opt for a treatment that proves to be ineffective or harmful because the pharmaceutical company has deliberately concealed information about its impact or because too little research had been done initially into the effects of the drug.

Again, I might argue that allowing low standards of research is unfair on patients and benefits pharmaceutical companies at the individual's expense.

Perhaps I have suffered because I waited too long for treatment. It might have happened because the resources given to my local health services were insufficient due to inaccurate projections of demand. Or it might have happened because government agencies have misappropriated the funds and used them to employ incompetent cronies. In our definition of transparency, these are all potential causes of behaviour that an individual might reasonably claim is unfair to them. Transparency in our definition occurs to the degree that I have access to information that allows me to evidence whether or not any of these things have occurred.

By defining transparency in this way, it does not apply primarily to organisations or individuals but to decision-making processes. Without saying that it should apply to all decision-making processes, we want a definition that can be applied to any process that requires information to be collected and a determination made as to how people should be treated as a result. Decision making is, in essence, nothing more than data processing. Transparency is nothing more than the rules over rights to create, store, access and manipulate information. By defining these rights in terms of decision-making processes we can identify how different arrangements are likely to end up with distortions in these processes.

Our contention is that a fair society can only exist where there is sufficient transparency to enable me to assent to the rules of that society and judge them as fair. Transparency is the means by which we can collectively agree that the allocation systems that regulate our lives – legal, administrative and market driven – are indeed fair.

The first and simplest way in which transparency can help ensure fairness is by allowing the public to play a role in ensuring that rules are applied correctly. The most basic form of corruption is the deliberate flouting of such rules for personal gain. Transparency of this sort is often used as an additional policing mechanism to support regulatory activity. To the degree that regulators are reliable and can be trusted, this process may not be seen as necessary. On the other hand, risks of regulatory capture (see Chapter 14) and the question of who guards the guardians are good reasons for believing that this level of transparency is necessary.

There is then a second way in which transparency ensures fairness – which is ensuring that the rules themselves are regarded as fair. But how do we judge if the rules are fair? Here, transparency is the *only* mechanism we have to try to reach a collective agreement. There is no expertise that can decide whether or not Gary Reinhart deserves a liver. It is a question we all have a legitimate stake in considering. It is only by knowing what the impact of the rules for organ transplantation means for individuals such as Gary Reinhart or across populations in different cities that we can decide whether we regard them as fair.

This same principle applies to questions over how much we spend on social support, health and education; how civil servants, teachers and judges are paid and managed; the rules that determine how financial services can be marketed; and the rules for determining when police can arrest people, how their behaviour is monitored and what determines whether they are promoted, sacked or pensioned off on full pay.

Some consequences of defining transparency in terms of fairness

Before setting out our model of transparency based on this definition we want to briefly address some issues that arise from it.

i. More information is not more transparency

One important consequence of this definition is that access to more information does not increase transparency. For example, if I can only access information presented in ways that support a particular narrative – a narrative that conflicts with what I believe to be true – it doesn't matter how much of it is put in the public domain, it does nothing to help me. Indeed, it can have the opposite effect of increasing the disadvantage I face in terms of access to information. We will in the course of this book look at some transparency initiatives which could be seen as doing precisely this.

Law courts are one of the few places that explicitly aim to create an environment of equal access to information in order to prevent either side in a trial having an unfair advantage over the other. In theory, anything material that one side has access to must be made available to the other. This is the law of discovery or disclosure in US and UK legal systems.

A tactic used by lawyers to undermine disclosure is over-disclosure. If you know that there is one file containing a vital piece of information that helps the other side's case, or one witness with a crucial statement to make, you can protect yourself by releasing not the one file but rather 15,000 files with that one hidden amongst them; and to release the name of the witness along with 15,000 names of other potential witnesses. That way you comply with the law but leave your opponent with little chance of finding the key pieces of information.

Equally, courts insist that statements made by one side must be open to cross-examination by the other. The same rules do not apply to political debate. A government can present evidence to support its policy case in such a way that no one else is able to check the validity of its statements. This can potentially have the effect of decreasing transparency by enabling the organisations supposedly being transparent to increase their informational advantage by placing claims in the public domain that cannot be challenged.

Transparency, then, is not the same as simply making more data available to people or increasing rights of access to information. If the form of the data is controlled by the organisation that I wish to be more transparent, or if the rights of access are sufficiently constrained by it, it will do little or nothing to enable me to hold it to account.

Transparency is not about the quantity of information available; it is about the relative degree of control over that information between parties with conflicting interests concerning what it can be used to evidence. Control of information is about much more than access. Control of information by organisations and individuals relates to the whole production and supply chain from the infrastructure that supports the recording, storage and use of information. Lack of transparency occurs when one side has an advantage that they can unfairly exploit at any stage of that process.

Selective disclosure or edited disclosure, in which the subject of transparency has been able to exercise control over the information to their advantage, can reduce transparency rather than increase it. What matters is transparency that gives me equal or similar narrative power – the ability to build a case, whether in a court of law or in the press. For transparency to work it needs to put narrative power into the hands of those who lack executive power.

ii. Fairness underpins the wider benefits of transparency

Defining transparency in terms of fairness is not intended in any way to diminish the importance of many other benefits that have been ascribed to transparency, including economic growth, more efficient public services and more empowered individuals and communities. We go into the benefits of our approach in more detail below, but at this stage want to point out that we see these viewpoints as wholly consistent with fairness providing the strongest underpinning principle.

We would argue that from the point of view of society – where the priority is the most efficient way to deliver social benefit – the fairest arrangement is also the most efficient.[9] If I am taxed to pay for a public service or a public good it is unfair on me if I am taxed more than necessary because the money is not used as efficiently as possible. Equally, it is unfair on the service users if they receive a substandard service as a result. Similarly, in a fair competitive market, more efficient providers of goods and services are able to offer me better value products and services. If something is preventing that from happening, it is unfair on me either as a consumer or as a competitive provider.

---

[9] It is important to distinguish between efficient and cheap. Cheaper justice will, in the main, be less accurate justice. Efficient justice is that which maximises accuracy within tolerable limits for the least amount of money. The degree to which inaccuracy is tolerated is a matter for society to determine.

Corruption occurs when governments hand contracts to the less efficient companies, when police arrest the innocent, when money allocated for vaccines is spent on presidential swimming pools or students are denied an education because absent teachers are promoted. These are all examples of unfairness and inefficiency.

Efficiency occurs when investors correctly categorise investments according to their likely return, consumers correctly categorise products according to the benefits and harms they produce, employers correctly categorise employees for promotion or redundancy according to their value, government departments correctly categorise services for funding allocations. For a health system to be efficient doctors must correctly categorise patients and treatments to allocate medical resources to those most in need, while those in charge of budgets must correctly categorise doctors and healthcare organisations according to their effectiveness in order to fairly allocate resources. In the same way, local planners correctly categorise applications according to their impact on the local community in order to allocate building permits fairly.

Allocative decisions apply to how people use their time and resources in work as well. Job roles are defined by rules around how time should be used and what behaviours are expected at different times, as well as rules about what constitutes acceptable performance in a role and ways of determining when and how people are removed from jobs. All of these decisions will be looked at from the point of view of transparency and how transparency can make the rules fair.

iii. Transparency as a right must be weighed against conflicting rights

Transparency is about assigning rights over control of information. This will at times conflict with other rights, such as ownership rights over information that may lie with governments, professionals, companies or other individuals as well as rights to privacy. There are numerous instances in which these rights directly conflict with each other. Defining transparency in terms of fairness provides a basis to weigh up the relative merits of transparency as a right, in so far as it is necessary for people to assure themselves that they are assenting to a fair system as opposed to the rights of others to limit their access to information. So, for example, there are instances where arguments of commercial confidentiality are outweighed by people's rights to ensure that they are not being sold unsafe products or that regulators are adequately protecting them from that risk.

Efficiency is not an ethical issue. However, to the extent that inefficiency results in me getting rough justice, an inadequate education or pot-holed roads when it was not necessary, then I have a grievance. And if transparency could have spared me that, I have a legitimate reason to question why the necessary information is not used appropriately.

Fairness is the relevant issue when it comes to considering the impact of transparency, because unfairness is the ethical justification for imposing the costs of transparency and for overriding other ethical imperatives such as privacy or commercial confidentiality.

iv. Fairness is relevant to scientific transparency

Fairness is also the relevant consideration when considering other benefits such as knowledge and accuracy. For example, in diagnosing patients – that is, assigning them to particular diagnostic categories – the question of fairness might seem irrelevant compared to the issue of whether or not the diagnosis is correct. But to the extent that I am entitled to competent medical treatment and the effective use of publicly funded healthcare, incorrect diagnoses result in unfairness if I die because of poor quality decision-making processes when others do not. If I myself am paying, I am entitled to a certain level of proficiency for my money.

The reason for fairness being the overriding concept is that accuracy, as well as inaccuracy, has a cost. All decision processes – from criminal courts to genetic tests – operate at a level of inaccuracy and error. In judging what level of inaccuracy is tolerable, according to what is achievable or potentially achievable within the constraints of technology and cost, the question cannot be answered technically. It can only be answered by considering the degree to which the cost/benefit ratio of a given level of error is undesirable – that is, the degree to which the unfair consequences of error, such as people receiving the wrong treatments, are regarded as intolerable.

In other words, the question of whether money and resources should be put into improving the accuracy of diabetes diagnoses, or whether the threshold for public assistance is too high or too low, or whether we should lower the threshold of proof for incarceration, depends on what I consider fair given the balance of risks and benefits.

v. Complete transparency is unachievable

It is not possible to ever have enough information to definitively evidence whether someone's treatment is fair or not. It is possible to be wholly transparent about the rules by which decisions are made, but beyond that there are important limitations. First, the degree to which it is possible to know whether people have been improperly influenced is limited. In other words, where any decision process grants discretion to people, there is a degree of potential procedural unfairness that is essentially unknowable. Second, it is impossible to fully describe the impact and outcome of any allocation system. In the case of organ transplants the aim is to maximise the health benefit in terms of life expectancy. But the best that can be done is to maximise the expected benefit based on the information it is possible and reasonable to know about patients and, from that, derive imperfect forecasts based on typologies of patients that treat groups of similar but not identical individuals as the same, while trying not to take into account any factors that might be unintentionally discriminatory. It is a process that by its nature is imperfect. The best we can do is to maximise the opportunities to identify harm and expose unfairness.

4

Fair allocation systems

In *Tragic Choices* two law professors, Guido Calabresi and Philip Bobbit, outline the various options open to society in allocating scarce resources.[1] They describe four basic mechanisms – markets, politically accountable systems of allocation, lotteries and 'custom'. The book points out that the last is really an attitude that informs the other three. To the degree that politically accountable systems operate in ways that are not accountable, or markets operate in ways that are not open, they could be said to be working according to custom and practice.

The authors were interested in 'tragic' allocations such as the allocation of donated organs or the imposition of military service - situations where the inevitability of inflicting serious harm on someone make us question our 'ultimate values'. These decisions expose the unavoidable inconsistencies in our values – that human life is priceless, and yet society must put a price on life; that all are equal before the law, yet money can buy you a better chance before the judge.

The book says: 'Honesty is the most influential brace in the tragic equilibrium. Though subterfuge may bring us peace, for a while … honesty permits us to know what is to be accepted and, accepting, to reclaim our humanity and struggle against indignity' (p 26).

The conflicting values that make tragic allocations difficult also make trivial allocations difficult. We tend to not worry about the latter because the consequences are trivial. However, an individual's life can be shaped by a series of trivial decisions

---

[1] Guido Calabresi and Philip Bobbit, *Tragic Choices,* W.W. Norton, 1978.

in ways that can have equally tragic consequences. For that reason, we believe that honesty, in Calabresi and Bobbit's words, is important to all allocation systems. Honesty here is the degree to which we acknowledge the failures we tolerate and the trade-offs we make. Honesty is about transparency.

We want to extend our definition of fairness as follows: fairness is the correct application of fair rules – where fair rules are the rules found to be those most in sympathy with the values of the individuals within a free society assuming a fair exchange of information. Transparency is the means by which we ensure a fair exchange of information.

When a school decides whether a child should go up to the next grade at the end of the year or stay down for an extra year they consider a range of evidence and make a decision. The child or the parents may feel that they have made the wrong decision and may protest. In some cases the decision will be wrong and may have an effect on the child's life. It may be wrong because the school is incompetent in making the decision. It may be wrong because the information they had in front of them at the time was insufficient or inaccurate. It may be wrong because the rules by which such decisions are made are inadequate and don't take account of important factors. Or they may have made the decision because they are corrupt – because they have given the space in the next grade to another child whose parents have recently donated money to the school library.

The question of whether such a decision is fair or not can be assessed first by reference to the rules by which the decision is supposed to be made. Is the school entitled to decide or does the parent have a say? If the school can decide what evidence should it consider if any? Does it have to follow a particular process – for example, to inform the parents of its reasons? If the decision was made in a way that did not comply with the rules we can say that is unfair. In some circumstances we might say it is corrupt.

Then there is the question of whether it is fair by appeal to some broader notion of fairness. Maybe the decision did abide by the rules but nonetheless is regarded by many as unfair because following the rules produces results or outcomes that strike us as not what was intended. In this case, perhaps the rules are unfair and need to be changed. Or perhaps the rules are seen as being the fairest that can be realistically achieved.

Whether or not your child goes up at the end of the year starts with the decision of the class teacher. If you were unhappy you might lodge a complaint with the head teacher, which might then go to the school governors or, if still not resolved, to an independent review panel. If the decision goes the wrong way this may lead to a challenge in the courts or a campaign to have the school governors replaced, which if it fails may lead to a campaign to change the law, which may lead to a political campaign to repeal the existing legislation.

Transparency is the degree to which access to information is liable to result in a fair outcome.

A model of allocation systems

Lotteries are rarely used in allocation systems. The two basic drivers of allocation systems are individual agency and decisions by politically accountable authorities – bodies granted legal authority to act in particular ways. Markets are where allocation decisions are driven primarily by individual agency – decisions for which people or organisations do not have to account to anyone but themselves – decisions about what one person wants to offer and another wants to accept. 'Adjudications' refer to allocations driven by decisions by politically accountable authorities tasked with policing the permissible range of individual agency, authorising controlled activity and preventing that which is banned.

Every allocation involves a combination of markets and adjudications. In the UK, shoes are allocated primarily by the market and healthcare is allocated primarily by adjudication (by both administrators and doctors). But while one may be more salient than another in any situation, *all* allocation processes involve a combination of adjudication and market.

In the market for shoes, regulators determine the scope of what is a safe product to sell; the terms on which people can be employed in shops and factories to make and distribute shoes; the mechanisms by which shoes can be advertised, priced and sold; and a host of other relevant factors. Within those constraints, people can buy whatever shoes they can afford. The market element is the more salient feature because the individual's wealth and tastes and the success of companies in meeting public demand at a low price are the most obvious drivers of who gets what shoes.

In university applications the balance between market and adjudication is more balanced. There is a market in that students choose to apply to particular institutions. There is adjudication in that there are rules around who can offer university degrees and within this, how admissions officers determine which students to accept – a role that must be performed according to certain rules of fair access. Adjudication plays at least as big a role as individual agency because universities get more applications than they have places and they are not free to distribute them in any way they choose (for example, by selling them to the highest bidder).

The allocation of negative goods such as tax obligations or jail time is primarily an adjudication process, but agency still plays a role. Indeed, the aim of such systems is often to incentivise individual agency – that is, to persuade people not to commit crimes or to stop particular activities.

There is very rarely if ever a single organisation that gets to determine the end result of an allocation process.

Transparency in allocation systems

Transparency is used to describe three different types of information flow in relation to such systems. These are:

1. Input information transparency.

   These are efforts to improve the accuracy of allocation systems by improving the quality and completeness of information available to people making decisions. It is used most often in relation to market mechanisms. Forced disclosure is intended to improve the agency of buyers by enabling them to better identify goods that will meet their needs. However, regulatory disclosure requirements in some industries are there primarily to inform the regulator rather than the public. The request for such information by the regulators is designed to improve the quality of input information used in their decisions. The publication of such information provides procedural transparency around the operations of the regulators.

2. Procedural transparency.

    This refers to the degree to which the application of rules and the operation of allocation mechanisms are observable in order to ensure that everyone is playing by the rules. This relates primarily to political forms of transparency around adjudications being carried out in a public manner, whether through open courts and legislatures or through making the documentary records of executive bodies open to public view. However, procedural transparency can be important in markets as well. For example, in financial and commodity markets visibility of the trades by other market participants can be part of ensuring a fair and efficient market.

3. Outcome transparency.

    This refers to the degree to which the results of allocation processes are observable. This is seen most often today in government efforts to measure and publish information about its performance and its success in, say, increasing employment or reducing public debt. It is seen in the measurement of the education and health system to try to understand how public resources are being used to bring about public good. It is seen in publications of key performance indicators (KPIs) by market regulators.

Arguments to increase input transparency are commonly made on the grounds that lack of input information is distorting the outcome of market allocation processes – customers are unable to identify correctly the products and services that meet their needs.

Within public services, transparency is promoted on the grounds that public services organisations are misallocating resources, sometimes corruptly, and are failing to provide adequate services either through ignorance or insufficient incentive. This leads to calls for more process transparency about the way decisions are made or the way in which resources are allocated – for example, are everyone's requests being processed within an acceptable time.

Figure 4.1: Information flows and allocation systems

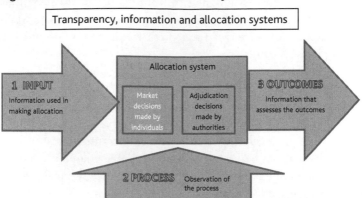

The same piece of information can play a role in different ways. For example, the more that adjudications are based on specified input information, the more it is possible to observe the decision-making process. If a committee meeting has no paperwork and a vote is simply taken after a brief discussion to demolish a park, it would be very hard to observe the thinking behind the decision since it has largely happened inside the heads of the members or in discussions elsewhere.

In many areas of public regulation, the 'input' information used to inform decisions about the performance of organisations is also used as the 'outcome' information to assess whether the system is working. So, for example, educational attainment data is used both to inform regulatory actions and to assess the impact of regulatory actions. These situations create *conflicts of interpretation* which distort the information and the allocation process (see Chapter 14).

Calls for transparency tend to focus on points 1 (inputs) and 2 (process) because people who are concerned about unfairness reckon they have identified the mechanisms by which they are being duped. They either believe that information is being withheld from them as voters, consumers or investors or they believe that people are concealing nefarious actions from view and that by being forced to open up their processes to observation it will be possible to stop this.

There is a natural tendency to be sympathetic to such calls since it seems likely that improving transparency in the form of inputs and process will also improve 3 (outcome). But as the critics of transparency have pointed out, this is not necessarily true (see Chapter 2). There are situations where changing the input information will make the allocation system worse. There are many examples from regulation where making the process more data driven has diminished the quality of the allocation system by creating easily gameable rules, that waste resources and give misleading signals to regulators. In some markets increasing information has led to perverse results (for example, disclosure of executive pay). Making some decision processes observable has also constrained the quality of deliberation (for example, central bank interest rate setting).

Process transparency has the appealing characteristic that, in theory, you can spot the unfair allocation while it is happening and prevent it. In contrast, outcome transparency can only occur, by its nature, after the decision has been made – which often means after it is too late to do anything about it. However, outcome transparency has the advantage of being less disruptive to the process of allocation and less prone to creating perverse incentives.

Four ways of evidencing unfair allocations

We can broadly categorise four different ways in which someone might evidence unfair treatment. First, there is the question of whether they are claiming that the rules were ignored or the rules themselves are unfair. This is in effect arguing that the process was not followed or that the outcome is indefensible.

Unfair processes and unfair outcomes can each be evidenced in two ways. First there is evidence drawn from individual cases such as Gary Reinbach's. Then there is evidence based on populations, such as the evidence showing that people were more likely to get a liver transplant if they lived in an area with competing hospitals.

This gives us four different possible ways of evidence unfairness which are set out in Table 4.1. Individual evidence aims to show that in a specific case somebody has been treated unfairly or that a particular decision has been made unfairly, either on the grounds of the process not being followed or because the outcome is unsupportable. Population evidence does not necessarily prove that a specific individual has been unfairly treated but provides evidence that somebody almost certainly has been mistreated. It is not always helpful to try to draw a distinction between the use of population data in demonstrating that the process is not being following or that the outcome is unfair. Often the latter is used as evidence that the process must be failing. Also, particular pieces of information can be viewed as the outcome of one particular process (getting the tests done in time) but one step in a broader process (treating the patient).

Table 4.1: Ways of evidencing unfair allocations

	Individual	Population
Process	One or more patients wrongly refused treatment because incorrect information was used. *Examples of transparency in this area* Publication of rules, trials held in public, committee meetings held in public Disclosure of commission that reveals a broker's conflicts of interest Disclosure of individual records showing incorrectly recorded information Providing marked examination papers back to pupils	Evidence that doctors in towns with competition were more likely to list patients for transplantation. *Examples of transparency in this area* Evidence that politicians taking donations from companies are blocking changes in relevant safety regulation Publication of waiting times for processing applications/treating patients by district Class sizes by district that exceed maximum limits
Outcome	A decision affecting an individual or group where the outcome seems wrong despite being correct within the rules. *Examples of transparency in this area* Access to credit ratings Gary Reinbach being denied a liver	Evidence of systematically worse outcomes for population groups, such as that the transplantation rules disadvantage African-Americans *Examples of transparency in this area* Rates of university access, job appointments by ethnicity Rates of government contracts going to smaller businesses Rates of air pollution by city

A more useful distinction to make is between what we might term the 'allocation outcome' of a process and the 'social outcome'.

- *The allocation outcome* is the direct results of a specific allocation – how long a case took to deal with, what they received and what they were denied.
- *The social outcome* is the supposed benefit or disbenefit that the allocation is intended to deliver.

So, for example, an allocation outcome might be somebody receiving an education inasmuch as they are given a place at school. But if they leave without knowledge or skills, the intended social outcome has not occurred. Someone may be jailed for a crime – the correct allocation outcome – but if they regard jail time as a normal part of life rather than a hardship, and if they are in no way dissuaded from future crime, it is debatable whether the intended social outcomes such as punishment and deterrence have been achieved.

If we look only at the allocation outcomes in assessing the fairness of social arrangements, we are likely to miss the point. It is of little use if society meets some technical criteria of fair allocations if the real outcomes are widely regarded as intolerable. The challenge for transparency is making visible the complexity of real world outcomes.

USING DATA TO EVIDENCE UNFAIRNESS: CAR LOANS
People often don't know they are being treated unfairly. And those treating then unfairly may be equally ignorant of what they are doing. The idea that people's lives might be tragically constrained not by large dramatic decisions but instead by a succession of small apparently insignificant decisions is illustrated by the story of Betty and Robert Cason of Tennessee.

The unfairness that they suffered was to take out a loan on which they were overcharged $3000. In the grand scale of injustice that may not seem much. But it provides an insight into how decisions can be biased in ways that are not obvious and which cumulatively could have a big impact.

The loan in question was for a Nissan car. They were pleased to be offered a loan to buy the car and accepted the offer of an 18% interest rate unaware that this was not the rate they would have been offered had they been white and not African American.

The first evidence that the system was stacked against them came from the work of Ian Ayres, a professor of both law and management at Yale. He arranged for researchers to approach car showrooms and, using a standard script, get the best offer they could on a car loan. The resulting papers published in 1991 and 1995 showed that researchers from African-American and Hispanic backgrounds were given consistently higher quotes than white applicants with the same details.

Ayre's research provided evidence that, in theory, there was a problem but it was not enough to make a case in court that any specific person had been discriminated against. However it did prompt people to come forward – people such as the Casons – which led to the filing of a class action suit against the Nissan Motor Acceptance Company (NMAC).

Evidence that, in general, there may be a problem with racial discrimination does not prove that a particular organisation has discriminated against a specific individual. Key to making the case against Nissan was the court's decision to make NMAC hand over complete records of its loan book to analysts working for the plaintiff.

An amicus brief from the Department of Justice pointed out the need to do this, saying: 'The Casons propose to establish a prima facie case of discrimination using statistical analyses based on data derived either from NMAC's business records or from public sources. The district court should be able to decide the validity of the Casons' statistical proof without conducting individualized hearings for each class member', and adding: 'a class action is superior to individual litigation in adjudicating the sort of disparate impact claim presented here' because of 'the enormous complexity and expense of proving such a claim; the financial disincentive for claimants to pursue individual actions; and the likelihood that most class members will never know about their alleged injury unless notified in connection with the class action'.[2]

---

[2]   www.justice.gov/sites/default/files/crt/legacy/2010/12/14/cason.pdf

In other words, if we left it to every individual to try to correct relatively minor but systematically unfair allocations they would, most likely, never get corrected. It would allow the possibility that a society could, with impunity, significantly disadvantage certain groups through a proliferation of small insults.

The way in which the discrimination in auto loans operated is instructive. It is not clear that anyone at any time acted with racist motivation or with deliberate intent to disadvantage certain people. Sales staff in car showrooms had leeway to mark up interest rates above the rate offered by the lender and total discretion as to how they used this. No one intended that such a mechanism would be used to the detriment of ethnic minorities.

Mark Cohen, a professor at Vanderbilt, worked with Ayres and a group of plaintiffs to take a class action against the industry. Crucially, this then enabled them to demand access to the underlying raw data about loans. As Cohen explains:

> During the course of the legal discovery process, the defendants in these cases were compelled to provide plaintiffs with individual customer records including information maintained on their credit application, loan details, and payment history. Overall, more than 20 million customer records were analyzed, covering six captive auto lenders and five financial institutions between 1993 and 2004.

He had only been able to look at the data because of the court case:

> Because of proprietary and consumer privacy concerns, these data were not available to the public. Instead, they were made available to both plaintiff and defence experts under strict court orders not to divulge confidential information or to use the data outside the confines of these lawsuits. Thus, the information reported here is based solely on reports made public throughout the litigation process.

The data themselves did not contain any record of the race of the borrower. On its own it was useless. But having it in this raw format along with the social security number as an identifier, Cohen was able to link the data to public records of drivers' licences. In some states this information is confidential. In 14 states it is not, including California with a population of over 30 million people. The driving licence data included both social security number and race. By linking them, Cohen was able to create a data set for millions of transactions that included full details of the transaction plus the ethnicity of the driver.

His analysis revealed a very clear pattern. African-Americans were typically charged around double the mark-up that white borrowers paid.[3] The car loan companies settled the cases, imposed caps on mark-ups and made payments back to disadvantaged borrowers.

The case put together by Cohen was challenged on the grounds that his analysis did not take account of all the factors that might have influenced the different rates. The level of detail in the data he held enabled him to rule out many explanations – for example, he could see how many different quotes were obtained for each borrower in some data sets, enabling him to confirm that higher rates did not reflect more work by the salesmen finding a quote. Similarly, he could see that the amount of time it took to get a quote – which might have reflected additional risks or complexities in particular cases – did not explain away the bias. Among people given instant quotes, African-Americans were still systematically disadvantaged. Despite this, before settling, the defendants called into question how reliable this evidence was and argued that there might be many other factors that needed to be considered, such as the overall package including the model of car being bought and the total price paid.

Access to detailed granular identifiable or re-identifiable data is essential for this type of work. It is difficult to isolate a particular relationship between events from observational data across populations. Whatever explanation you come up with for particular patterns, it is impossible to rule out the possibility of other explanations and wholly different drivers for the patterns seen. Creating robust narratives from population data needs to be done from disaggregated data sets that contain the important and relevant variables for each event.

---

3   Mark A. Cohen, *Imperfect Competition in Auto Lending: Subjective Markup, Racial Disparity, and Class Action Litigation*, Vanderbilt University Law School Law and Economics Working Paper No 07-01, 2008, pp 8, 9.

5

Population-level transparency

Two children, faced with a single slice of pie, have developed what is, perhaps, the world's most perfect allocation mechanism: 'you cut, I choose'. One child cuts the pie in two, the other picks the piece they prefer. It does not guarantee that they will get equal slices, but it does guarantee that neither party can complain afterwards they were unfairly treated. If you feel you got too small a slice, it can only be because you failed to cut the pie evenly or you picked the wrong piece.

A fair society is built on fair institutions – institutions that do not guarantee a particular outcome for any individual but which embody a natural justice and which can be seen to be fair. 'You cut, I choose' works because it combines complete transparency and the appropriate separation of powers - the building blocks of fair systems.

More complex allocation decisions require more complex mechanisms. The idea of a jury trial is simple – separation of judge and jury powers to assess contested evidence from conflicting parties. But this simple idea requires complex implementation with reams of detailed rules and precedents that determine who is allowed to testify, how juries are selected, who is allowed to plead a case, what evidence is admissible and so forth. As institutions get more elaborate, the process becomes less transparent.

Despite their complexity, court rooms and elections are among our most transparent institutional arrangements for politically accountable allocations. This makes them expensive. Most decisions in life cannot be given that much time and attention. Instead decision making is handed to politically accountable executive bodies that make assessments and determine allocations. We attempt to ensure fairness with elaborate systems of operating rules and oversight procedures, including transparency requirements.

But, unlike the 'you cut, I choose' example, in more complex scenarios transparency around the rules and the process are insufficient to assess the fairness of the system. It is impossible to tell from an examination of the rules of such systems whether they are fair or not. This is for a number of reasons.

First there is the impossibility of objectively defining a mechanism that produces a uniquely fair outcome from a set of conflicting and inconsistent desires. This may seem common sense today, but when the institutions of the modern state were being first conceived in the rationalist thinkers of the 17th and 18th centuries there was optimism that this might not be so. One of the key moments in undermining such beliefs was economist Kenneth Arrow's demonstration that different ways of designing a voting system will produce differing results and none can be said to be a truer reflection of the underlying preferences of the population. Knowing that, how do we choose a voting system? By voting! Fair systems are organic and shifting social arrangements, not scientific or logical solutions to problems.

There is an additional problem that we might call the *perfect implementation fallacy*. The fairness of systems depends on how the rules work in practice. For example, assigning an individual the responsibility to act impartially and to consider various issues in making a determination does not cause this to happen. People are imperfect. To defend an allocation process as fair, it is necessary not only to show that it would be fair if it had all been implemented exactly as intended. It also needs to be shown that people do implement it in this way.

This fallacy disappears when we consider purely machine-driven allocation systems. The error rate in such systems is clearly a function of the design of the algorithms that determine the allocation. When humans are involved, there is a temptation to regard failures that occur through human error as something that is not a function of the design of the system but the result of human weakness that should not be tolerated. This is flawed as the whole system of responsibilities and regulations is designed to produce appropriate decisions from the people involved. Rates of human error – whether driven by corruption, ignorance, prejudice or other inevitable human frailties – should be viewed as an aspect of the design of the allocation mechanisms. To do otherwise is to disown appropriate responsibility. This is not to say that accountability, blame and punishment will not form part of the mechanisms used. It is only to argue that it is not an adequate response to say, once such arrangements are in place, that their failure to produce perfect outcomes reflects only on the individuals and not the on the allocation system.

This viewpoint can be uncomfortable because of the 'tragic' nature of certain allocations. Accepting that a rate of false conviction is a necessary and inevitable part of any judicial system is less comfortable than maintaining that such a system could, in theory, operate perfectly. We are sometimes tempted to argue from the fact that no one intended any particular false conviction to occur that it is reasonable to say that 'the system is not intended to produce any false convictions' or that 'the system will not necessarily produce false convictions'. Both statements are disingenuous as it is certain that the system will produce false convictions given enough time – and that 'enough time' can be a very short period. What matters is not our intentions but the way that the system works in the real world. Our responsibility is to try to understand the rate of false convictions and to minimise it, while accepting that it cannot be eradicated. This cannot be ascertained by looking at the rules.

Not only is it impossible to assess the fairness of a system from observing the rules, it is impossible to assess it by observing the processes of executive authorities. This is because those operating the process can, in many circumstances, conceal corrupt motivations such as prejudice, favouritism or bribery. In some cases they will not be aware of these themselves. Furthermore, the intention of the allocation system is often to produce a social outcome that is not observable until some time after the process has occurred.

Calls for transparency are often driven by a belief that executive authorities are being improperly influenced, that they are concealing evidence of their failings or that they are prejudiced in their actions. None of these things are permitted under the rules. However, the degree to which they occur or are prevented by particular arrangements of rules, punishments, appointment systems or oversight is unpredictable. The degree to which process transparency limits such activity is open to question as all of these things can occur without being visible in any way by observing public committee meetings or reading the records of such meetings.

The benefits of population level transparency

The argument that observation of the rules and processes is rarely sufficient to assess fairness is not an argument against implementing this form of transparency. In many situations, this will be the most effective form of transparency. However, there are a number of situations where population-level transparency and outcome transparency are more effective in evidencing the fairness or otherwise of systems.

i. Population-level outcomes can reveal concealed motives and policies

When the Kenyan victims of British rule took their case to the high court, a key part of getting their case heard was not just their own testimony but the historical research conducted by Caroline Elkins in interviews with hundreds of people. Their case rested on demonstrating government complicity in the events. Evidence that hundreds of people had experienced the same treatment gave credibility to the claim that mistreatment was systematic and orchestrated. It seemed improbable that mistreatment would be so consistent if it were not being guided by some degree of central policy. The ability to demonstrate that the abuse is systematic can be a central part in presenting any case of human rights abuse.

ii. Some biases in allocation systems are unobservable except in population outcomes

Process transparency is designed to prevent people secretly conspiring to misapply the rules. But this only works if the behaviour is deliberate. In some cases, it is enough just to show that processes are systematically producing a particular outcome, with or without any evidence of deliberate intent. This is what happened when the car hire industry was shown to systematically charge higher rates of interest to African-Americans and other minority ethnic groups.

A number of cases were taken against the car hire industry which resulted in the courts ruling that information had to be handed over to academics working with the plaintiffs. They were able to successfully demonstrate that African-Americans were typically charged around double the mark-up that white borrowers paid.[1] The rental companies settled the cases, imposed caps on mark-ups and reimbursed disadvantaged borrowers.

It is entirely unclear whether salespeople were consciously and deliberately charging higher rates to African-Americans or whether they were acting on some other impulse. It may have been entirely subconscious for some dealers – they may have simply offered their best rates to those they felt warmest towards, or those they felt were likely to be the most knowledgeable customers. Subliminal racial bias did the rest. However, the law – the moral principle – is clear that the intentions are not what matters. What matters is the result. Allocation systems are fair to the degree that they are not prone to error and bias, regardless of the cause of that bias.

iii. Accuracy of assessment and categorisation is essential to fair allocations and is best assessed from population data

Adjudication systems put people and objects into different categories or score them in ways that allow them to be processed. People are categorised as guilty or innocent; approved for a second interview or not; eligible for medical treatment or eligible for a tax break. They are put through a series of processes that generate information about them (interrogation, blood tests, examinations, form filling) which is then used to put them

---

[1]   Mark A. Cohen, *Imperfect Competition in Auto Lending: Subjective Markup, Racial Disparity, and Class Action Litigation*, Vanderbilt University Law School Law and Economics Working Paper No 07-01, 2008.

into various categories (diabetic, guilty of speeding, eligible candidate and so on).

These processes are the same from an abstract formal point of view, but we treat them very differently. Categorisations from different sources are treated as if they are qualitatively different when they are not. Some categorisations are regarded as impositions – for example the categorisation of people by marketing companies into groups with a propensity to buy certain types of products. Some categorisations tend to be regarded as 'facts' about a person – for example a diagnosis. Others as seen as being 'assessments' of that person or 'decisions' about that person – for example an exam grade is an 'assessment' of an individual.

With an exam grade we are more conscious of the fact that it is an imperfect attempt to put someone into a category, whereas with a diagnosis we would prefer to think of it as a truth about that person. We would like to believe that diagnostic processes can be 100% accurate and error free whereas there is something disquieting about the idea that an exam system could produce an error-free and wholly truthful assessment of your abilities.

The way we speak about verdicts highlights our discomfort with this situation and our desire to believe in perfect allocation systems. Court verdicts are sometimes regarded as a 'fact' about the person and sometimes as a 'decision' about that person. Natural language is not good at distinguishing between 'he is guilty', meaning he was found guilty by a court, and 'he is guilty', meaning he is *really* guilty.

From the point of view of social allocations, they are all probabilities the accuracy of which can only be assessed in the light of future evidence by looking across populations. The accuracy of a diagnosis is the degree to which it identifies a set of people who share the characteristic of responding to a particular treatment. However accurate a diagnosis is in terms of the attributes that define it (for example, the blood pressure measures used to define hypertension), what matters is the degree to which it accurately identifies a medically homogenous group of people who benefit from a particular treatment. While some diagnostic processes are relatively precise and reliable, many others are not. A doctor signing something saying you have bipolar disorder may be a far less reliable categorisation of your mental health than a SAT[2] score is of your intellectual abilities.

Formally, they are identical – an assignment of a definitive categorisation to an individual based on data that is not wholly reliable. Both systems will have a rate of error in them. They will also, almost certainly, have various biases whereby the rate of error is higher and skewed when applied to certain groups of people.

With most allocation systems, we can get some fix on their level of accuracy and bias because in the period following the allocation decision, further information will come to light that will either confirm or refute the allocation.

In some cases this happens very quickly. In areas such as the marketing of products it is relatively easy to discover whether a particular categorisation of people is effective in identifying those most likely to respond to a particular sales pitch. There is a large industry devoted to it. In those areas where customers are able to correctly identify products that meet their needs this works to our benefit. In others, such as financial services, the ability to work out how customers tick can be used to their disadvantage.

In areas associated with public service, such as health, social care and education, our ability to understand how allocation systems are affecting people's lives is increasing rapidly. We are developing a better understanding of whether public resources are being allocated fairly for the benefit of populations and this is an area where we could do much more to identify error and bias. This is being achieved by the growth of data sets that let us see in more detail how interactions work at the individual level rather than relying on gross generalisations about averages.

In medicine, the information to assess whether we are diagnosing people accurately is increasingly available and growing exponentially. It has at times proved shocking in the degree to which it reveals inaccuracy in areas that had been considered relatively scientific. In some instances this is due to the lack of precision in the rules used for categorisation (for example in

---

2   SAT scores, or Scholastic Aptitude Tests, are standardised tests commonly used for admission to higher education in the US.

mental health). In others it is due to unreliable implementation of diagnostic processes resulting in error.

In education, the growth of public data sets and longitudinal surveys about the progress of pupils into adulthood is starting to give us a better insight into the degree to which education and qualification systems are working as we would hope.

Law enforcement, by its nature, is the area where it is hardest to assess the fairness of allocation systems because there is no mechanism which guarantees the future availability of information that would allow some assessment of past decisions. The guilty who evade conviction will most likely take their secrets to the grave.

However, occasionally, changes in technology have altered the boundary of what is knowable. When this happens we get some visibility of the accuracy of the system. The development of DNA technology in the 1990s made it possible, in some circumstances, to rule out certain suspects from rape cases[3] using the genetic profile of the assailant. The new technology made historical cases reviewable and resulted in a number of people in jail being found to be innocent. It has been estimated, based on the rate at which DNA evidence has consistently ruled out the prime suspect and on rates of conviction, that hundreds of people would have been jailed without this new form of evidence – the implication being that, in the past, such people have been wrongly jailed.

The increasing efforts being put into reviewing cases – particularly of those facing the death penalty – has led to estimates that 4.1% of people on death row in the US are there mistakenly.[4]

Such arguments do not mean that we abandon our system of justice because it is flawed (although it makes justification of the death penalty challenging). Instead it argues for concerted

---

[3]   Edward Connors, Thomas Lundregan, Neal Miller and Tom McEwen, *Convicted by Juries, Exonerated by Science: Case Studies in the Use of DNA Evidence to Establish Innocence After Trial*, Department of Justice, June 1996.

[4]   Samuel R. Gross, Barbara O'Brien, Chen Hu and Edward H. Kennedy, *Rate of False Conviction of Criminal Defendants who are Sentenced to Death*, Proc Natl Acad Sci USA. 2014 May 20; 111(20): 7230–7235; doi:10.1073/pnas.1306417111

efforts to monitor the degree to which courts are acting in a biased fashion. One group in New York has started an initiative to collect information on the parole system in order to 'enable data-driven research that will help identify existing problems and position decision makers well to solve them'.[5] With a clearer understanding of the behaviour patterns of different parole boards it will be better able to recognise biases or unfair variations.

iv. The level of absolute error and the level of bias need to be assessed separately in population data

The fact that a judicial system will result in false convictions is no reason not to have such a system. The degree to which such a system is fair depends on two things:

1. Is the overall rate of error reducible at a reasonable cost?
    The fact that a judicial system or any allocation system results in mistakes does not make it unfair. Society can only invest so much in court hearings and policing and we have no option but to tolerate a degree of error in such systems. We can still take the view that the system is fair so long as there is no systematic pattern to those errors. If the error will fall randomly on the next person, there is an argument for saying it is not unfair. If it is as likely that I will end up wrongly jailed as you will, then the unavoidable unfairness is distributed fairly and if as a society we chose to tolerate that risk, so be it.
    This does make inefficiency a matter of fairness. To the degree that we spend large amounts of time and money on regulation, courts, assessments and so on, and fail to achieve the lowest rates of error, people are entitled to feel unfairly treated. The question whether regulations are fair or not, the degree to which it is reasonable to impose restrictions on people, depends crucially on whether the time and effort spent enforcing those regulations is effective in resulting in a fairer allocation of goods across society. If they look correct

---

5   The Parole Hearing Data Project, http://www.lizday.com/parole-hearing-data-project-ideo/

in principle but in reality are achieving nothing, then they are unfair, not only on those regulated but on those whom the regulation is designed to protect since it wastes time and effort that might otherwise have been used effectively.

2. Is there a systematic bias against a community?
   Systematic rather than random error in a judicial system or any allocation mechanism provides a prima facie affront to natural justice. For example, if the error rate in the law courts was skewed so that the people being wrongly jailed were predominantly from one ethnic group, then it would fail most people's sense of fairness.

Fairness requires us to distinguish between systematic and random error. This is well understood by anyone operating an allocation mechanism and it is why failures are often ascribed to 'one-offs', temporary problems or 'bad apples'.

We have seen that population outcomes are essential in trying to understand the bias and skew in the errors of allocation systems. Without population-level transparency we cannot assess whether mistakes are systematic or random. Without assessing these aspects, it is not possible to judge whether they are fair or not.

But population-level transparency is also, we will argue, the best mechanism to identify the overall rate of error in allocation mechanisms and discover cost-effective ways to reduce it. Far more people die every day as a result of errors in diagnosis than errors in the conviction rate. The degree to which individuals are culpable is often tested in courts when doctors are sued and the process by which a decision was reached is examined in detail. Increasing obligations on health systems to share individual health records and impose a duty of candour on doctors, as has recently been introduced in the UK, may be helpful.

v. The skew of errors towards false positives and false negatives is an important aspect of the fairness of allocation systems

The error in all such systems can be described in terms of a number of dimensions. First there is the absolute scale of error – how often wrong categorisations are made. Second there is the question of whether these errors are random or systematic – does there seem to be some pattern that suggests a specific cause or a specific group affected? Lastly there is distribution of errors between false positives and false negatives – how many times are people excluded from a category who should be included and vice versa?

The degree to which a level of error is acceptable depends on the extent to which it is skewed towards false positives or false negatives. So, for example, it is generally agreed that the test of whether or not someone should go to jail should err on the side of avoiding false positives (innocent until proven guilty). The test of whether someone should hold a public position should err more towards avoiding false negatives, on the grounds that wrongly preventing a good man from becoming a judge is less problematic than allowing a corrupt man to become a judge.

There is no correct answer to the question of how allocation systems should skew the error rate. It is a question for societies to decide on the basis of transparent information. Take, for example, the question of acceptable levels of error in allocating credit through the market. There are significant social consequences that flow from misallocation of credit. The question of the right balance of risks, however, varies according to the market. In personal credit markets we may favour a skew against the risk of lending to people who cannot pay back their loans as personal debt can leave society picking up the tab. With business lending, by contrast, we may favour more of a skew towards higher risk loans because of the potential social benefit from economic growth.

The credit industry often employs the perfect implementation fallacy to argue that the market-clearing, profit-maximising rate of credit will be socially optimal since 'banks don't want to lose money by making bad loans'. This would only be true if banks could perfectly identify credit risk. The most profitable customer is often the customer who borrows the maximum they can, is unable to pay back the capital for a long period but just manages to make the interest payments. Given the imperfections of credit scoring, maximising the return from such people would require lenders to make a significant number of loans to people who borrow more than they can afford and end up bankrupt.

There is a logic in introducing responsible lending rules to combat this risk. However, it is not possible to tell from reading the rules or even from observing the individual decisions of loan officers whether they are having the desired effect. This can only be sensibly assessed by looking at the outcome across whole populations.

Our ability to know whether the regulation of markets, public services and government – including the imposition of transparency requirements – are resulting in fair allocation processes depends on the quality of our understanding of population outcomes.

The use of population outcomes in assessing fairness

There has been a long philosophical debate about the dangers of using the outcome of an allocation process as a consideration in determining the fairness of rules. Two US academics led opposing camps during the debate in the 1970s. John Rawls argued that a fair set of rules should be defined as one that produces a fair outcome.[6] Robert Nozick argued that you cannot both support a belief that a particular outcome determines whether or not rules are fair and support the view that some processes are inherently unfair.[7] Otherwise the ends can justify the means and excuse any act. If you regard certain ways of doing things as inherently wrong – such as torturing people – you cannot also hold the view that the fairness of a system depends on the outcome. At some point the two will conflict and you will have to pick one or the other.

Few would disagree with Nozick that a fair decision at any point in time must be one that results from applying the rules as agreed. Changing the rules in real time if you don't like the results you are getting fails the basic test of fairness. Most people would also agree that certain processes, often defined in terms of protection of human rights, are protected whatever the outcome that results.

---

[6]   John Rawls, *A Theory of Justice,* Harvard University Press, 1971.
[7]   Robert Nozick, *Anarchy, State and Utopia,* Basic Books, 1974.

It is also true that the imposition of rules designed purely to generate a given outcome – such as minority quotas – are uncomfortable. We want university places to be awarded on individual merit and quota systems cut across this. That does not mean quota systems cannot be justified. But such methods are always an ungainly kludge adopted when we cannot work out how to correct biases in the system too subtle for legal controls. They inevitably conflict with other values.

But while there are ways in which referring to the outcome in designing rules can be problematic, it is equally true that it is not possible to assess the fairness of rules without reference to the results they produce. Retrospective assessment of the outcomes produced by a set of rules is an important piece of evidence in assessing whether it is fair or not, and to refuse to consider it would be equally unjust. Achieving a particular outcome can never be the sole criterion by which rules are judged, but outcomes are an important consideration in assessing their fairness.

The main problem in Rawls' approach is that it assumes there is such a thing as 'the outcome' of a set of allocations. In reality, there are an almost infinite number of outcomes that all differ in the time frame you look at and what you choose to measure. This is the practical obstacle to using outcomes in assessing rules and one that requires new institutional arrangements.

It is essential to consider the outcomes of allocation systems to assess their fairness. But for that process to be fair, the way in which outcomes are defined and measured must be an open and democratic process. Whether a process appears to be fair or not depends on how you define an outcome, how you cut the data and what story you choose to tell. If the power to assess outcomes is monopolised or concentrated in the hands of particular institutions, we should not be surprised if we find ourselves in a society where a public narrative about how our society is fair jars with the experience of our own eyes and ears.

6

Equality of narrative power

Helena Hofbauer began trying to access information in Mexico in the 1990s. This was before there was a right to information law. She decided to try to find out how the government was spending public money. At the time, information on government budgets was hard to come by. She went to the offices of the comptroller three times a week to ask for more and more detailed information. 'They always gave me the wrong information. Incomplete information. So I would ask again. In the end they got so bored they gave me a desk in the building and left me to it.'[1]

She set up an organisation, Fundar, to start to compile and analyse budget information in order to expose unchecked discretionary spending. A key target was the practice of 'pork barrel' budgeting. This is the practice of legislators, representing particular constituencies, writing line items into budgets allocating money to their projects and interests – in effect using public money to reward their supporters. What should happen, she explains, is that representatives decide the overall budget and the principles as to how it should be allocated. The executive decides the particulars. Earmarking or pork barrel politics, as it is called, has been a prominent feature of both Mexican and US political systems. The US has had a moratorium on it since 2011, although some commentators continue to identify billions of dollars of spending they describe as earmarks.

The case that drew her particular concern arose from a congressional decision to spend more money on women's health.

---

[1]   Interview with author.

Extra funds were allocated, but the president of the budget committee wrote in line items detailing which organisations the money should go to. Fundar and five other groups campaigned around this case for several years, and used the new freedom of information (FOI) law to discover exactly where the earmarked money had gone.

One allocation was particularly concerning. The president of the budget committee had written in a provision of $30 million to an organisation called Pro-Vida. Fundar made a request under the new law for all documents relating to Pro-Vida. The information was provided to them in the form of boxes of receipts.

They were lucky. The law was new. 'It is fair to say they would not make the same mistake again. All the mechanisms that government has developed to hold back information - they had not even begun to imagine let alone put them in place.'[2]

With the raw receipts, Fundar was able to piece together exactly how each dollar had been spent. What emerged was an organisation that was spending money not only on lavish expenses and entertainments but also, more importantly, on programmes to directly undermine stated government policy. Health programmes were encouraging the use of contraception while Pro-Vida was using public money to actively campaign against the use of contraception.

The resulting report and furore prompted a government investigation. Although the government was embarrassed at the scandal, it had no sympathy for Pro-Vida. The audit confirmed Fundar's findings. The case established a new legal precedent - that someone running a private organisation spending public funds could be held to the same level of accountability as a public servant.

While that was a success, Helena recognises the limitations of what was achieved. Although at the end of the court case, the head of Pro-Vida was required to repay $10 million, 10 years later it has not happened. More importantly, the original objective of the campaign - to prevent legislators from having discretionary power over budgets - is entirely unchanged.

---

[2]   Interview with author.

This campaign has been highlighted as an example of transparency and access to information (ATI) working. But, as Helena points out, the truth is that Pro-Vida got away with it and the fault in the system of budget allocation that allowed it to occur remains unchanged.

When she reflects on what has been achieved, since she started there are areas of real progress. There is far more public information now available in Mexico, particularly in areas like budgets. But any idea that this might have a sudden and transformative effect is misjudged. 'This is a long hard war', she says.

But her key conclusion is that 'Information is not enough'. On its own it achieves nothing. Information has to be used in particular ways to leverage change. Campaigning for access to information needs to go hand in hand with putting in place the legal and constitutional arrangements that will enable people to act on information and bring about change.

Information can be used in many ways. It can be used to build cases against corruption that can be taken to court. But if the courts are corrupt, it will have no effect. Information can be used to help communities to engage with government consultation processes. But if the consultation processes are sham, it will not work. Information can be used to create opposition through stories in the press. But if the media are suppressed it will not work. Information can be used to shame the wicked. But if the wicked are shameless, the information will have no power.

Whether or not transparency can reduce government corruption depends on a range of factors. The belief that transparency can help reduce corruption is based on a particular view of corruption best summarised by economist Robert Klitgaard's[3] formulation that corruption is the consequence of monopoly minus accountability. If a person or organisation has a monopoly of discretionary control over a particular allocation, such as the awarding of a contract, and no accountability for how that power is used, we should expect corruption to occur.

---

[3]   Robert E Klitgaard, *Controlling Corruption*, University of California Press 1988

Many anti-corruption policies focus on the first part of the equation, reducing incentives by reducing discretionary monopolistic powers. E-government policies have been used to put government contracting onto transparent websites which have clear contracts and qualification criteria with all bids made public. A requirement that the best qualifying bid should win removes the possibility of corruption. Choice in public services takes away monopoly control over which services are used.

Transparency plays a role in these mechanisms, but it is more often advocated as a way to increase accountability. If my decisions and the reasons for my decisions are public, I can be held to account and punished if I am found to act corruptly.

But some types of corruption are less likely to be affected by transparency, at least in the short term. For example, clientelism or cronyism – where the political stability of the state is maintained by using revenue streams to illicitly pay off particular constituencies – is not something that is likely to change if exposed to public view, since the whole power structure is invested in these arrangements.[4] The most likely response to exposure is to do no more than restructure the illicit payments in order to remove them from public view.

It is beyond the scope of this book to explore the political dynamics that bring about the societal and institutional points of leverage necessary for transparency to have any impact. We hold on to the belief – the faith perhaps – that within every society there is some minimal point of leverage upon which information can work. Even in the most repressed societies, the gradual seeping of samizdat information from individual to individual, like ice breaking rocks, can help to build the force necessary to eventually break the grip of power. However, it is important to acknowledge the evidence that certain situations are much less likely to be affected in any short period of time by changes in control over information.

---

[4]   Mushtaq H. Khan, 'Determinants of Corruption in Developing Countries: The Limits of Conventional Economic Analysis' in *International Handbook on the Economics of Corruption*, ed. Susan Rose-Ackerman, Edward Elgar (2006), Cheltenham, p 216.

There is a chicken and egg relationship between the free flow of information and the institutions in a free society that can be used to turn information into pressure for change. Societies that are less corrupt tend to have greater freedom of information. But it does not follow that one causes the other to come into being. Rather, each one leverages the other. Information that reveals corruption in the courts can help to make courts a little less corrupt. Such courts can then use information to put corrupt judges behind bars. The hope is that, inch by inch, information and institutional reform will eat away at the abuse of the ignorant by the powerful and even spare us from our shared delusions.

In their review of transparency initiatives for the UK Department for International Development, Rosemary McGee and John Gaventa say that transparency policies often assume that information will result in some good without an explicit 'theory of change'. Theory of change, an idea that has come from the world of non-governmental organisations (NGOs) and aid donors, addresses the fact that people spending money - often public funds or money held in trust - to benefit others need some mechanisms to ensure that their actions are genuinely benefiting others and not just expressing good intentions.

A theory of change should be plausible, feasible and measurable. It is plausible if there is a sound logic as to how someone might benefit from a particular policy; it is feasible if, considering all the obstacles, there is decent chance that this logic will work in practice; and it is measurable if it is possible, in retrospect, to tell whether or not it did work.

Information is not enough

One way to address theories of change in relation to transparency is to consider how individuals or communities that believe they are being treated unfairly might be able to do something about it. We can think about this in terms of three questions:

1. *Access.* Do they have access to information that is, in theory, capable of being used to evidence whether someone is being treated fairly or not?

Are they capable of identifying whether allocations have been made in contravention of the rules? Are they capable of showing how outcomes from allocation decisions are likely to be unfair on them?

2. *Leverage.* How might they use that information to counter the problem they have identified?

   Could they use it to take the government to court, as the Kenyans did over torture? Could it be used to galvanise a community into political action? Could it inform people's choices of which services to use? Could it persuade a regulator to intervene?

3. *Capability.* Do the people who might wish to make this case have the capability to use the information in the way described?

   Capability starts with the ability to identify your own interests as an individual or a group and become organised. Even if communities are well organised or are represented by powerful regulatory organisations, there is a question as to whether they have the skill necessary to produce the information required to argue their corner. Can they turn information into evidence that would stand up in court? Can they turn it into a media story that would galvanise political action? There are specific skills needed in each case.

Table 6.1 lists a number of points of leverage through which access to information might result in some sort of change for the better. In each case, there are implications both for public policy (in terms of ensuring that the proposed point of leverage is effective) and implications for the capabilities in civil society to make use of that point of leverage.

The key point that we want to emphasise is that all of these mechanisms require more than just information. Information does not win a court case; information does not prompt an insurrection; information does not change my view of the world. No document, no data point, no single record has any particular impact unless it forms part of a narrative. It is when information is turned into a narrative that it has power.

If information is to be used to generate political support for change, it needs to be turned into a narrative setting out why the information implies that particular policies need to be opposed or reformed and how different communities would benefit as a result. If the target of such arguments is the broad population, the narrative will take a different form from that if their target is the much smaller number of people with executive power inside government.

Table 6.1: Ways of using information to produce change

Programmes	Instigator	Relevant areas	Civic society action	Government action (= ensure ATI+)
Consultation/ participation	Government	Budget allocation, policy formation, design of public services	Participate	Establish consultation mechanisms
Social audit/ public expenditure tracking	Government/ citizen	Delivery of public services	Conduct audit, take part in information collection and review, engage with local service provision	Act on the results of audit, correct errors and restore where there has been default
Political opposition	Citizens	Anything and everything	Protest, organise community representative and campaign organisations, voter organisation	Establish rights to free speech, rights of association, ensure diverse accessible media
Complaints/legal challenge	Citizens	Rights violations, unconstitutional actions, delivery of public services	Challenge executive actions in courts or through ombudsman	Establish appropriate citizen rights for example, to standards of public service and mechanisms to seek redress
Consumer and citizen choice	Citizens	Consumer goods and services, public services, utilities	Make informed choices. Discriminate between service providers or types of services	Establish effective markets, for example contested public services and utilities
Research and discovery	Government/ citizens	Anything and everything	Fund research, participate in research, establish effective media organisations	Support development of skilled research community

To work through market mechanisms, information needs to be turned into a marketing communication that promotes the benefit of one option over another. People rarely buy products or choose schools on the basis of a particular fact. Instead they have a narrative that explains why one option is better for this person than another. Consumer guides will often contain tables of information about different products, but they will also include a 'narrative' that summarises the details into a story of why this product is good and that product is bad.

The way that science and academia work is by testing hypotheses against available information. A hypothesis is a narrative. This might be a historical narrative of how political insurrection was quelled in Kenya or a medical narrative about how a particular form of therapy affects patients.

The power of transparency lies in the extent to which it gives different people the ability to create these narratives to make use of the various points of leverage. But the creation of such narratives is a complex area that requires specific skills.

This view of transparency argues that direct forms of transparency, in which organisations are required to give their own account of their activity, are of far less value than transparency that aims to enable others to put together their own narratives. Transparency fails if information is not amenable to the construction of any sort of useful narrative, whether it be about unfair political decisions, reasons to buy particular products or testing particular hypotheses.

The creation of useful narratives requires independent intermediation. A model of transparency based on Locke's view of conflicting interests, rather than Rousseau's view of honest government, implies that government cannot act on behalf of the people, not simply because it may have interests that conflict with citizens but because citizens have interests that conflict with each other. The aim of democratic accountability is to allow conflicting potential narratives to be created that are equally grounded in evidence. This can only work effectively if the power to create narratives is surrendered to a plurality of organisations within society.

The need for independent intermediation is not simply an issue of conflict of interest. It is also an issue of complexity. The examples cited throughout this book illustrate the degree to which effective transparency depends on the creation of specific narratives suited to different types of leverage – media stories are one type of narrative, direct marketing campaigns are another (see the Romania case study, Chapter 12). A case presented in court is an entirely different sort of narrative, a research report different again. The range and diversity of types of narrative required for the many different constituencies and interests within a society mean the task could never be done adequately without independent and specialised intermediation.

Evidence that direct transparency lacks effectiveness and independent intermediation is necessary comes from a range of sources. The evidence for the effectiveness of participatory development interventions suggests that 'induced participation' – where the government sets the terms of engagement and recruits citizens to participate – are ineffective whereas organic participatory projects can work.[5] Organic projects depend on the existence of independent community and civil society organisations (CSOs). If transparency is to play a role in such participatory programmes, it follows that the information should be channelled through such organisations.

In a review of ATI laws, Transparency International concluded that:

> In countries where the law is good on paper but has been introduced as part of a top-down government reform plan (Albania), international initiative (Bosnia), or lobbying from a civil society elite (Peru), implementation has proved slow. By contrast in countries such as Romania and Bulgaria, where broad-based coalitions pressed for access laws, the less-than-perfect statutes were then hungrily used by civil society, journalists, and members of the general public alike.[6]

---

[5] Ghazala Mansuri and Vijayendra Rao, *Localizing Development: Does Participation Work?*, World Bank, , © *World Bank*, https://openknowledge. worldbank.org/handle/10986/11859 License: CC BY 3.0 IGO.

[6] *Using the Right to Information as an Anti-Corruption Tool*, Transparency International, 2006.

Alina Mungiu-Pippidi's work for the EU on the impact of FOI on corruption also finds evidence of the importance of civil society organisations, concluding that: 'transparency is a highly significant predictor of corruption at equal levels of rural population, informality and civil society. This also implies that in highly informal and rural societies, with fewer civil society organizations, its role is weaker or might be cancelled'.[7]

This is challenging for governments, which fear that access to data by political opponents will allow them to twist the information and deliberately create false narratives to undermine the government. Direct transparency has the appeal of placing the government in a heroic light whereas intermediated transparency tends to have a bias in the opposite direction. A key strategy for CSOs is to make transparency effective by making a clear distinction between 'civic' political action and 'party political' activity.

But at this stage we simply want to set out the view that for most of the mechanisms capable of having any influence on government a necessary component is the construction of a narrative independently from government.

The creation of effective narratives requires specific information. To make a case in court, you need the key pieces of evidence that together make a convincing argument. If just one crucial piece is missing, the case collapses. To make a political argument, you need information that is relevant to the specific argument you are making about particular constituencies. General information is of no use to you. For a scientist to test one hypothesis against another, the data required is entirely specific to that hypothesis. Related information in the same topic area but captured in a slightly different way is not partially useful or of some interest — it is wholly useless.

For transparency to be effective, it is not just that you need both information and a mechanism of change but that the two need to be complementary. If you have information and a

---

[7]   Alina Mungiu-Pippidi, *FOIA as an Anti-Corruption Tool*, European Research Centre for Anti-Corruption and State-Building Working Paper No 34, 2013.

mechanism, but the information does not fit the mechanism, transparency will achieve nothing.

We will make the case that fitting the information to the mechanism can only realistically be achieved by abandoning direct transparency and recognising that it will only work through civil society organisations. We will further argue that it is only by allowing such organisations access to data in its raw form that we can achieve the sort of pluralistic society in which citizens have the possibility of telling their narratives and control of information is not used to control public discourse.

Plural and equal access to data

Outcome transparency in particular requires a democratisation of narrative power. Consideration of outcomes is essential to understanding the fairness of rules. However, the problem with this position is that it is impossible to define and measure the outcome of any set of allocation processes. It is truer to say that there are an almost infinite number of outcomes, none of which are knowable at the moment when you determine and apply a set of rules. From a practical perspective, the best you can do is weigh up evidence of the likely distributions of different outcomes at different time periods as a result of a particular set of allocation rules.

For any person at any moment there are many different positive and negative aspects of their situation which will shift over time. My wealth at any one moment could be viewed as the outcome of a process or as a contributing factor to a future outcome which may be beneficial or harmful.

So, for example, one justification for welfare to work programmes has been the evidence that unemployment benefits for people with depression have increased the individual's wealth at that time but reduced the rate at which they return to work. This latter effect can result in prolonged depression and reduced wealth in the longer term. If people think it is fair to raises taxes to pay these benefits in order to stop people living in unacceptably deprived circumstances, then the relative weight put on the more certain immediate outcome and the less certain long-term outcome is an important consideration.

Putting objective values on particular outcomes is another challenge. We now live in an age when even life itself is no longer regarded as necessarily desirable. Many people with long-term health conditions now opt for death over a life of prolonged pain. The development of measures such as 'healthy life expectancy' and happiness surveys reflects a concern that the outcome measures, such as national wealth and life expectancy, which have been used to assess the impact of public policy for most of the last century may be leading us in the wrong direction.

Even if we could agree on the use of a particular measure as a reasonable proxy for benefit to the citizen, we face great difficulties in measuring it accurately. The ability to measure people's real wealth in terms of access to resources is obscured by, amongst other things, the extent of the informal economy as well as the nature of support networks within families and communities. Recent revelations that many of Japan's centenarians are, in fact, dead have shown how hard it can be even to keep accurate records of which citizens are alive and which are dead.[8]

If we want to use the outcome as a consideration when assessing the fairness of a particular process of allocations, we need to be able to judge the extent to which that outcome has resulted from that process. Even if we felt able to collect information about any outcomes likely to be affected by these arrangements, demonstrating the degree to which they have, in fact, brought about desirable or undesirable outcomes is something that we can at best manage imperfectly with hypotheses and statistics.

There are many other technical complexities to this question. For example, in trying to predict the likely outcome of a process for me, the best that can be done is to see what has happened in the past to people like me. But 'people like me' are never exactly the same as me, and future events are never exactly the same as past events.

This problem of the uncertainty and complexity of outcomes is a central consideration in thinking about transparency policy. We want to define transparency as the extent to which I can

---

8   See e.g. Martin Fackleraug, 'Japan, checking on its oldest, finds many gone', *New York Times*, August 14, 2010.

evidence whether I am being treated fairly by a particular system of allocation where there are conflicting interests. We have further said that we think the outcome of such systems is a relevant consideration. But we are also saying that the outcome of any system of allocation is something that is essentially uncertain and where the range of possible narratives is extremely large.

This implies that, by our definition, transparency requires not only access to information but also an ability to analyse and interpret this information. If transparency is about fairness, it must democratise the ability to construct such narratives and to evidence the impacts of policy – to produce a society in which people with competing interests are in a reasonably equal position to put forward their case for what constitutes fair treatment.

Transparency has traditionally been conceived of in terms of processes and activities being publicly visible. In government, transparency has been about us being able to see decisions being made; about organisations informing us what they are up to. In markets, it has been about ensuring we can trust the information available to us when we are making decisions. We need a definition of transparency that applies equally to situations where it is information about the outcome that most needs to be visible; one that works as well when applied to processes driven by big data and machine learning as it does to legislative processes. By defining transparency in terms of the ability to evidence fair treatment, we hope to achieve that.

7

Transparency in an age of big data

We are now in the middle of a second wave of transparency policy. The first wave saw most countries around the world adopt freedom of information (FOI) legislation between 1960 and 2000. This has now become an expected feature and marker of democratic regimes, with over 75 countries now having laws covering general public access to government documents and information excluding personal information (normally referred as FOI) and individual access to personal records whether held by government or non-government organisations (normally referred to as data protection or privacy protection legislation). Most countries deal with these different data access regimes with separate legislation, but in some jurisdictions an overarching legal framework is in place. At the same time, consumer transparency became a growing concern, pushed forward by consumer advocacy groups and governments' increased willingness to enforce transparency on companies.

In the past couple of decades the focus has shifted to widening access to public data sets and the idea of open government. The Open Government Partnership (OGP), a collaboration between 69 countries, is very much in this mould. It describes itself as: 'a multilateral initiative that aims ... to promote transparency, empower citizens, fight corruption, and harness new technologies to strengthen governance'.[1]

Where access to information (ATI) was about stopping abuse of power, open government is as much about finding better ways to govern. In that sense, open government is at times more

---

[1] www.opengovpartnership.org/about#sthash.QDITOvb6.dpuf

closely in tune with the scientific tradition of transparency than the political – with the idea that by sharing data and knowledge we can collectively uncover new knowledge and better ways of doing things more quickly.

The spread of ATI legislation and the enthusiasm of governments for transparency – along with corporate efforts to adopt transparency as a business virtue – could be seen as evidence that the world is becoming more transparent. This idea chimes with another popular notion – the idea that privacy is dead. Put someone's name into Google and you will usually learn something about them.

The continuous scrutiny of public institutions through 24-hour news, the growth of continuous commentary on politics and institutions, the rise of blogging and in particular the anonymous 'insider' blog, the growth in availability of official data, the spread of ATI and the increasing protection afforded to whistleblowers – these trends might lead one to conclude that the world is becoming a more transparent place.

A world of diminishing transparency

However, we want to put forward the opposite argument. We start from the point of view that transparency should not be measured by the amount of information in the public domain but in terms of the information balance between individuals and groups with conflicting interests. Transparency fails us when one side is able to take unfair advantage of the other through better access to information. From that perspective, what matters is not the amount of information in the public domain but the relative access to information between people on opposite sides of an argument, negotiation or transaction.

By that measure, there are reasons to suppose that far from becoming more transparent, the world is, in fact, becoming ever more opaque. Information technology may have increased the level of information in the public domain. But that increase is as nothing compared to the increase in the information assets available to the organisations and agencies with which we interact. The growth in computerised processing of individuals by companies and governments has altered our relationship with information. Data is no longer a useful tool for implementing decisions; data is increasingly driving decisions, with a rapid feedback loop between what the data tells an organisation about us and the way that the organisation then chooses to process the data in future. Power over information today consists more in the control of big data assets than in the ability to conceal specific documents or pieces of information. By that measure, the world is becoming less, not more transparent.

There was a time when laws introducing freedom of speech and freedom of press did much to even up the informational balance between the public and those within government. It reduced the gap between what those in power were allowed to know and what the public was allowed to know narrowed. The ability of those in power to control what I could know largely vanished. This did not result in power being distributed equally – those with a printing press or the gift of the gab had more power than those without either. But the tables were made more even.

Move forward 400 years and that gap between the state and the individual is once again widening. What the state can know about the population and the state's ability to control what is publicly known from these data resources puts it in an enormously privileged position with regard to large swathes of public policy. Similarly, the corporate advantage in the marketplace in terms of what a company knows about us compared to what we know about them is widening, not narrowing.

Transparency is not just about the relative access to information – it is also about our ability to shape that information, to determine what the total pool of data and information consists of. In both markets and public policy, it is companies and governments that have largely determined the format and nature of data – whether that be about our health, our finances or any other aspect of our lives. This has enabled these bodies to further extend their informational advantage over customers and citizens. The stuff we know about in terms of public policy is dominated by what those in power have determined is of most interest. The informational advantage of power does not just reside in access to data, or in the capacity to interpret that data, but also in the control over what data is created and how it is held.

Until very recently media organisations had the capacity to interpret and disseminate information about the institutions around us. They could do this because the information came in formats they were able to examine and question – hearings and committees, public meetings and demonstrations, documents and press releases, briefings and leaks. Today, an ever growing proportion of the information of most interest about our institutions comes in the form of large data sets that require specialist skills to interpret. The challenge of holding to account such institutions is beyond the capabilities of even the most sophisticated media organisations and requires, we will argue, new types of organisation.

We live in a surveillance society. Surveillance, using data to understand customers, is a central driver of modern capitalism.[2] It can be a powerful way to identify people's needs. But it is just as useful as a way to identify their psychological weaknesses. Surveillance is central to the state's ability to maintain public safety. It can be used to meet our expectation to be protected from those around us who wish us harm. Equally it can be used to suppress dissent.

The central challenge for information-driven societies is how to create institutions that allow us to benefit from the astonishing opportunities that data technology offers without allowing it to be turned against us. At one extreme there is an argument that protection lies in regulation and legal oversight. At the other extreme is the argument that we must all forgo the ability to know the society we live in and must accept privacy as our only protection – a deal which forces us to either reject surveillance outright or accept it only on unequal terms.

Our interest is in trying to define arrangements in which the ability to see our society for what it is allows us to enjoy the vast benefits of surveillance but on terms that we can trust to operate fairly.

This is not simply about access to information. If transparency is about trying to create a level playing field between parties

---

2 Shoshana Zuboff, 'Big other: surveillance capitalism and the prospects of an information civilization', *Journal of Information Technology* Vol 30 (2015), 75–89.

with conflicting interest, it follows that transparency is not just about access to data. It must also encompass individual and institutional capabilities to use that data. Freedom of speech in a modern democracy would mean little without the existence of media organisations. It is their role in collecting, analysing, disseminating and commenting on information that leads to an effective public discourse about political arrangements. In the 400 years since John Locke we have reached a sophisticated level of understanding about the market dynamics of a pluralistic press, and desirable and necessary qualities for media organisations. There are established principles around, for example, the protection of sources, separation of advertisements from editorial content and regulation of political bias. Media organisations are recognised in law and accorded specific treatment that recognises their public function.

Transparency requires the development of a similar set of institutional arrangements. Over the past 20 years they have started to come into existence. The authors were involved in one such experiment and in the following pages we will describe many others. However, the ground rules for how such organisations operate have still not been established and remain a contested area. We will set out some proposals as to what, in our experience, is likely to work most effectively.

If it is true, as we are suggesting, that using data in more sophisticated ways to inform decisions is making the world more opaque and forcing us to put more and more trust in institutions, it is also true that we are often entirely sanguine about the issue because the rewards seem to be worthwhile. Although, at the fringes, there is strong agitation from the privacy lobby to limit, in particular, commercial use of data about individuals, the political traction that the campaign can generate is limited by the degree to which people feel that the good has outweighed the bad. The fact that Google finds what I am looking for seems more important than any concern about how they did it. I may not know how they use information about me but it seems to work and that's good enough.

Objectors, such as US author Frank Pasquale,[3] have identified the fundamental problem here – that we are not actually able to assess whether this trade-off is worthwhile because we don't know what we have lost in the process. We actually have no idea to what degree the Google algorithm is in fact leaving out or downgrading results that would in fact be of most interest. But, even though we agree with such objections in theory, we may not care much in practice.

In medicine, growing sophistication in the collection and analysis of data about people's state of health is, in the main, credited with being wholly beneficial. We are quicker to spot emerging outbreaks and new diseases. We are more precise in our diagnoses. We are discovering new treatments. There are downsides, however. It means that it is increasingly unlikely that an individual doctor could ever be expected to have a complete understanding of my healthcare. It means there is a greater risk that I will not benefit from all that is known about how to best care for me – I am more likely to receive suboptimal care because optimal care is so complex and difficult to ascertain. But that loss may feel rather theoretical compared to, say, the gains in cancer survival rates that, over a single generation, are plain for all to see.

Ben Goldacre has written with great power about the lack of transparency within the pharmaceutical industry and the very real costs in terms of lives and ill-health that result.[4] The risk that someone knows I am taking something that is harming me or not healing me and opts not to expose that information is increasing every day. As the range of data about health increases with gene sequencing, phenotyping and wearable sensors, the failure to correctly interpret the data has the potential to become one of the major risks to my health.

While the urgency of delivering effective transparency grows, the task of being transparent is becoming exponentially harder. We currently live in a world where the algorithms that use data to decide whether we should be treated one way or another are reasonably fixed over time. They may develop and shift. But at

---

[3] Frank Pasquale, *The Black Box Society: The Secret Algorithms that Control Money and Information,* Harvard University Press, 2015.

[4] Ben Goldacre, *Bad Pharma*, Faber and Faber, 2012.

any one moment you can ask to see how data is used and the statistical evidence that supports or undermines a particular policy, prescription, financial judgement or clinical diagnosis. This is true even of the more sophisticated machine-driven systems, whether it be an algorithm that assigns a penalty to a number plate caught on a police camera or an algorithm that determines whether your blood pressure puts you in a category needing medication.

Machine-learning systems change that relationship. With machine-learning algorithms, only the initial parameters within which the machine creates the algorithm are fixed. The algorithm itself can be allowed to constantly adapt to new information. There is no longer a relationship between data about an individual and a fixed algorithm which is justified by reference to a fixed data set. Instead we move into a world where the data is continually shifting and the algorithm applied to information about an individual may be entirely unique – the one-off product of that individual's data in relation to a constantly adapting data set at a specific moment in time. Assuring ourselves that we are happy to consent to be governed by such systems becomes both a more complex and simpler task. More complex because interpreting information in such circumstances can be harder. But simpler because there is less that you *can* feasibly know about such systems.

There are huge benefits to such technology and we should embrace its ability to learn and improve. But one thing it does not do is increase transparency. Working groups are currently wrestling with how to develop principles for delivering sufficient transparency to allow these mechanisms to be employed in ways that allow regulators and companies to fulfil their legal obligations to act responsibly. How can they demonstrate that they know such algorithms are not resulting in actions that infringe their legal duties – if they don't know what's happening, how can they be regarded as accountable?

We will argue that the best way – quite likely the only effective way – to police this is to end commercial or governmental monopoly control over data assets. There will be some instances where such control is necessary for national security reasons and there may equally be instances where such control is trivial and the costs of ending it outweigh the benefit. But where there are significant public risks and limited public benefit from such control, we need to have a mechanism by which it can be broken. The only surety that society can accept these powerful and valuable technologies as beneficial is an opening up of access to and control over the underlying data assets used.

This argument challenges governments and companies in different ways. For governments, the principal challenges relate to ensuring a fair political debate and protecting the privacy of citizens. For companies the main challenge relates to investment capital tied up in data assets and the potential to damage market incentives to create such data assets.

We recognise these concerns but also believe that we would be very unwise to continue to consent to being governed by ever more opaque information systems that underlie government and corporate decision making without demanding a level of transparency that provides genuine assurance that we are not being abused. To safely make use of the astonishing power of data and machine learning we need to start preparing now to fundamentally alter our individual, commercial and governmental rights over data access. We hope to persuade you that this can be done in ways that are not as challenging as they might at first appear. We also want to offer some proposals to governments, civil society organisations (CSOs) and companies about the viability of different strategies to navigate these challenges.

Three degrees of transparency

The use of data sharing to underpin transparency does not supersede existing methods of transparency. It is important that rules are published and processes open to public view. However, in an age of big data that is not enough. As decision systems are increasingly driven by large data, there is a significant risk that systems will define outcomes that suit those with executive control of the process yet disadvantage citizens more widely. Conversely, the ability to make such information transparent has greatly increased the potential to identify and reduce unfairness, improve efficiency of government and markets, empower individuals and communities, and lead to new knowledge.

This requires a model of transparency that deals explicitly with the issues relating to data and how data can be used to evidence unfairness. Having defined transparency in terms of fairness, we now want to describe three models of transparency to illustrate how it can help in the assessment of the fairness of allocation systems.

We should stress that these are models – highly simplified diagrams of complex information flows that have numerous relevant features not captured here. However, we want to use the models to highlight the weakness in many current transparency initiatives and to give an outline of what is needed if transparency is to be more effective.

In these models we have identified three actors. First a decision-making authority labelled 'allocator', which might be a government agency or a business. The second actor is labelled 'challenger' – we discuss the types of entity that can play this role in Chapter 16 but they might be a non-governmental organisation or an infomediary business. Finally, we have the citizen who is concerned to know that he or she is being treated fairly.

Figure 7.1: Zero degrees of transparency

No transparency: Citizen provides data to allocator, allocator tells them result
Eg, Citizen sends tax return to government, government informs them of their tax bill

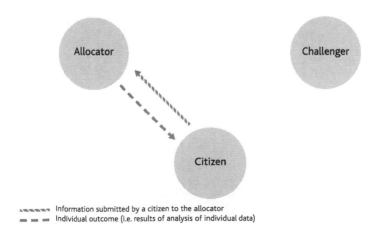

Information submitted by a citizen to the allocator
Individual outcome (i.e. results of analysis of individual data)

i. Zero degrees of transparency

The first illustration is a situation of zero transparency. The citizen provides information (for example, an application for insurance, a tax return), the allocator processes it and issues a decision (for example, a tax bill, an insurance offer).

In this scenario, there is very little opportunity for the allocation to be challenged. The best that the citizen can do is complain if they feel it is unfair, but there is little ground on which they can base their claim.

ii. Transparency 1.0 or Direct Transparency

Transparency 1.0 or Direct Transparency is the term we use to describe most of transparency in evidence today. It occurs when the allocator agrees to publish information about its processes and outcomes. This might include publication of the rules by which decisions are made (enabling people to make an assessment of how decisions about them ought to be made) as well as analyses of the effectiveness with which these rules have been implemented in terms of compliance and outcomes. Often

Figure 7.2: One degree of transparency

1D transparency: Allocator publishes rules and aggregate analysis about the population
Eg, Average time taken to process tax returns, % of citizens paying different levels of tax

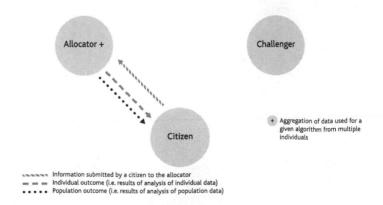

Information submitted by a citizen to the allocator
Individual outcome (i.e. results of analysis of individual data)
Population outcome (i.e. results of analysis of population data)

this will be in the form of requirements imposed by regulators to provide a particular form of account. However, the ability of citizens and challenger organisations to challenge this account is severely constrained by lack of access to the information on which it is based. In particular, lack of access to the raw data used by government severely limits both the scope to question the degree of accuracy in any assessment of the levels of systematic and non-systematic error and any attempt to challenge narratives about the outcome of such processes.

In Part One of the second section of this book, we will look at the state of transparency across the globe today and argue that, in the main, it consists of this sort of direct transparency. We will contend that one of the reasons for its limited success is that it leaves very little room for challenge and does not enable those who feel that the system is unfair and inefficient to access evidence on how and where this is occurring. To put it more bluntly: what is given to people who would want to use information to improve systems is mainly of little use. The most that can be done is to try to raise doubts about the official account by looking for inconsistencies and implausible statements or to speculate about the information that is missing.

iii Transparency 2.0 or two degrees of transparency

Transparency 2.0 is increasingly common around the world. It occurs when the raw data used by an allocator is shared in sufficiently raw and machine-readable formats that a challenger can test the fairness of the allocation and present alternative narratives.

Transparency 2.0 occurs in two quite different ways – first by sharing the data about the citizen with the citizen. This should ideally comprise not just the information the citizen has provided but the processed information including risk and propensity data such as diagnoses or segmentations used for marketing purposes. This allows a challenger to assess the way the rules have been followed.

The second form occurs when raw data for the whole population is shared. This allows a challenger to see the

Figure 7.3: Two degrees of transparency – shared individual data

2D transparency at individual level: the allocator's determination of the individual allocation is open to alternative narrative by the challenger

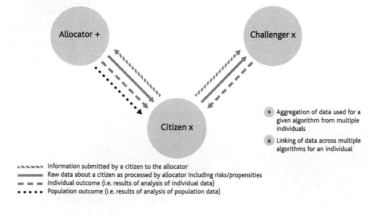

Figure 7.4: Two degrees of transparency – shared population data

2D transparency at population level: the allocator's analysis of population outcomes is open to alternative narrative by the challenger

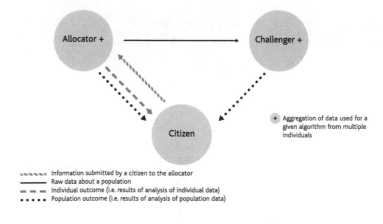

differential impact of the rules on the citizen compared to the rest of the population.

These both allow a challenger to provide a much more effective assessment of the fairness of the allocation process and the degree to which it is harming the individual. However, the challenger may have problems making a full assessment because in the first case they lack the population data for comparison or, in the second case, they lack the specific processed information about an individual.

Challenger organisations can address this by attempting to construct their own population data sets or to make their own estimate of the individual's processed data based on the data submitted by the citizen. But these mechanisms are costly and will reduce the accuracy of the assessment.

Transparency 2.0 is being strongly promoted in a number of areas but not always implemented effectively.

A number of laws and initiatives have been established to try to give individuals full and unfettered access to data held about them by both companies and governments. In many areas policies to try to promote individual transparency – health, criminal justice (pre-trial), utilities, financial services, telecoms – organisations holding data have been successful at undermining these rights. Furthermore there is considerable dispute over the degree to which I have rights over information about how my data has been processed to calculate propensity scores and categorisations. Despite this, there is a small but growing number of examples of success (see Chapter 14).

Sharing of population-level data has been promoted in public services in some developed countries with success. However, this remains one of the most controversial areas with disputes over the degree to which individuals can refuse to allow information about them to be used in this way (see Chapter 18)

However, it is almost unheard of to find both individual data transparency and population data transparency occurring at the same time around the same decision process. This is unfortunate as we hope to show that this is the standard to aspire to if transparency is to play the role it should in ensuring a fair society. This hoped for scenario we call Transparency 3.0.

Figure 7.5: Three degrees of transparency – equality of narrative power

3D transparency: the challenger organisation is in the same position as the allocator in assessing the fairness of the allocation system

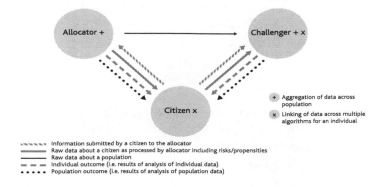

iv. Transparency 3.0 or three degrees of transparency

To assess the fairness, accuracy and efficiency of allocation systems, an individual needs to be able to assess both that their case has been handled correctly according to the rules and that the rules are fair overall. Transparency 3.0 occurs when the data used by allocation systems is also available directly to the individual concerned, in standard electronic machine-readable formats, while system-level data is available to independent organisations able to assess that the handling of the individual is fair and can be compared to the handling of other people in similar circumstances.

This then allows me to know not only how I have been treated but also how that compares to how others have been treated, from a source that is independent of the decision-making system. This represents a genuine stripping away of the power of executive decision-making bodies to disguise the impact of their actions – it represents true transparency.

This approach to transparency is designed to cope with a data-driven world. It is of greatest value where decision processes are well structured. It is most effective in high turnover decision-making processes that are relatively information intense. It is also of most interest in situations where it is possible to capture information about the outcome of allocations on individuals. It has less to offer in situations where the information used to make decisions is less well structured, less frequent and where there is concern not at systematic corruption but that one individual decision has been made corruptly. However, the review of current approaches to political transparency in the next section of this book would suggest that all forms of access to information are less effective in those situations.

There are, we suggest, large areas of public administration and commerce where Transparency 3.0 could yield significant benefits in terms of fairer, more efficient, high-quality services. However, progress towards this has been slow. It is common to see systems that allow Transparency 2.0 to develop so long as they do it in a way that dodges Transparency 3.0. In commercial markets the push has been for individual access to data and regulatory access to population data sets has been minimal, although powers often do exist with regulators. In contrast, in public services, where government has control over aggregate data sets, we have seen population-level Transparency 2.0 develop while strong resistance to individual-level transparency remains.

My ability to know whether the prosecution of a legal action is progressing as I should expect, my ability to know the basis on which a diagnosis has been arrived at, my ability to know whether my financial arrangements are incurring fees at unreasonably high levels compared to others in a similar situation – these are all questions that will only be effectively answered by moving to Transparency 3.0.

There are, of course, countervailing considerations of rights to commercial confidentiality and individual rights to privacy that will make this approach inappropriate in some circumstances. But this level of transparency occurs when the citizen is able to access independent assessment both of the aggregate impact of a decision-making process and also the individual impact on their case. The information used by the allocator needs to be accessible to the individual in the same form as was used by the allocator in order to enable an assessment of its accuracy and the degree to which this information has been processed in a fair way in line with the processing of other information.

The benefits of Transparency 3.0

Our argument is that Transparency 3.0 creates a circumstance in which transparency can cease being a well-meaning government policy that achieves less than hoped for and can start to become a self-sustaining system that is essential to the functioning of a fair society.

One of the problems we will look at with regard to Transparency 2.0 is the question of how challenger organisations are funded, what gives them their legitimacy and what rules they follow. There is no prospect of satisfactorily resolving that issue if Transparency 2.0 is all that exists. Transparency 3.0, however, opens up the opportunity of transparency ceasing to be an awkward extension of democratic institutions and instead becoming a part of each citizen's life and their relationship with government, public services and markets.

Innovation and discovery can be boosted by sharing data but remains limited by issues of recruitment, consent and by the need to collect ongoing information from people. Transparency 3.0 provides the mechanisms by which these obstacles might be overcome.

Lastly, Transparency 3.0 holds out the possibility of people self-organising around data both to share information and to support each other. That might be people in a neighbourhood sharing concerns about the upkeep of public land and agreeing to do something about it, to patients who share a rare condition deciding to share data in the hope of finding new and better treatments more rapidly.

But before we get too far into the future we want to step back and look at the state of transparency policy now.

Section B | **Practice**

This section looks at how transparency operates in the current world.

- Part 1 looks at the most common forms of transparency in use today
- Part 2 looks at some of the examples of data-sharing transparency that currently exist
- Part 3 looks at the emerging issues and technologies that could enable a more complete form of data-driven transparency.

Part One
Transparency 1.0

This section looks at examples of how transparency operates currently, focusing particularly on transparency around government and public services. It is organised as follows:

- Chapters 8 to 12 look at the most common current mechanisms for access to data and their record of success as a way of reducing corruption within government.
- Chapter 13 looks at the way in which these methods of information sharing are undermined by the editorial control wielded by government and argues that the same is true wherever such methods are used.
- Chapter 14 looks specifically at the tension between regulation and transparency and at the tendency to regard more transparent regulation rather than data sharing as a way to provide public assurance. We set out why regulatory capture and the monoptic view of regulators prevent this approach from providing effective transparency.

8

Every day is a fight for information

War veterans in Croatia enjoy many privileges. They can import a car without paying duty, their children can attend any university in the country regardless of school grades, and they enjoy substantial pensions of often more than the average salary. In 1995, when the war in the region finished, there were 350,000 registered veterans. In 2010 there were more than 550,000, an inflation of 60% during 15 years of peace. 'Everybody knew somebody who was claiming benefit, but not part of the war effort', said Marko Rakar,[1] a former printing entrepreneur who has become the country's most outspoken open government activist.

On 7 April 2010, an unofficial website appeared which offered citizens the opportunity to enter a person's name and review their war record, or type in a unit's name and obtain a list of veterans. The website became a cause célèbre after it revealed that the minister of war veterans himself had not told the truth about his service (he served 300 days less than he had maintained) and that there were many 'veterans' who had no war service record at all.

Rakar was arrested that day and held for nine more. The story dominated the news media. 'When the Pope died the newspaper printed a special edition', he said. 'When I was arrested, they printed two special editions.' The police had no evidence for his involvement in the website, but his arrest followed a widespread (unproven) assumption that he had been responsible for the leak of a similar government database on registered voters the year before.

---

[1]   Author interview.

In this earlier case, it emerged that Croatia had 4,750,000 registered voters – rather more (by 45,000) than its actual population. On the website, which allowed interrogation of this data, you could type in the name of your village or if you lived in a city you could select the street where you live and find the top 100 addresses with the largest number of registered voters per address. There was one building of 400 people at a non-existent address in the mountains; there were people living in police stations and in public schools. In addition, it seemed that there were many people who were registered in both Croatia and neighbouring Bosnia, and media commentators alleged that this was deliberate gerrymandering and conferred electoral advantage on the ruling party. Since the disclosure, Croatian law has changed to close the loophole on multiple places of residence and also regulates the number of people who can vote. Solving the problem of veterans' fraud is more complex. There are many court cases challenging individual claims – but the former 'saintliness of the war veteran is over', said Rakar.

Rakar was never prosecuted – but the sites did come down after his arrest. In 2011, given the level of public interest and outrage, the newly elected government published its own online versions of both the electoral and veteran data. The unidentified open-data digital activists had used transparency to bring official focus on – and acknowledgement of – post-war political and welfare corruption in Croatia. 'These changes would have happened', he said. 'But this was an important event in forcing it.'

Rakar's point is that corruption is hard to uncover, but often the answer can be transparency – making more information more widely available so that people can look for suspicious activity and start to find ways to combat it. Since these leaks, one former president has been convicted for taking large bribes from transnational corporations, voter registration lists have been corrected and the administration of veterans' benefits cleaned up.

Rakar became a global open-data celebrity when the Croatian websites were published and in July 2011, much to his surprise, he was invited to address the inaugural meeting of a new international initiative called the Open Government Partnership (OGP) at the US State Department in Washington DC. He had operated in isolation in his own country for many years – one of few people prepared to challenge local political accountability – but was shortly to discover that the new digitally enhanced potential of transparency had become a global agenda and a preoccupation of the Obama White House.

Rakar was there when Hillary Clinton, secretary of state, opened the meeting with a call to action for world leaders to embrace transparency:

> When a government invites people to participate, when it is open as it makes decisions and allocates resources, when it administers justice equally and transparently, and when it takes a firm stance against corruption of all kinds, that government is ... far more likely to succeed in designing and implementing effective policies and services.[2]

This event brought together senior leaders from more than 50 countries, along with some of the world's most influential civil society activists and digital pioneers, including Sir Tim Berners-Lee, inventor of the World Wide Web. There was a sense of history, an outburst of multinational idealism. It felt like a fresh start for a new kind of collaboration between government and civil society. Even Rakar was convinced and he joined OGP Croatia (his country having become one of the first member states).

People like Rakar seemed to embody a potential solution to government corruption. Government just needed to harness this power of data and transparency in order to reinvigorate democratic politics. But this narrative rather overlooked the key fact about Rakar's story – the fact that the Croatian websites had used stolen government information. The proponents of open data were arguing that this same effect could be created by governments voluntarily ceding control of information through transparency. Rakar's story was evidence of what could be achieved when governments involuntarily lost control. But

---

[2] Hillary Rodham Clinton, Secretary of State Remarks at the Open Government Partnership High-Level Meeting, July 12 2011. http://www. state.gov/secretary/20092013clinton/rm/2011/07/168049.htm

it offered no evidence that any government would voluntarily hand over the evidence of its own failings.

Three months later, heads of state from the 12 countries on the OGP's founding steering committee took their place in a formal meeting to launch the new body during the meeting of the UN general assembly. One of the co-authors of this book, Tim Kelsey, was UK government director of transparency and open data at the time and he was the official responsible for UK membership – and subsequently co-chairmanship – of the Open Government Partnership. Francis Maude, the British cabinet minister responsible for making the machinery of central government more productive, said in that launch meeting, which was hosted by Obama: 'Transparency is not easy for politicians. It is not comfortable.'[3]

Since its inception, the OGP has grown to include 69 nation states and a larger number of global civil society organisations as members. It has its supporters and its detractors, but nobody will deny that the vigour and excitement of its launch has given transparency a certain kudos in many of the capitals of our planet.

Transparency is in vogue. There is currently a boom market in global initiatives to foster transparency. There is the Aid Transparency Initiative, the Medical Supplies Transparency Initiative, the G20 anti-corruption Transparency initiative, the Organisation for Economic Co-operation and Development (OECD) has one, and there are many others.

But Marko Rakar is nonplussed. He has left OGP Croatia because he says it is self-serving and a career vehicle for some government officials. Only around 25% of the OGP member countries are committed to the project, judged by a simple fact: that they have, according to one observer, actively given officials the task and capacity to work on their national action plan (a requirement of membership is to publish an action plan and for this to be subject to periodic independent audit). Another 20% have 'never really committed', says the same observer, which leaves around 50% 'who are willing but don't have the capacity'.

Rakar's work has made transparency of government data a political priority in Croatia. But he is sceptical of the depth

---

3   Author's contemporaneous notes.

of the political commitment. Rakar himself has collaborated with the administration on developing various proposals for publication and the finance department now publishes daily data on spending and revenues, an initiative he proposed direct to the minister of finance.

An online portal has also been launched, publishing raw data on government activity in digital formats to allow non-governmental organisations and citizens to develop their own analysis. 'The finance website is hardly usable, poorly presented; they took four years to build the open data portal and there's hardly any useful data', according to Rakar. 'Officials are not moving fast enough and still don't understand the value of opening up data: seven years ago we didn't know corruption existed, and now we do and it is everywhere. There is much greater awareness, transparency has caused that. They say: why do we need transparency when we have a department of government analysts?' But he has some sympathy: 'Transparency is difficult for government: there is the backlash and initial bad press. Politicians must hold their nerve, but what's important is the comparison over time.'

'Transparency is not easy for politicians'

Rakar's words will ring true with anyone working in transparency. It is common to see governments investing in data portals and transparency initiatives that yield plenty of data but often little that is usable.

Downloading the spreadsheet of OGP commitments in July 2015, we identified 425 that were categorised by OGP as relating to wider provision of information and described in English. Of these, we then attempted to identify the number that committed to publication of specific information and, in particular, any commitments to make available specific information in raw formats either as data to the individual or as population data.

Overall we found eight that committed to disaggregated population data and four that committed to provision of individual data. The four commitments to let individuals access data about themselves were all from Indonesia, which wanted to let people track the progress of their complaints to the police, their applications for government jobs and their applications to the land register.

Commitments concerning raw or disaggregated data across the population included a UK commitment to publish the underlying data behind survey results and, in Albania, to publish 'the list of payments made daily by all general government units since January 2012' – including 'such details as: the beneficiary, invoice number, description, the institution to which the treasury branch makes the payment, the respective amount and the date of registration of this bill in the Treasury system'.[4] Four commitments were from Tanzania and included promises to post details of orders and receipts of medical supplies at facility level, quarterly disbursement reports from the ministry of finance, and water point mapping data.

Commitments this specific were a rarity. The largest category consisted of what we would term 'access' commitments – projects to make data easier to find. This included the creation of web portals, enforcing open data standards, creating open data interfaces or building data inventories. These are all useful things to do. But the fact that there are many more commitments of this sort than there are to the release of specific information in reusable formats highlights the problem that Rakar has identified. Building a web portal is easy. It is particularly easy if you don't put much useful information there.

The enthusiasm of politicians is sincere. President Barack Obama made strong public commitments to transparency from the start of his tenure. Obama has specific, longstanding views about open political jurisprudence and he gave trusted advisers in his administration the latitude to develop concepts of open government and indeed recruited advocates like Cass Sunstein, co-author of *Nudge*, and Beth Noveck, a long standing advocate of open data, to the new administration for that purpose.

On 21 January 2009, on his first full official day in office, Obama issued a memo across government: 'In the face of doubt, openness prevails ... sunlight is said to be the best

---

4   Taken from descriptions of commitments on the OGP website. Details of all OGP commitments can be found at http://www.opengovpartnership. org/irm/ogp-irm-database-12

of disinfectants'.[5] This unprecedented presidential missive talked of 'accountability through transparency' and said such 'accountability is in the interest of the government and the citizenry alike'. He made open and machine-readable data the default setting for government.

In the UK, David Cameron was equally committed. Immediately after his election as prime minister in 2010, he issued the first of two public letters on transparency to the British cabinet:

> Greater transparency across government is at the heart of our shared commitment to enable the public to hold politicians and public bodies to account; to reduce the deficit and deliver better value for money in public spending; and to realise significant economic benefits by enabling businesses and non-profit organisations to build innovative applications and websites using public data.

This letter ordered the publication of raw data for – among others – all items of central government spending over £25,000, local government spending over £500 and crime statistics. In his second letter, he ordered publication of a range of other datasets with a particular focus on making available the raw data that supported independent analysis of comparative public service outcomes.

The emphasis on transparency is not just the preserve of developed nations. It has been a recent focus for a number of newly democratic nations – from Brazil and Indonesia to Liberia and Mongolia – who have wrestled with the challenge of trying to increase tax revenues from exploitation of natural mineral assets which had historically been the subject of endemic (often government sanctioned) corruption and build public confidence in the social benefit of multiparty politics. Warren Krafchik, who heads the International Budget Partnership, a

---

[5]   Barack Obama Transparency and Open Government: Memorandum for the Heads of Executive Departments and Agencies https://www.whitehouse. gov/the_press_office/TransparencyandOpenGovernment

non-governmental organisation that works with budget-focused CSOs in over 100 countries to promote transparency of national budgets, comments: 'It was this – the energy unleashed in a number of countries dealing with the challenges of democracy and their need for fiscal accountability – that contributed to the tone for OGP and, in a bottom-up way, built the case which the Obama administration embraced'.[6] Krafchik is also a campaigner for communal audits to improve the accountability of public spending (which we shall see has been an important success of the first phase of the transparency movement) and was also the first civil society co-chair of the OGP.

The difficulty governments face in becoming transparent is not publishing more information, it is publishing data in ways which genuinely improve accountability and deliver other benefits, including public service effectiveness. Some governments are committed in practice as well as principle to release of machine-readable data for this purpose, but international initiatives like OGP have yet to persuade most governments to do so.

In 2014, Mexico took over as chair of the OGP. President Enrique Peña Nieto described open government as a 'new paradigm' which 'revolutionizes the way in which citizens and governments collaborate in order to design and evaluate public policy'.[7]

He has made an impressive list of commitments which include joining the Extractive Industries Transparency Initiative, publishing a database of mining projects, publishing more information about budgets, including school budgets, and publishing information about potential human rights violations, including databases of people who have disappeared and people who have been detained.

Transparency, accountability and anti-corruption are key elements of Peña Nieto's reform agenda. The digital strategy unit has the task of trying to use data and technology to make Mexico's political system more transparent and to encourage greater

---

[6] Author interview.

[7] OGP press releases Nov 24 2014 announcing that Mexico was taking over the chair of the partnership. http://www.opengovpartnership.org/blog/open-government-partnership/2014/09/24/mexico-lead-open-government-partnership-press-release

participation. Mexico has taken on the chairmanship of the Open Government Partnership and has made 26 commitments, including many that relate to release of government data.

Alejandra Lagunes is running Mexico's national digital strategy as part of the president's executive office. Her team is based on the 14th floor of a high-rise government building, with a view across town to the mountains. The windows are covered in flow charts and plans, written in coloured marker pens, setting out strategies for open government and open data.

Mexico is an international leader in the use of data-driven evaluations of policies. It is currently conducting the world's second largest programme of conditional cash transfers where the poor are given additional social security payments if they do certain things, such as making sure their children go to school. This programme includes the use of randomised controlled trials – a process where different types of incentives are tested on randomly selected groups of citizens to see which ones are most successful at improving their lives.

They are currently conducting a trial on how to improve outcomes for pregnant women to address Mexico's high rates of death in childbirth. Ania Calderon is head of the national digital strategy's open data initiative. She and her team have sourced as much information as possible from the health ministry. Health systems generate large numbers of records concerning births, deaths, doctor's appointments and medical treatments. In the past this data had been used purely for administrative purposes.

The data was sent to academics in Chicago who identified a series of problems and possible solutions. Three of these approaches are now being trialled – giving women more information by mobile phone about how to care for themselves; putting them in touch with a local community worker who can support them; and giving healthcare workers perks if outcomes improve. Administrative records are then being monitored to see whether measures such as the weight of children at birth or mortality rates across the three test groups improve compared to the rest of the population.

This impressive programme is an excellent example of the use of data in government – of digitally informed evidenced-based policy. Furthermore the entire programme is wholly transparent.

The data that was used is published in full, including details of every live birth – from time of birth to the number of previous pregnancies, the educational attainment of the mother as well as every maternal mortality.[8] In addition, Chicago University has published in full the code used to analyse the data and to produce its results.[9]

For Calderon, digital government and transparency are about helping the state function more effectively and she is optimistic about the progress being made. Mexico is becoming an innovator in digital government, using mobile phones to deliver healthcare and data to track the impact of government policies in real time. It wants to become a leader in technology.

The government's digital strategy is designed to achieve many things. It is intended to result in more effective evidenced-based delivery of public services; greater economic growth both as a result of more effective government and also by creating opportunities for digital innovation; greater public participation in democratic decision making; and less corruption. Some of these goals are easier to achieve than others.

A key requirement of the OGP is that government works with civil society to determine what information is made public and how. The national digital strategy sits between departmental ministers and government officials who are fearful of how open data might undermine their authority and civil society organisations frustrated at the barriers put in the way of transparency.

They are working with each government department to identify how more information can be released in useful formats to the public. Part of their programme is to adopt international data standards for government information so that the data from one country is immediately comparable with data from another.

There's a careful path to tread. Calderon says that government officials need persuading that this is a good thing to do. They are aware that publishing data is likely to lead to negative press

---

[8] http://busca.datos.gob.mx/#/instituciones/salud
[9] http://dssg.uchicago.edu/project/reducing-maternal-mortality-rates-in-mexico/ or in Spanish, http://datos.gob.mx/impacto/historias/mortalidad-materna.html

commentary and put pressure on them. Her job is to try to show them that the process of releasing data can help them as well as the public. She gives the example of the hydrographic office which now publishes information about hydro-meteorological hazards in standard formats. Organising the data in this way has enabled them to greatly reduce the time they spend creating forecasts by being able to computerise the process. Communicating alerts to the public has improved as both Twitter and Google now take the data and publish it.

However, flood alert systems are not an area of political danger for the government. There is not widespread social disquiet that collusion between government and vested interests within the system are resulting in substandard flood prevention processes. Areas such as education, health, natural resources and criminal justice are where the real tensions lie and where access to information becomes much more disputed.

IMCO (Instituto Mexicano para la Competitividad) is one of the leading CSOs involved in negotiating greater openness. It is a highly respected organisation that boasts some of the country's most senior figures from government and business on its board. They have done a great deal of work on identifying failures in education – work that supports the government's current efforts to reform education. Despite this, the relationship remains at times difficult.

Alexandra Zapata (see the case study below), who has led on much of the work in education, says: 'It is a struggle every day to get data'.[10] At times, it has only been irregular access to data that has enabled the truth to come out. She and her colleagues have been threatened simply for disseminating information that the government had itself officially published.

Article 19 is a civil society organisation working with government on releasing data about the disappeared and the detained in Mexico but is having to fight every inch of the way to get access to information in a format that they believe will be of some use in combating the problems of human rights violations (see Chapter 12)

---

[10] Author interview.

Fundar, an economic and civil rights group, is working with the government on its commitment to greater transparency in extractive industries. It has found it hard to get the information of most use to those affected by the mining industry, although data on mining concessions has now been published and has been one of the most widely downloaded data sets on the government website.[11]

They all recognise that the government is sincere in its overarching belief that greater openness is a good idea. But when it comes to the crunch in areas where there is a degree of political sensitivity, the government lacks either the will or the capacity to release the information that is most likely to be of use to citizens. The president and the president's office might be wholly committed to transparency, but they have to work through the ministries, the civil service and the layers of local government and public service administration which are populated by many people who have little or nothing to gain from greater transparency.

Anyone who has worked in transparency outside of government will have their tales of the ways in which governments – even those with a strong commitment to transparency - create constant obstacles to the free flow of information. The authors were engaged in an argument for more than eight years with the Office of National Statistics (ONS) in the UK over the issue of whether it was legal to release information from the national deaths register. This is information that in some parts of the world (e.g. California) is public information. In the UK, each individual death record is a public document, but the dataset of all deaths is not. After eight years of debate, the ONS finally agreed that they did in fact have the legal power to release the information.

In accessing information, the IMCO (see below) had to work around both minor and major obstacles put in place by the education ministry in Mexico – even in situations where there was a public commitment to transparency and where the information being published by IMCO was sympathetic to the

---

[11] http://busca.datos.gob.mx/#/conjuntos/concesiones-mineras or http://busca.datos.gob.mx/#/conjuntos/cartografia-minera

policy of government, albeit treading on the toes of powerful interest groups.

The appeal of ineffective transparency

This constant battle over information is a feature of transparency policy, but it is an unequal battle. In the next few chapters we want to describe the dynamics of the various mechanisms currently used to increase transparency and access to information, and to explore why they tend to result in limited access to useful data and limited impact on measurable improvements in accountability or public sector effectiveness.

This occurs because governments can often find benefits in creating the maximum appearance of transparency, while ensuring that the minimum possible is done to enable people to evidence unfairness or corruption in allocation systems.

Calls for transparency are driven by a concern that one person is pulling the wool over the eyes of another – it may be corporates disguising the truth about the safety of their products, utilities hiding their true levels of profitability, public servants hiding poor-quality service delivery or governments concealing corrupt decisions. Whatever the issue, the matter at stake is not transparency in itself – it is concern about safety, low-quality public services, tax avoidance and criminality.

There are many policy responses to these disputes. Transparency is often the most appealing because it can feel like the safe option – it is taking action without taking sides. Who can argue with a call for more information and more clarity to help resolve the dispute?

By agreeing to greater transparency politicians can fend off pressure to take more direct action or pick sides in the dispute. They can buy time because it will take some time before it becomes clear whether the specifics of the information being made transparent is sufficient to address the needs of either party in dispute. With any luck, by the time that happens, public interest and pressure for change will have dissipated.

That is not to say transparency will not have the desired effect. As we shall illustrate later, however, the technical intricacies of making it work mean that is very easy to establish transparency initiatives that are so undermined in the detail of the requirements placed on organisations that while they appear to address an issue they do no such thing.

It is impossible to know if such policies are caused by cynicism or – as seems more likely in many cases – whether they are simply due to the fact that the holder of information has such a natural advantage over the person seeking information that, unless policies are very tightly drawn, those holding information can very quickly run rings around those seeking to reveal it. As a result, the harm the policy was intended to address continues unabated, while an additional and pointless cost has been added to the workings of a particular government department or industry. Often the route of least political resistance is to concede to one side the need for greater transparency and to the other side the control over how it is implemented. The end result can be the costly production of information deliberately designed to be of little or no value to anybody.

Low-income developing countries where foreign aid constitutes a significant percentage of GDP (gross domestic product) have a particular reason to implement transparency programmes of limited effect. Donor organisations favour countries that can evidence higher levels of transparency. Creating a false appearance of transparency can yield a high financial value to such governments and avoid the inconvenience of real transparency.[12]

The same effect can be seen in commercial environments where government is asked to address concerns about risky products or questionable behaviour by companies. A standard policy response is to make use of 'forced disclosure' and argue that, once the information is made available to the public, they have been adequately protected from risk of harm.

For these reasons we should be wary of government claims for transparency. Agencies have an incentive to create a false appearance of transparency by publishing information or requiring the publication of information that is of little use to

---

[12] Liz David-Barrett and Ken Okamura, *The Transparency Paradox: Why do Corrupt Countries Join EITI,* Working Paper, European Research Centre for Anti-Corruption and State Building, 2013.

people – information that fails the basic test of transparency in that it gives the citizen little or no usable ammunition in evidencing unfairness or raising grievances.

Groups calling for transparency report that, even where government adopts a high-level policy to support their objectives, individual agencies are able to frustrate policy through the provision of information that falls short of what is needed.

In summary, there are good reasons why transparency is more often promised than delivered and claims that transparency has been achieved as a result of the publication of information should be regarded with suspicion.

IMCO: EDUCATION IN MEXICO

In 2014, on the day before Mexico announced it was chairing the OGP, Alexandra Zapata walked out of the offices of Instituto Nacional de Estadística y Geografía (INEGI), Mexico's national statistics office, with a briefcase full of a computer discs containing state secrets. She was nervous. Four months earlier she had received a series of threats from the ministry.

The information that led to such heavy-handed threats did not concern military deployments or details of intelligence operations. It was a list of which teachers taught at which schools in Mexico.

Zapata and her boss, Juan Pardinas, are not what you would normally regard as a threat to the state. They work at a think tank called El Instituto Mexicano para la Competitividad (IMCO) – Mexico's institute for competitiveness. It aims to promote growth by making Mexico a place that 'forges and attracts talent and investment'. Its headquarters are in the upmarket Polanca district of Mexico City and many of Mexico's most successful business people sit on the board.

IMCO is interested in schools because they believe that the poor quality of Mexico's education system is holding back the country's economic growth and contributing to enduring poverty. Despite spending 5% of national income on education (in line with the US and Canada) and having an income per capita slightly above the global average, Mexico's education system is ranked in the bottom quartile by the World Economic Forum. In the OECD's programme for international student assessment (PISA) tests, Mexico came 53rd out of 65 for maths.

Zapata had been working on a website called 'mejora tu escuela' – improve your school. The website was set up to help the public find better information about education locally. The first information they decided to publish was the standardised test results for each school in a way that was easier for the public to understand. They then began to look around for what other information might be available. As well as test results, the government published information about every teacher's salary. However, it was presented in a way that made it hard to use. Each school published their own data but, Zapata explains, 'some of them were literally photos take on phones of old documents with thumb prints and stains uploaded onto the government website'.

It was a significant piece of work to transcribe all the documents into a database. When it was done, they found some curious results. Some teachers were earning millions of pesos a year. Others were employed by schools that did not exist. In the state of Hidalgo, more than 1000 teachers were over 100 years old. Odder still, they all shared the same birthday – 12 December 1912 or 12.12.12.

In Mexico if you are born on 12 December, the celebration of the birth of the Virgin, you are traditionally given the name Guadalupe or Lupito for short. The idea of thousands of centenarian Lupitos teaching in schools in Hidalgo caught the public imagination and created a media frenzy focusing on corruption in the education system.

The story broke on a Wednesday. By the end of the Thursday the ministry of education had had enough and started issuing threats that Zapata stop doing press interviews immediately. But by then the press had got their teeth into the story. It went on for two weeks.

For the governor of Hidalgo it was intolerable. He called both Zapata and Pardinas to his office. He said the suggestion of impropriety was a slander. All that had happened was a simple clerical error. Officials were using 12.12.12 as an administrative convenience, he said.

But media outrage heightened when it emerged that the government had conducted an accurate census of teachers but refused to publish most of the results. INEGI, the national statistics institute, prides itself on its independence and had been deeply unhappy at having to sign a contract with the department of education that forbade it from releasing the results of the survey. The news coverage of IMCO's findings was what persuaded someone at INEGI to leak the discs with the census data.

To understand why such information about teachers is so sensitive, it is necessary to understand the peculiarities of the Mexican education system. In Mexico, teachers are not just teachers. They are an important part of the political power structure. Raising the issue of 'ghost' teachers – non-existent teachers on the payroll – strikes at the heart of that structure.

Sindicato Nacional de Trabajadores de la Educación (SNTE), Mexico's main teaching union, is the largest union in Latin America. Until 2006 it had consistently supported the Institutional Revolutionary Party (PRI) which ruled Mexico as a one-party state from 1929 until 2000. In 2006, the union switched sides and sold the support of its members to the opposition National Action Party (PAN) for a reported $30 million. A team of researchers from Harvard and New York University have analysed the data on voting and concluded that the deal won PAN the election.[13] They found that where the union controlled the local education system and the polling station was located in the school, the SNTE delivered an increase of two percentage points in the vote – enough to swing the result in an election won by a margin of only 0.58% of the vote.

This is not just an issue of political influence. What Pardinas and Zapata care about is the damage to education. Pardinas explains that in Oaxaca a child might expect no more than 100 days' schooling a year. The rest of the time the teachers are protesting or striking or doing union business. According to one study, between 1998 and 2003 a total of 434 teaching days were lost to strikes – 87 days a year or close to half of all school

---

[13] H.A. Larreguy, et al, *The Role of Labor Unions as Political Machines: Evidence from the Case of the Mexican Teachers' Union*, March 2014 www.iq.harvard.edu/files/iqss/files/updated_march_6_paper.pdf

days. Much of the budget that is supposedly used for educating children is being redirected into operating a political machine.

One of the ironies of their fight with the education department was that they are really on the same side. The government is engaged in a major battle with the union to reform education. In 2013, the head of the union was jailed for embezzling $130 million.

'Right now, the army is on the streets in Oaxaca',[14] said Pardinas. They were there to quell rioting teachers who had invaded polling stations, burnt ballot papers and blockaded the streets to protest against a reform bill which strips them of power over the education system – and therefore of much of their political power too.

The media is a key part of the strategy to generate pressure for change. The explicit goal of IMCO is to try to bring hard data and facts into the public debate by presenting them in ways that engage the public and raise awareness of the issues facing the country. But this needs to be done without getting involved in party political disputes or attempts to undermine the government. A news story exposing corruption in education can help a government trying to reform education or it can undermine it by giving the appearance that it is incompetent. The art, Pardinas explains, is to apply just enough pressure for change without provoking a backlash.

The media is only part of the strategy. Exposing ghost teachers might have made one particular channel for corrupt funds slightly harder to operate, but it is not difficulty to substitute alternative methods for subverting public money. The media stories may have helped political forces trying to reform teachers, but if the political winds change, the politicians and the teachers would not find it hard to make new, equally corrupt arrangements. The media on its own is not sufficient as a watchdog.

IMCO wants the 'mejora tu escuela' campaign to do more than prompt media stories. They want to directly engage the population in trying to address the fundamental corruption in schools. 'We want to catalyse

---

[14] Author interview.

parent involvement in education. We need parents to change the balance of power', says Zapata.[15]

The aim is for the website to engage parents through four stages. The first part of the site is the simplest level of engagement. It gives useful information about the school – location, the name of the principal, contact details – stuff that anybody might want. The next part gives comparative information about tests scores and encourages parents to consider that the school their child is attending may not be providing the level of education they should expect. The third step is then to get parents to rate their school, to get them to pass their own judgement on the education their children are receiving.

This is harder than it might seem. When they first invited parents to rate their schools the average score was 8.7 out of 10. Zapata explains: 'If children got to 9th grade and the parents had only got to 7th, they felt the school must be good'. The problem was their expectations were too low.

The final step is to get parents engaged as activists. This is the hardest level to achieve, but they are having some success. As an example of the latter, when the test results are published each year, some schools are identified as having cheated because so many kids have filled in exactly the same answers. 'The teacher dictates the answers to the children during the exam', Zapata explains. So the website helps to recruit parents to become 'citizen invigilators' who go to the school on exam day and check that it is done properly.

In the state of Baja California parents are becoming even more active and have started to make use of the courts. Legally, teachers' rights to strike are limited and persistent absence is a reason for dismissal. But as it is the union or union members who are responsible for enforcing this, it rarely happens. In Baja California, parents have collected their own information on teacher absences and gone to the courts to demand action.

This is a brave thing to do. 'They are often scared that the teachers will then mistreat their children, so solidarity in numbers is important.'[16] But

---

[15] Author interview.

[16] Author interview.

the fact that it is happening at all is, according to Pardinas, a sign of hope. This country is changing so fast, he says, 'I never would have believed that we would see parents taking on the teachers union in the courts.'

9

Access to information laws (ATI)

Kwame Kilpatrick is the former mayor of Detroit who was sentenced to 28 years in jail for a range of offences, following a string of allegations about misuse of public funds.

Kilpatrick was brought down by a campaign run by the *Detroit Free Press* which unpicked a sensational web of secrets. Kilpatrick's downfall starts with rumours about an alleged party with strippers at the mayor's mansion held while his wife was away. The rumour ran that his wife had returned unexpectedly and assaulted one of the strippers; and that the stripper was thought likely to testify in court. What we do know for sure is that a few months later the stripper was found dead, shot several times in her car.

Kilpatrick ended up in court after two whistleblowers from the Detroit police department alleged he had closed down an investigation into the shooting of the stripper. The *Free Press* unearthed text messages that showed Kilpatrick was having an affair with his chief of staff – something he had categorically denied in court. Freedom of information requests from the paper then uncovered a secret agreement Kilpatrick had reached with the whistleblowers, requiring them to keep their knowledge of the texts secrets.

Loren Cochran, writing on the website of the Reporters Committee for the Freedom of the Press, said:

> The *Detroit Free Press'* marvellous investigation into the veracity, or lack thereof, of testimony by Mayor Kwame Kilpatrick and Chief of Staff Christine Beatty during a multimillion-dollar whistleblower retaliation

trial was all made possible due to Michigan's open records laws, and *The Free Press'* dogged pursuit under the law to obtain these public employee's text messages.[1]

This account glosses over one rather important detail. The texts that proved Kilpatrick had perjured himself – the texts that were the key to breaking the scandal – were leaked, not released under freedom of information (FOI) laws. The City of Detroit had successfully resisted information requests from the *Detroit Free Press* for a number of years. After the leaking of texts and their publication in January 2008, demonstrating that Kilpatrick had lied about his affair, the city council voted 8-1 to release further information and the *Detroit Free Press* successfully progressed a range of information requests through the courts.

It is also worth pointing out that Kilpatrick believed his mobile was a personal communication device exempted from the Freedom of Information Act (FOIA). The courts decided otherwise on the grounds that when the City of Detroit paid for the phones they stated explicitly that communication on these devices would be regarded as public information. But if Kilpatrick had been smart enough to use a personal device – as other politicians do – Michigan's open records laws might have been largely powerless to uncover the truth.

Michigan's laws on freedom of information were certainly helpful. But it is far from clear that they could ever have brought down Kilpatrick without the unauthorised leaking of information.

Media organisations overclaim for the power of freedom of information (ATI) laws as they are some of the primary users of such laws. In the UK, the 2010 scandal of members of parliament is regarded as a success for the UK Freedom of Information Act. But, as with Kwame Kilpatrick, the full story gives a rather different picture.

The UK was held captivated in 2010 by the *Daily Telegraph* newspaper's gradual revelations of exactly what our politicians

---

[1] www.rcfp.org/browse-media-law-resources/news/mayor-shows-why-all-government-e-mails-should-be-public

had been spending taxpayer's money on in their expenses claims. The information had come into the public domain after a long FOI campaign led by journalist Heather Brooke. The details that emerged were entertaining. There was the conservative minister who had claimed that having his moat cleaned qualified as an expense 'wholly, exclusively and necessarily incurred for the performance of a Member's parliamentary duties'. His colleague claimed the cost of a duck house on the lake in his garden was similarly essential to his work as a representative of the people. By the time the dust had settled, the home secretary had resigned and six Labour members of parliament, including a former minister (Eric Illsley, Elliot Morley, David Chaytor, Jim Devine, Margaret Moran, Denis MacShane) and two conservative peers (Lord Hanningfield and Lord Taylor of Warwick), were charged with crimes in relation to false accounting. Five of the seven have been jailed. Over £500,000 of wrongly claimed expenses were paid back.

The members of parliament (MPs) expenses scandal started with two FOI requests made in 2005 shortly after the UK's Freedom of Information Act came into force. The MPs had not seen it coming and immediately tried to retrench. The House of Commons at first refused the request as being an intrusion into the privacy of MPs. The High Court overruled this. The Commons responded by attempting to change the law to exempt parliament from the act, but when this attempt failed they appeared to concede defeat, announced that they would publish the information and started doing so.

In 2008 the first details were made public for 14 senior politicians. And nothing happened. Referring to this publication, Jeremy Hayes, in a working paper on FOI for the Reuters Institute for the Study of Journalism, said: 'The first batch of expenses yielded few shocks'.[2] He then goes on to say that 'further publication in 2009 presented the home secretary, Jacqui Smith, 32 and the employment minister, Tony McNulty, 33, in an embarrassing light. The resulting row led to a review by the Committee on Standards in Public Life and moves by the

---

[2] Jeremy Hayes, *A Shock to the System: Journalism, Government and the Freedom of Information Act 2000*, RISJ Working Paper, 2009.

prime minister to reform the system for these expenses'. Jacqui Smith, whose expenses included a subscription porn channel, was forced to resign.

Just as with the Kwame Kilpatrick case, this account fails to mention a rather crucial detail. This first batch was released in response to the FOI requests – and had been carefully redacted before publication. The revelations that led to a review of the expenses system and the downfall of the home secretary were the result of information leaked to the papers. Crucial to the leak was that it included information about Jacqui Smith's home address in London. Addresses were redacted from the official information releases as sensitive information. Only the amounts paid were known. Jacqui Smith's downfall came about because she was paying her £20,000 a year London living allowance to her sister with whom she lodged. She claimed that this house was her main residence so that she could maintain her family home in Birmingham at the taxpayer's expense. Without the address information none of this would have come to light.

The Campaign for Freedom of Information in the UK cites the parliamentary expenses scandal as one of the successes of FOI legislation. But while FOI played an important role at the outset, what led to the expenses scandal was not the official release of information but the leak of the unredacted records to the *Daily Telegraph*. The importance of having the address information was summed up by Ian Watson, BBC political correspondent at the time, who said: 'by obtaining the information unofficially - the Commons authorities say potentially illegally - the *Telegraph* has been able to check which properties politicians designate as a second home. In doing so, they highlighted the practice of "flipping"'.[3]

Flipping, the biggest abuse of the expenses system, is when politicians use their entitlement to claim the expense of maintaining a second home (i.e. one in London, one in their constituency) to pay first for the renovation of one home and then 'flip' their claims to the second home and claim for the renovation of that also. Some politicians flipped their claims back

---

[3] Iain Watson, 'Risks and gains of expenses leak', BBC, 9 May 2009, http://news.bbc.co.uk/1/hi/uk_politics/8041591.stm

and forth a number of times and sold properties at a significant profit.

ATI legislation is an essential part of any democracy. However, there is a temptation to overclaim for its successes. It is striking that many of the biggest stories described as scalps for ATI are no such thing. Often, they reveal the extent to which ATI has proved unable to winkle out the key information and it is only through leaks or disclosure of information to courts in pursuit of other claims that information is forced into the public domain.

Evidence that ATI reduces corruption

Despite this, the evidence would suggest that ATI does contribute to anti-corruption efforts. A number of studies have tried to show a connection between having an FOI law and having lower levels of corruption. These studies tend to look at perceptions of corruption as the measure of corruption (since true levels of actual corruption are hard to measure by their nature). Some find a connection between FOI and lower corruption and conclude that FOI may be causing a reduction in corruption.[4] Others find that the introduction of FOI is associated with raised levels of perceived corruption, particularly in the immediate aftermath, and conclude that FOI may be exposing corruption.[5] Yet others find that FOI is associated with higher levels of perceived corruption in developing countries but not in developed countries – where there is found to be no connection between FOI and corruption.[6]

The evidence from these studies is mixed and hard to interpret, since the patterns described above are consistent with FOI being a symptom of a low-corruption society rather than a cause of reduced corruption. It might be that FOI reduces corruption. But, equally, it could be that countries which achieve lower

---

[4] Roumeen Islam, 'Does more transparency go along with better governance?', *Economics and Politics* Vol 18, No 2 (2006), 121–167.

[5] Samia Costa, *Do Freedom of Information Laws Decrease Corruption?*, December 2009, www.biu.ac.il/soc/ec/seminar/data/29_12_2009/costa_foi.pdf

[6] Monica Escaleras, Shu Lin and Charles Register, 'Freedom of Information Acts and public sector corruption', *Public Choice* Vol 145, No 3 (December 2010), 435–460.

levels of corruption through, say, better policing are the countries which tend to introduce a freedom of information law.

Rising perceptions of corruption and a reduced instance of corruption can be consistent. An interesting US study argues that we should expect an increase in transparency to cause prosecutions to rise initially as more is exposed and then fall as the true rate of corruption is reduced.[7] It compared rates of prosecution for corruption in each state both before and after the introduction of state-level FOI laws. There was a strong pattern where the introduction of the law led to an increase in prosecutions followed by a fall to a level below that seen prior to the law. The resulting hypothesis was that the introduction of FOI led to the true rate of corruption being revealed and higher rates of prosecution. That then led to a fall in the true rate of corruption.

This may well be the case. But it may equally be that the introduction of the act exposed corruption that had previously been hidden. And that this then led to more sophisticated ways of concealing the evidence. Helena Hofbauer was lucky to get the Pro-Vida receipts (see Chapter 6) because the law was new and people were not wise to what might happen. After Kwame Kilpatrick's conviction, politicians will have noted the need to check whether or not they are communicating on a personal device.

Analysis for the European Union by Alina Mungiu-Pippidi finds a similar pattern, but in this instance a range of measures of corruption are used including the international country risk guide (ICRG) corruption index – an assessment of overall corruption by political risk consultants assessing risk to business investment – as well Transparency International's survey of perceived levels of corruption among the population.[8] She finds strong evidence that in the years following introduction of

---

[7]   Adriana S. Cordis and Patrick L. Warren, 'Sunshine as disinfectant: the effect of state Freedom of Information Act laws on public corruption', *Journal of Public Economics* Vol 115 (July 2014), 18-36, http://dx.doi.org/10.1016/j.jpubeco.2014.03.010

[8]   Alina Mungiu-Pippidi, *The Good, the Bad and the Ugly: Controlling Corruption in the European Union*, Advanced Policy Paper for Discussion in the European Parliament, 9 April 2013.

ATI legislation corruption falls. Furthermore, she looks at FOI alongside three other possible interventions – the establishment of an anti-corruption unit, the creation of an ombudsman service and signing up to the UN Convention against Corruption (UNCAC). ATI is the only one that is found to have an association with a fall in the measures of corruption. The fact that it behaves differently from other moves to reduce corruption is compelling evidence.

A different story has emerged from the work of Robert Hazell and Ben Worthy, two academics at University College London who have spent several years studying the impact of FOI in the UK.[9]

In advance of the new law, they first analysed all the statements about FOI made by politicians and in policy documents and summarised the claimed benefits as follows:

- Increasing openness and transparency of government
- Increasing accountability of government
- Improving quality of decision making
- Improving public understanding of government
- Increasing trust in government
- Increasing participation in government. [10]

They then surveyed FOI requesters, reviewed media articles and conducted 56 interviews. The results, in this first ever summative systematic evaluation of FOI legislation anywhere in the world, find that only one of these benefits has clearly been delivered to a significant degree. They find that government has

---

[9] R. Hazell, Benjamin Worthy and M. Glover, *The Impact of the Freedom of Information Act on Central Government in the UK: Does Freedom of Information Work?*, *Understanding Governance*, Palgrave Macmillan, 2010.

[10] Note in passing the difference in language between benefits of FOI identified by the UK government and the benefits of publicity listed by Bentham. The former is far kinder to government but diminishes the role of the public. Instead of more honest government we have more accountable government and improved decision making. Where Bentham hoped that people might be better able to express their grievances, the UK government hopes people will benefit from an increased 'understanding' of government and ability to 'participate'.

become more transparent at least as defined in terms of a net increase in the amount of information available to the public.

On everything else – on the substantive benefits – the evidence is less reassuring. They conclude that FOI has not increased trust in government, nor has it led to improved public understanding; it has not increased participation in government, nor has it improved decision making. The best that can be said is that it has had a marginal effect on accountability,[11] with some clear examples of evidence coming to light through FOI that has revealed how decisions were made and identified individual responsibility for particular actions. In some cases, it has uncovered errors in previous accounts of decision making. However, these instances do not reliably occur with sufficient timeliness to carry consequences for those found responsible for errors.

Transparency International UK conducted an analysis of 95 instances of corruption identified on its database drawn from press reports.[12] It found that the highest number of corrupt incidents were disclosed by law enforcement (34%), followed by investigative journalists (25%), FOI requests (14%) and whistleblowing (13%). Open data was identified in 7% of cases. The FOI cases were successful primarily in uncovering legal activity, that was nonetheless corrupt, rather than illegality.

ATI, the media and the public interest

ATI legislation is currently in retreat in many parts of the world. This has been informed by evidence that lack of deliberative privacy – a space in which people can discuss ideas in confidence – is damaging to effective decision making.

A further charge laid against ATI is the view that it has itself become corrupted and used by the media and special interest groups to distort public debate. This is the argument that the UK

---

[11] With reference to the discussion in Chapter 2, Hazell and Worthy use the term accountability to mean the ability to get an account of how decisions were made and who was responsible. Accountability in their usage does not imply that there must be consequences if this information reveals culpability.

[12] *How Open Data can Help Tackle Corruption*, Transparency International UK, 2015.

government has put forward to justify a review of the law. The minister announcing this decision, Chris Grayling, described the use of the UK's freedom of information law to research stories as 'unacceptable'. Not surprisingly, his words prompted a fair degree of ridicule from media commentators, who pointed out that this was precisely what the law was supposed to enable. It was the media using ATI to hold government to account that prevented people like Chris Grayling getting away with things.

That, at least, is the theory. And there are clear examples of FOI being used effectively in this way. However, there is evidence to suggest that most of the time this is not what is happening. The *Guardian* newspaper ran a story after the government announced its review, listing 103 stories which, it said, showed Chris Grayling was wrong. Below we have taken the first 10 and analysed them. The results are typical of any 10 selected at random from the list. Our analysis does not support the view that ATI is leading to the sort of informed debate and the holding to account of power that the *Guardian* claims.

ATI and data

As the analysis of the *Guardian* stories shows, ATI is now being used increasingly to try to access data sets from the administrative records of government. A successful example of this was a group of investigative journalists across Europe who successfully collated a data set on the distribution of farm subsidies which showed how the bulk of the money was not going to small farmers. Public rhetoric in defence of farm subsidies had often emphasised the need for taxpayers to support such people. The evidence gathered by Brigitte Alfter and the International Consortium of Investigative Journalists (ICIJ) showed that the biggest recipients of this money were large agri-businesses and very wealthy landowners.

There are other outstanding examples in the work of journalists. We looked at all the winners and nominees for the Pulitzer Prize for investigative reporting between 2005 and 2014. The first thing to note is that ATI plays little or no role in the vast majority of cases. However, there are exceptions. Revelations by the *Birmingham News* of corrupt appointments of politicians to sinecures in the Alabama state two-year college system[13] was done through careful and persistent use of FOI to create a data set of political appointments to colleges. The pattern that emerged showed a string of politicians in posts with limited duties and high remuneration. It might have been possible to defend one or two as unfortunate errors of judgement, but the widespread and consistent pattern that emerged provided strong evidence of systemic corruption.

An inventive use of public records access laws was *The Sacramento Bee*'s successful attempt to get information about bus tickets booked by a Nevada mental hospital which enabled them to reveal a pattern of patients being discharged and dumped out of state.[14] Public data, rather than FOI, was also important in some Pulitzer Prize-winning stories – such as the *Sarasota Herald-Tribune* analysis of insurance accounts to expose regulatory failings[15] or the *Seattle Times* analysis of death certificates to identify the dangers of prescribing methadone.[16] In each case, an individual failing would have little resonance. A single patient dying of methadone is just unfortunate. It becomes discrimination when you can show consistently higher death rates amongst poorer patients put on methadone than wealthier patients on higher cost drugs.

The difficulty with the ATI mechanism is that it was designed with the idea of making documents available to public view, not as a mechanism to drive the release of data sets. Consequently, most requests end up with very limited amounts of information. Data is useful for establishing patterns of activity, trends and relationships. But to do that, you need data at scale produced to sufficient standards of accuracy, in consistent formats. Using the combative ATI process can mean months, if not years of request, clarification and further request before a coherent data set can be compiled. The work of Brigitte Alfter and the ICIJ to collect data on farm subsidies in the EU took months of complex work by teams of journalists across the European Union to extract a

---

[13]   2007 Pulitzer Prize-winner by Brett Blackledge.
[14]   2014 runner-up by Cynthia Hubert and Phillip Reese.
[15]   2011 Pulitzer Prize-winner by Paige St John.
[16]   2012 Pulitzer Prize-winner by Michel J. Berens and Ken Armstrong.

single consistent data set. If someone inside the bureaucracy had requested the same data, we might imagine it would have been produced much more quickly and at much less cost.

ATI and privacy

ATI is a poor mechanism for accessing data in part because of the nature of the mechanism. It is also poorly suited to this task because it provides no means to deal with privacy issues. Access to detailed data or raw information in any form will often give rise to privacy concerns – as happened with requests for information on farm subsidies. When farmers complained that this was personal financial information, they won the right to have certain information restricted.

Many of the issues that the stories identified by the *Guardian* aim to address could only be properly addressed through analysis of much more granular information. But that more detailed level of information would be unavailable to the journalists because it would raise issues of privacy.

Similar issues have arisen with the use of ATI to try to get hold of dashcam (or dashboard camera) footage from police officers in the US. The appearance of this footage in the public domain has provided evidence not only of individual cases of civil rights violations but of a culture within the police that is tolerant of such violations. Its dissemination through social media has had an enormous effect in galvanising public protest in a way that access to documentary or statistical information never could.

The footage of interest will by its nature tend to relate to incidents that form part of an ongoing investigation or a trial which can be used to justify non-disclosure under ATI (although the legal basis of this is subject to question). The most controversial footage has been released as the result of the judge in such court cases overruling police requests that the evidence should be sealed on grounds of public interest.

The law is currently in flux, with some states bringing in legislation to restrict the degree to which such footage can be subject to FOI and other states strengthening legislation to prevent deletion of material or to require flagging of material of potential public interest. We would argue that on the principles set out earlier, such information should be automatically and routinely shared with the citizen and the technology should be built with this in mind.

ATI and access to personal data

ATI legislation (often in the form of separate data protection legislation) also enables people to access their own records. While this is seen most often as a mechanism to check what information is held about an individual it can also be used as a means of ensuring people are deal with fairly.

In Indonesia, two of the commitments made as part of their Open Government Partnership plan were of this sort – a commitment to allow people to know about the processing of any complaint made to the police, including the name of the officer responsible, and a commitment to let people know about the progress of any application made for a government job.

It was this approach which produced perhaps the single most convincing piece of evidence that ATI can stop corruption. An academic research study by Leonid Peisakhin looked at whether individuals could use ATI to ensure that their own dealings with government were handled honestly.[17]

In India, registration on the electoral roll is needed not just to vote but also to get a voter identification (ID) card which is needed for a host of other important tasks such as job applications or receipt of government benefits. Legally, applications are supposed to be processed within 60 days. The reality is very different and it is common practice for people to bribe officials in order to get their applications processed more quickly.

For the study, the researchers recruited groups of urban poor (income: $1.50/day) and middle class (income: $10/day) to register on the electoral roll. Some simply put in an application and waited. Others put in an application and enclosed a 1000 rupees (the usual level of bribe). A third group put in an application but followed up with a request under the Right

---

[17] L. Peisakhin, 'Transparency and corruption: evidence from India', *Journal of Law and Economics* Vol 55, No 1 (February 2012), 129-149.

to Information Act, asking 'What is the current status of my application?' and 'What is the average waiting time?'

The results were remarkable. They showed that an ATI request was about as effective as a bribe, with both resulting in the wait falling by more than half.

At the end of the 11-month period, most of those who had simply put in an application were still waiting. The urban poor were the worst treated, with 74% of applications still outstanding after 11 months, while the middle classes fared better with only 43% of applications still unprocessed.

Those who paid a bribe saw their applications processed in 100-150 days, although within this group the urban poor still waited longer than the middle class applicants. The group that put in information requests received similar waiting times to those paying a bribe and saw no significant difference in the treatment of rich and poor.

The authors conclude that this provides clear evidence of how FOI requests can indeed reduce corruption by making bribes unnecessary and that furthermore it can reduce class differences in government services.

That seems a fair conclusion and points towards how transparency can be made to work more effectively. Here transparency is being used to make sure that the handling of one individual is fair, not to try to bring down a politician through media exposure of deceit and corruption.

It might be argued that there is a problem with Peisakhin's study because, while it did expose system level corruption, and while it did enable some people to get their applications sorted more quickly, it did nothing to change the system. On the other hand, a mechanism by which people could individually circumvent the corruption, if used enough, might perhaps be a more effective way to change the system. In Chapter 14, we will explore further the relationship between 'personal level' transparency – that is, access to information about the handling of your own case – with transparency about the workings of whole systems.

Summary

Summarising the evidence, there is a persuasive case that ATI legislation has played a role in reducing corruption. But its impact is highly variable and it appears to be less effective than other mechanisms such as leaking, whistleblowing, criminal investigation and investigative journalism. Arguments for ATI as a democratic human right provide a more secure basis to defend these laws than evidence of efficacy.

The ability of ATI to act as a mechanism to expose unfair allocation systems, corrupt decision making or ineffective public institutions is limited in its effectiveness because of the degree to which those being held to account control the production of the information that can be accessed through ATI. In Chapter 8 we set out the view that the impact of ATI is blunted by the extent to which organisations are able to control the recording and format of information. While steps can be taken to try to reduce the freedom to do this, there is a limit to what can be done without infringing the privacy of public servants or undermining the effectiveness of government by eliminating deliberative freedom.

Finally, although not much used in this way, rights to individual data access requests may be as important as – if not more important than – a mechanism for collecting information that identifies unfair allocations and corrupt processes.

STORIES THAT PROVE THE VALUE OF FOI?

When Chris Grayling, the Conservative minister, announced a cross-party review of the use of the Freedom of Information Act in the UK because of the media were misusing it to research news stories, the *Guardian* published its list of stories that 'prove Chris Grayling wrong' and which were 'all in the public interest'.

A closer look at the first 10 stories in the *Guardian*'s list does identify a problem with this process, however (see Table 9.1). For each we have asked four questions:

- Is it in the public interest?
- Is there a broad point being implied by the story?
- Does the information substantiate the point being made?
- Is there a conflict of interest that affects the reporting of the story?

With the last question we exclude the natural political leanings that any media organisations will quite properly exhibit and we consider only more immediate conflicts.

All these stories are clearly matters of public interest and bring additional information into the public domain about those issues. However, in six of the 10, the implications of the data are incorrectly reported as the data does not support the suggested interpretation. The *Sun* story argues that more than 40 out of 250 UK citizens returning from fighting in Syria and Iraq should have been prosecuted. This is a conclusion that it cannot substantiate as it knows nothing further about the individuals who were not prosecuted. It is an appeal to 'common sense' and/or public prejudice, depending on your point of view. The *Sun* is conflicted in its reporting as it argues that this reveals a bias in the prosecution, which has opted instead to prosecute *Sun* journalists.

The *Mirror* report that 49,000 claims for damage to cars as a result of potholes means that we are not investing enough in roads. Again, nothing in the information provided could substantiate such a claim. To do this, there would have to be a view on what was an acceptable level of pothole damage. The view that it should be zero is unlikely, since the level of investment that this would require is unlikely to be optimal. Even if it was zero, the *Mirror* presents no reason for supposing this to be true. Instead, the reporting plays on the unspoken but false assumption that if something is bad, it ought never to occur. There is a clear conflict of interest as the information has been collected and analysed by a research group linked to a roadside assistance business and is used in the article to argue for less investment in rail and more investment in roads. Furthermore, the most important implication of the figures quoted in the article is that the total cost of compensation has fallen, suggesting that things are improving. This, however, is not clearly stated and instead the rather smaller increase in the number of claims is said to be the most important fact. This increase of less than 10% is very likely to be random year-on-year variation. The bias in the reporting is consistent with the interests of the organisation sponsoring the research.

The *Guardian* reports that the BBC has used its powers to look at emails of 150 staff members and reports the NUJ (National Union of Journalists) view that this 'casts doubt' on the BBC's claim that this is only used in criminal or disciplinary cases. Why? What number would the NUJ have said failed to cast doubt on their claim? Why is 150 an unlikely number to be caused by investigations into criminal and disciplinary cases?

The reporting by the *Manchester Evening Guardian* of the number of crimes committed by children is a standard technique advocated in media guides on how to get an easy story from FOI. Whatever the number reported, it is said to be 'shocking'. Clearly it is shocking that children commit crimes. But as a news headline 'children commit crimes' would not be shocking. The addition of the number with the word 'shocking' implies that we should expect fewer offences to be taking place. But there is no reason to believe this on the basis of the information presented.

In the *Guardian* report of BP's donation to the Tate, no broader unsubstantiated conclusions are drawn from this figure. It is simply presented as useful additional information in relation to the debate over whether or not the Tate should accept certain forms of corporate sponsorship. Similarly, the *Times* report that there has been an increase in cheating on driving tests draws no further conclusions from this fact. Finally there are two stories on use of public funds – one to pay expenses for an executive and one to pay for flowers for the grave of a paedophile who died in jail without any family. It is perfectly legitimate to express the view that public money should not be used for such purposes and readers are able to come to their own conclusions.

This last story might even be seen as a perfect example of FOI in action. The public were made aware of an issue they had not previously known about. Disapproval was voiced in the media which, quite likely, reflected accurately public opinion. After the story ran, government policy was changed. A victory for the people, it would seem.

The stories that the *Guardian* proffer as evidence of the value of FOI could equally be construed as demonstrating the inadequacies of FOI as a mechanism to investigate many serious questions. Rather than a penetrating insight into areas that government has attempted to conceal, we are offered a profusion of stories based on a handful of data points that are rarely sufficient to make any argument objectively. They are only convincing to the degree that they are deployed to bolster existing prejudices.

It would be very hard to take someone's expense account data and argue that they ought to be spending more in order to do their job effectively. It would equally be hard to take figures for the number of children who have committed crime and run a headline extolling the effectiveness of our police and our schools in keeping child crime rates so low.

The result is a form of transparency that works most effectively only when it reinforces existing belief systems and the power structures that have given rise to them. Such transparency might be regarded as the enemy of an open society rather than its ally.

Table 9.1: Ten stories cited as evidence of value of Freedom of Information

Headline	Quotes/key facts	Comment
Only 40 of 250 returning jihadis in UK face prosecution: *The Sun* (www.thesun.co.uk/sol/homepage/news/politics/6288118/Only-40-of-250-returning-jihadis-facing-prosecution-while-CPS-orders-retrial-of-Sun-journalists.html)	'Feeble action on alleged traitors [fighters returning from Syria and Iraq] emerged yesterday as the CPS [Crown Prosecution Service] ordered a £5 million retrial of four *Sun* staff'. 'The relentless pursuit of journalists over jihadis was last night slammed as a huge waste of public money.' 'The low number of those [jihadis] facing prosecution will alarm Brits.'	*Public interest:* Yes *Implication:* More should have been prosecuted *Implication substantiated:* No *Conflict of interest:* Yes
Tate's BP sponsorship was £150,000 to £330,000 a year, figures show: *The Guardian* (www.theguardian.com/artanddesign/2015/jan/26/tate-reveal-bp-sponsorship-150000-330000-platform-information-tribunal)	[It was wrong for Tate to take the money, given] 'BP's horrendous environmental record, and their role in obfuscating climate science and slowing down a meaningful response to climate change.' 'BP has a lot of money and Tate is an important gallery and it would be nice if BP gave more. Tate should be asking for more. I have no problem with oil companies, we need them'.	*Public interest:* Yes *Implication:* None made (the story does not suggest that the new information – the sum paid – has any bearing on whether it was right or wrong to accept it) *Conflict of interest:* None

Headline	Quotes/key facts	Comment
Pothole Britain: 49,000 people demand compensation for damage caused to vehicles by worn-out roads: *Daily Mirror* (www.mirror.co.uk/news/uk-news/pothole-britain-49000-people-demand-5042100)	'It is the equivalent of a claim being submitted every 11 minutes day and night 365 days a year and an increase on the 2012/13 figure of 46,139 claims, according to the RAC Foundation.' 'The average payout for a successful claim in 2013/14 was £286, down from £357.' Professor Stephen Glaister, director of the RAC Foundation, said 'This is about prioritisation and our roads should be at the top of the list.'	*Public interest:* Yes *Implication:* Too many potholes because of lack of investment in roads *Implication substantiated:* No. In fact figures support the opposite conclusion as the total cost of compensation is going down, but the presentation obscures this. *Conflict of interest:* Yes
Clare's Law: 1,300 domestic abuse disclosures made: BBC News (www.bbc.co.uk/news/uk-30977759)	A scheme allowing people to find out if their partner has a history of domestic violence has been used more than 1300 times in less than a year. Clare Wood's father said he was 'quietly delighted' the law was being used.	*Public interest:* Yes *Implication:* The law is being used *Implication substantiated:* Yes

Headline	Quotes/key facts	Comment
BBC accused of 'spying' after nearly 150 staff emails accessed or monitored: *The Guardian* (www.theguardian.com/media/2015/jan/14/bbc-spying-staff-emails-accessed-monitored)	The BBC said 37 staff email accounts had been monitored because of leak investigations in 2013 and 2014. Other staff accounts had been looked into as a result of … allegations of fraud, assault, harassment and disciplinary cases.	*Public interest:* Yes
		Implication: Powers are being misused
		Implication substantiated: No
	Michelle Stanistreet, general secretary of the National Union of Journalists, said: 'The BBC has previously denied any significant monitoring of staff email accounts, and only in criminal or disciplinary investigations, but these figures cast doubt on that explanation.'	*Conflict of interest:* Two related issues here. One: journalists reporting on their own working conditions. Two: *The Guardian*, reporting this, is not subject to the same FOI requirements as the BBC
Prison service spends over £2,500 on funeral for child-killer: ITV News (www.itv.com/news/2015-01-25/prison-service-spends-over-2-500-on-funeral-for-child-killer)	Raymond Morris, originally from Walsall, died at HMP [Her Majesty's Prison] Preston in March 2014 while serving a life sentence for the rape and murder of a seven-year-old girl.	*Public interest:* Yes
		Implication: More money is spent on prison funerals than author believes is acceptable
	The Ministry of Justice (MoJ) said a single floral tribute provided on behalf of the prison service was considered a 'reasonable' cost of prisoner funeral arrangements.	*Implication substantiated:* Yes
		Conflict of interest: None
	'Prison Service Instruction 64/2011 advises that prisons must offer to pay a contribution towards reasonable funeral expenses of up to £3,000. This is considered to be moral and decent in the circumstances.'A MoJ source said, in a story update: 'Taxpayers' money should not – and in future will not – be spent on flowers for offenders who die in prison.'	

Headline	Quotes/key facts	Comment
Two children aged 7 and 8 suspected of rape as figures reveal almost 1000 alleged child criminals last year: *Manchester Evening News* (www.manchestereveningnews.co.uk/news/greater-manchester-news/two-children-aged-7-8-8370917)	'Shocking figures ... show the extent of crimes those under the age of 10 were suspected of committing last year in Greater Manchester.'	*Public interest:* Yes
		Implication: There is too much child crime
	'Because of their age, they will never be charged or taken to court for their crimes.'	*Implication substantiated:* No. The 'shock' of the figures being too high rests not on the belief that there is a lower acceptable figure but on the unstated and indefensible assumption that we should expect the rate to be zero.
	David Spencer, research director of the Centre for Crime Prevention, said: 'In cases when children of this age are committing such offences, they have often been the victims of criminal behaviour, neglect, or worse, in their home lives. It is right for them to be punished for their actions, but difficult to hold them criminally responsible if they have never been taught right from wrong themselves.'	*Conflict of interest:* None
Driving test fraud: More learner drivers caught cheating: BBC News (www.bbc.co.uk/news/uk-30989499)	More novice motorists in Britain are being caught trying to cheat the written and practical driving tests by hiring lookalikes, figures show.	*Public interest:* Yes
		Implication: Driving test cheating is increasing
	From April to the end of December 2014, there were 677 reported cases, compared with 554 for the whole of 2013–14 and 628 in 2012–13. Criminals are charging up to £1,800 to sit an exam, according to the *Times*.	*Implications substantiated:* Yes
	The DVSA said this type of crime was a serious offence but extremely rare.	*Conflict of interest:* None

Headline	Quotes/key facts	Comment
TfL boss charges taxpayers for £40 bottles of wine and meals at the Groucho: MayorWatch (www.mayorwatch.co.uk/tfl-boss-charges-taxpayers-for-40-bottles-of-wine-and-meals-at-the-groucho)	Transport commissioner Sir Peter Hendy has been urged to publish the names of those he entertains on expenses after it emerged fare-payers are picking up the tab for expensive wines and generous tips. Receipts since provided to MayorWatch include meals at the exclusive members-only Groucho Club where fare-payers, who this month saw the cost of their fares increase by up to 38%, treated Sir Peter and guests to bottles of wine costing up to £44 each. Sir Peter's party enjoyed a £32.50 leg of lamb.	*Public interest:* Yes *Implication:* Peter Hendy is spending more on his expenses than the author thinks acceptable*Implication substantiated:* Yes – to the extent you agree with the author's opinion*Conflict of interest:* None
NHS gives contraceptives to girls aged 10: *The Times* (www.thetimes.co.uk/tto/health/child-health/article4335708.ece)	Girls as young as 10 have been given contraceptive implants in the past five years, leading to fears among charities of widespread abuse. The implant, which has not been medically tested on under-18s, has been given to at least three 10-year-olds since 2010 and to almost 10,000 girls under the age of consent.	*Public interest:* Yes *Implication:* Doctors are making the wrong decision about the risks and benefits to the young people being given this contraceptive *Implication substantiated:* No *Conflict of interest:* None

10

Social audit and public reporting

Perhaps the best known example of using FOI to combat corruption is the story of Mazdoor Kisan Shakti Sangathan (MKSS, or the Association for the Empowerment of Workers and Peasants). Founded in India in the 1980s to fight for better pay and conditions for poorer people, the group identified that one of the principal difficulties it faced was misappropriation of social welfare funds. The group launched a campaign for access to information about welfare budgets, which led to the remarkable sight of peasants protesting outside government offices – calling not for work or housing or food but for information. All they wanted to know was where the money supposedly allocated for their welfare had gone.

The campaign led to two developments – the first, new laws granting rights to information in India; the second, a new method of using these rights. In its original incarnation, this was called Jan Sunwais or 'public hearings'. These events would take place after a successful petition for information relating to welfare spending in, say, a particular village. A public meeting would be called and the information would be read out, allowing an on-the-spot crowd-sourced audit of the accuracy of the information. Shekar Singh, who worked on the National Campaign for the Right to Information, has described how they work:[1]

---

[1] Shekar Singh, 'India: grassroots initiatives', in *The Right to Know: Transparency for an Open World*, ed Ann Florini, Columbia University Press, 2007.

The first jansunwai in Kot Kirana panchayat (December 1994) was held in front of an incomplete building with no roof. As the list of purported expenses was being read out, an item on which 30,000 rupees had been spent the previous year in constructing the roof of a government office came up for verification. Everyone burst into spontaneous laughter, for the roofless building nearby was that very government office. In another case, the name of a villager was read out as the recipient of hire charges for his bullock cart. The agitated villager protested loudly that he was never given any money and, in any case, he did not own a bullock cart. He added, for good measure, that if they still insisted that they had hired his bullock cart, could they please return it to him.

This campaign was the start of what has become a worldwide effort to develop social audit and public expenditure tracking – the idea that the public could stop the corrupt misappropriation of funds by policing the use of public money.

Evidence that Social Audit works in developing economies

In India, social audit was made a mandatory part of the Mahatma Ghandi National Rural Employment Guarantee Act (MNREGA), which guaranteed a minimum amount of employment for people volunteering for work in rural communities. Implementation was delayed in many parts of the country, for example in Rajasthan, because bureaucrats objected to the involvement of 'outsiders' in the supervision of their work.

The implementation of the scheme in the state of Andra Pradesh (AP) has been held up as a model example of how to do it. Audit teams were trained and given unrestricted access to the books of the project administrators. Public hearings were held regularly to review the audit findings. Compared to other states, Andra Pradesh's thorough implementation of social audit has been associated with an improved performance.[2]

Some assessments of the impact audits in AP were less enthusiastic. Work by Farzana Afridi and Vegard Iversen found only modest evidence of a reduction of misappropriation of funds.[3] There was clear evidence of reduction in the type of corruption easiest to detect – the failure to offer work or pay wages. But they saw a trend towards substituting harder to detect acts, such as purchasing low-grade materials but booking the cost of high-grade materials, for easy to detect acts such as not paying wages.

The problem, they suggest, is not simply that one is harder to spot than the other. The reason is also that the cruder forms of corruption are perpetrated by low-level local functionaries who could be effectively shamed and held to account in the meetings. In contrast, those higher up the chain were immune. If a scam was uncovered, that particular form of misappropriation might be put right. But official sanctions were rarely used against those discovered to have done wrong. For the officials involved there was little or no risk in simply coming up with some new system to divert the funds.

Similar conclusions were reached in Indonesia. There, efforts to engage local communities in overseeing the spending of money on road-building programmes had no effect on the levels of corruption or the efficiency with which public resources were used.

In contrast to these stories, there are some very clear examples of social audit working. One of the more celebrated examples was in Uganda of information where money paid to schools was published in newspapers throughout the country. The intention was that 'social audit' – the public noticing and complaining if they saw that the money for their schools was not being spent on their schools – would reduce the amount stolen en route as the money travelled through layers of bureaucracy from the

---

[2]   Shylashri Shankar, ,ASARC Working Paper 2010/09.

[3]   F. Afridi and V. Iversen, 'Social audits and MGNREGA delivery: lessons from Andhra Pradesh', in *India Policy Forum*, ed Barry Bosworth, Arvind Panagariya and Shekhar Shah, Brookings Institution, 2014.

national treasury to the local classroom. Analysis of the results showed a clear pattern in which the amount of money that 'leaked' along the way fell overall, and fell more the closer the school was to an outlet selling newspapers. Subsequent studies have shown that initial estimates of the impact of publication may have overstated the effect by failing to take account of other changes at the same time, including increases in funding and changes to the administration of education.[4] But even with the caveats, the publication of information does appear to have contributed significantly to preventing the theft of public funds.

Another project that was found to have a significant effect in improving services in Uganda was one that gave communities information about the performance of their local health services, together with a forum in which they express their views to providers.[5] This involved a structured process of public engagement facilitated by outsiders but did not involve clear repercussions in the event of failure to deliver improvements. Tested in 50 areas, it produced a sharp decline in infant mortality compared to other regions. Attempts to achieve similar improvements in the Indian educational system have been less successful, despite the fact that the failures within the service are highly visible (for example, teacher absentee rates of 25%).

Evidence that public reporting works in developed economies

Social audit is a term used most frequently to refer to programmes in developing countries to reduce corruption in public administration. In developed economies, similar programmes have emerged to improve the efficiency of public services, generally referred to as public reporting programmes. The target of such efforts has been more often described as low

---

[4]   Paul Hubbard, *Putting the Power of Transparency in Context: Information's Role in Reducing Corruption in Uganda's Education Sector,* Working Paper No 136, Centre for Global Development, December 2007.

[5]   Martina Bjorkman and Jakob Svensson, 'Power to the people: evidence from a randomized field experiment on community-based monitoring in Uganda', *Quarterly Journal of Economics* Vol 124, No 2 (2009), 735–769. DOI:10.1162/qjec.2009.124.2.735

quality services or inefficient use of public resources rather than corrupt misuse of funds. Problems such as staff absenteeism or theft of public funds tend to be lower in developed economies, although the point at which a high rate of staff absenteeism ceases to qualify as corruption and instead becomes described as inefficient management is open to debate.

The publication of information about service standards in health, education and policing has become common in the US and the UK, along with published data about the resources, levels of staffing and the pay of managers. This has been accompanied by policies to open up competition either through encouraging citizens to choose service providers or by allowing commissioners of services to run competitive tenders.

There is a difference in the political dynamics of transparency between developing economies and developed countries. In developing countries, international donors and 'contender' democratic parties tend to be advocates for transparency against the established power structures. In developed economies, transparency policies are more often seen as a left versus right wing issue in which such policies represent part of a broader programme to reduce state ownership of public service providers and weaken the influence of unionized labour. But below the surface the objectives and mechanisms of such policies are remarkably similar in all countries and are driven by the need to increase the productivity of public services in order to deliver more for any given tax take.

As in developing countries, the evidence of efficacy in developed economies is mixed, but the weight of evidence on balance is positive. In healthcare, systematic reviews of evidence have found good evidence of an association between publication of information on standards of care and improvements in quality of care.[6] The effect is not huge but, interestingly, studies suggest that paying healthcare organisations to improve their performance on particular measures of quality has only a slightly bigger effect than simply publishing information about the relative performance of different organisations.[7] In Education the evidence again suggests a positive impact although the contribution to this caused by individuals selecting schools is limited.[8]

The public rhetoric behind these programmes has often emphasised the right of the public to know about variations in quality of services and to be able to act on that information. However, the evidence from both health and education is that, while the public often view information about performance, it has little impact on the decisions about which services to use. Instead, it has been the response of professionals and managers that has, in the main, driven improvement.

In some cases, the professionals have themselves, led initiatives to increase transparency around their work. In the UK, Sir Bruce Keogh, a heart surgeon and now medical director of NHS England, persuaded his surgical colleagues to publish outcomes at individual level, including death rates, in 2008. Since then,

---

[6] Annette M. Totten, Jesse Wagner, Arpita Tiwari, Christen O'Haire, Jessica Griffin and Miranda Walker, *Public Reporting as a Quality Improvement Strategy Closing the Quality Gap: Revisiting the State of the Science*, Evidence Report/Technology Assessment Number 2085, Prepared for Agency for Healthcare Research and Quality, US Department of Health and Human Services AHRQ Publication No 12-E011-EF, July 2012; Paul G. Shekelle, Yee-Wei Lim, Soeren Mattke and Cheryl Damberg, *Does Public Release of Performance Results Improve Quality of Care? A Systematic Review*, The Health Foundation, 2008.

[7] Peter K. Lindenauer, Denise Remus, Sheila Roman, Michael B. Rothberg, Evan M. Benjamin, Allen Ma and Dale W. Bratzler, 'Public reporting and pay for performance in hospital quality improvement', *New England Journal of Medicine* No 356 (2007), 486-496. DOI: 10.1056/NEJMsa064964

[8] Jaekyung Lee, 'Is test-driven external accountability effective? Synthesizing the evidence from cross-state causal-comparative and correlational studies', *Review of Educational Research* , (September 2008), 608-644; S. Burgess, D. Wilson and J. Worth, *A Natural Experiment in School Accountability: The Impact of School Performance Information on Pupil Progress and Sorting* (CMPO Research Report), University of Bristol, Centre for Market and Public Organization,

research has suggested that performance has improved so that 1,000 fewer avoidable deaths occur from heart surgery in NHS hospitals.

Despite the limited degree to which citizens choose services, competition is still important and the effect of public reporting is stronger where there is more competition between services. Also, there is evidence that the response of citizens to information about services can be dramatically enhanced by the way information is disseminated.[9] Public reporting has proved itself most powerful as an additional mechanism by which governments and other regulatory agencies can apply pressure on public service providers to perform. The presentation of this information in the public domain adds legitimacy to this work. Furthermore, it acts as a form of pre-commitment for government. By staking its reputation on seeing improvement in published performance information, the government limits the possibility of service providers being able to bargain with it for less demanding terms.

More recently, initiatives such as Collective Impact originated in the US have tried to strengthen the voice of communities in holding services to account and expressing concerns. In that regard, the use of transparency in public services is moving more towards the social audit models first used in developing economies. This approach tries to bring together users and providers of public services in an environment where they can review evidence of how well those responsible for the service are meeting the needs of users and jointly assess whether resources are being used fairly and efficiently.

Reasons for social audit effectiveness

Jonathan Fox, professor at the School of International Service of Washington University, reviewed the best known cases of social audit in developing countries and concluded, first, that

9   Jeffrey R. Kling, Sendhil Mullainathan, Eldar Shafir, Lee C. Vermeulen and Marian V. Wrobel, 'Comparison friction: experimental evidence from Medicare drug plans', *Quarterly Journal of Economics* Vol 127, No 1 (2012), 199-235. DOI: 10.1093/qje/qjr055

the question 'does it work?' was asked badly.[10] Just as vaccines work, but not against all illnesses, social audits can work, but not against all ills in all circumstances.

He also points out that the benchmark for failure is not clear. When community oversight of food distribution programmes in rural Mexico was found to be ineffective in two-thirds of cases it was regarded as a failure. But for the third of areas where it worked, it brought enormous benefits.

Afridi and Iversen were cautious about the impact of MNREGA in India, pointing out that 87% of the money stolen had not been recovered. But they also pointed out that the social audit element of the rural employment programme accounts for about 1% of the cost. In terms of return on investment that might be regarded as rather good value. In the words of one of the managers of the AP scheme: 'saying that recovering 13% of the money is trivial is living in a fairy tale'. She then added that, unlike other parts of India, in AP activists involved in MNREGA social audit had not been murdered.[11]

Even if you take the view that the overall reduction in financial leakage is disappointing, for individual workers who as a result receive both the work and the wage they were due, it is unquestionably a success. Even if other forms of corruption result in an equivalent loss of public funds, there is still a benefit to those who have been spared mistreatment.

But Fox's central conclusion is that the key feature of successful social audit is bringing effective sanctions against those exposed by such audit. Unsuccessful social audit occurs when no proper mechanisms are established to move from the findings of the audit to sanctions against wrongdoers.

Fox argues that there needs to be better coordination between the work in releasing information and efforts to make public servants more responsive and accountable. This could take the form of managerial interventions such as stronger performance management, but if the system is sufficiently corrupt this will not

---

[10] Jonathan A. Fox , 'Social accountability: what does the evidence really say?', *World Development* Vol 72 (August 2015), 346–361.

[11] Jonathan Fox, *Social Accountability: What Does the Evidence Really Say?*, GPSA Working Paper No 1, September 2014.

work. Alternatives are the imposition of ombudsman systems to hear and rule on complaints or the extension of legal rights to citizens (and financial legal aid) to bring public servants to court.

He also makes the point that attempts to induce participation by disempowered people rarely work and tend to get co-opted by elites. Belief in effective sanctions and the willingness of people to engage in social audit go hand in hand. It is hard to persuade people to engage unless they have a sufficiently high degree of faith that doing something will result in action.

This issue is believed to lie behind the failure of a well-designed social audit system of the water supply in Tanzania. Irregular water supplies and the unfair distribution of water – with more resources going to better off communities – is a problem in many Tanzanians' lives. The Maji Matone project was set up to allow villagers to report failures in their water supply. Whenever the water pumps stopped working, people could text a free number to report the problem. The information collated was open for all to check. This was seen as being more reliable than getting the water administration to report its own service failures and would enable people to see that their complaints were being acted on. But it did not work. Too few people sent texts. Part of the problem was that mobile phones, while widespread, are more often in the possession of men while women collect water. In addition, there was a belief that nothing positive would happen, together perhaps with concern about complaining.[12] The result was that it never got off the ground and the programme was closed down.

Fox advocates a 'sandwich' strategy in which support for 'scaled up collective action and voice' are bolstered by government action to ensure that the state provides the necessary mechanisms whereby it can respond to such. For sandwich strategies to work there has to be both downward pressure from some form of authority that has oversight of the organisation being subjected

---

[12] Björn-Sören Gigler and Savita Bailur, *Closing the Feedback Loop: Can Technology Bridge the Accountability Gap?* World Bank, 2014. © World Bank. https://openknowledge.worldbank.org/handle/10986/18408 License: CC BY 3.0 IGO.

to transparency and upward pressure from the individuals and communities that are served by that organisation.

This analysis of social audit projects in the developing world is consistent with the evidence of public reporting in developed economies where the impact of the publication of information has been as much if not more due to upward accountability to payers, regulators and political overseers rather than downward accountability to citizens, students and patients.

This analysis highlights that there is a risk that public reporting and social audit can become divorced from the interests of citizens and communities to become little more than an adjunct to traditional top-down managerial control of public services. The primary focus of most of this book is on how the 'upward' pressure from society at large can be strengthened. Fox agrees with other analysts that such pressure cannot be artificially induced by the government. Government may be able to amplify such pressures, but if it is to work its basis must be the genuine expression of interest by individuals and communities. Part of that is the question of how civil society organisations are able to create the information they need to express their views.

The problem is the same for developed countries where faith in the ability for transparency to drive improvement in public services is high but where the hope is that there will be a shift from downward pressure from the top of the sandwich to upward pressure from the bottom. Jeremy Hunt, the current Conservative Secretary of State for Health in the UK, has said transparency should 'replace performance targets' and support the National Health Service (NHS) to become a 'learning organisation'. He has also tasked the National Information Board with implementation of a comprehensive data strategy across all services, so that more data can be shared more easily and made available for independent analysis of outcomes and research, as well as the online publication of a new public benchmarking tool, called MyNHS. He has described these initiatives as: 'nurturing a new culture in which the main driver of performance improvement is not endless new targets, but a culture of openness, transparency and continual improvement through peer-review'.[13]

His comments recognise that the long-term sustainability of transparency requires a shift in power over information – and the capabilities to use that information – to individuals, communities and civil society organisations. Often social audit and public reporting become seen as mechanisms for governments or international organisations to enforce new standards on organisations rather than a reflection of public demand for action. But if it is true that public services are failing the public, it must be public awareness of that problem and the desire to correct it which provides the motivating force for transparency programmes.

HAKI ELIMU

Godfrey Boniventura remembers his friend at primary school crying on learning he would not be going to secondary school. This was 1995 and out of 71 children only nine got a place in secondary school. While Boniventura did well enough to progress, his friend did not, and he knew even at that age that it would most likely limit the rest of his friend's life. Boniventura is now the programme manager for research and policy analysis at HakiElimu, an organisation that uses transparency to monitor budgets and improve education in Tanzania. His friend still lives in the village where they grew up together and sells clothes. He tried to get a job in mining but did not have the necessary education. However, he has three sons and they are all in secondary education.

HakiElimu began advocating for expansion in education so that all children can get basic schooling. The Tanzanian government also recognised the need for this and in 2001 initiated development programmes for primary and secondary education.

HakiElimu started to work on monitoring the implementation of these programmes. It was one thing for government to announce an increase in

---

[13] The Rt HonJeremy Hunt MP Innovation and efficiency. Speech delivered 13 November 2014, The King's Fund, London, https://www.gov.uk/government/speeches/innovation-and-efficiency

spending, it was quite another for the money to arrive at the school. The government had committed to $10 per pupil to cover books, stationary and minor repairs to improve the classroom environment. HakiElimu began visiting schools to check whether the money was arriving and what it was being spent on. Boniventura explains: 'We were going into the field seeing the schools, we would find a class with two or three desks and children on the floor. Or schools with no toilets. There was need for repair and maintenance. As we got this information we were trying to analyse it and disseminate it to the public.'

The most common thing to do in this situation is to produce a policy report highlighting the issues. HakiElimu did something rather different. It went on sports channels on TV and radio. It bought up advertising spots and made its own commercials highlighting what it had found. 'We wanted people to understand the real situation', Boniventura says.

In 2005 HakiElimu aired a commercial highlighting the problem of teachers' pay. To collect their wages, each month teachers had to travel to the district administrator's office – a journey that might take a day. When they got there they might have to queue or wait for two or three days before getting their money. By the time they got back they might have lost a week's worth of teaching. In other words, teachers could be spending one-quarter of their time simply collecting their wages.

The government was not amused. It regarded the advertisement as a distortion of the truth, an exaggeration. The president banned HakiElimu from entering any public institution offering education services. But protests in the media and from other civil society organisations persuaded the government to relent.

HakiElimu has now established a network of 'friends of education'. It has 40,000 of these citizens who with the agreement of the school and local government carry out regular inspections and information gathering exercises. A report sent in from one details the fact that money due two months ago has still not arrived. It then includes a number of hand-drawn tables showing teacher absentee rates and truancy rates from the school as well as the percentages of pupils going on to secondary school.

These reports are shared with the school and within the local community to drive up the learning and teaching standards in each school. But HakiElimu will also use the information to report on the state of affairs nationally or regionally if widespread problems are identified. This type of information is not available through the government administration.

HakiElimu only raises issues nationally when it feels it is necessary. Recently, says Bonaventura, a number of schools closed because they had not received the money to provide school meals. 'We then worked with journalists who covered the story – "Schools closed for lack of food". After four days, the minister said that this had happened without their knowledge, that money had in fact been sent and that teachers were not checking their accounts.' Regardless of the excuses, the money then turned up and the schools reopened. 'They would have paid the money', says Bonaventura, 'but it would have been later.'

'One of the things lacking is the recognition among people that they can be the one who brings change to their community', he continues. If more people got engaged 'we would minimise so many things that happen. There is a lot of corruption. Sometimes civil servants are not where they are supposed to work, sometimes they are not in the office when people are applying for services, teachers are sometimes not teaching. But if you have each and every citizen doing this kind of work, people will be accountable. People are getting more aware of their rights and their role as citizens'.

11

International initiatives

Social audit and public reporting can be effective as part of a 'sandwich' strategy – when an organisation being subjected to transparency is forced to be more open about its performance to service users while at the same time being held to account by a governmental authority overseeing it. But if the organisation being subjected to transparency is government itself then who can apply the 'downward' pressure? If the constitutional separation of powers has ceased to function due to high-level corruption, how can government be held to account short of violent insurrection? The development of international transparency initiatives is one approach in trying to solve this problem.

The extractive industries – oil, gas, mining, logging – have a history of corruption in which those in power appropriate large amounts of wealth either through direct government control of these assets or through corrupt deals with multinational companies. The resulting 'resource curse' has been remarkably destructive in terms of human life and opportunity.

To take one example, the amount of oil in Nigeria could have made it a rich country. Oil was discovered there in 1956 and, by 1973, Nigeria was exporting 600 million barrels of oil a day, making it one of the top oil producers in the world. But between 1965 and 2004, per capita income fell and the proportion of people subsisting on less than $1 a day rose. It has been estimated that 90% of revenues go to 1% of the population and that, in 2003, 70% of the country's oil wealth was stolen. It is not just that the population was robbed, it is also that the country has been run to enable the expropriation of this wealth and in the process it has been prevented from developing in other ways.

Extractive industries became a focus of activists, many of whom advocated transparency as a solution. The Publish What You Pay initiative aimed to halt corruption in the extractive industries, a sector notorious for high levels of bribery. The idea was that if companies were forced to publish what they paid to the government and governments were forced to publish what they received, there would be little or no room for backhanders, kickbacks and bribery.

The campaign led to the development of the Extractive Industries Transparency Initiative (EITI), an approach to transparency with a set of international standards that governments could subscribe to and put into effect in their countries. EITI is classified not as a social audit but as a 'multistakeholder initiative'. The project established committees that bring together people from government, the industry and civil society organisations (CSOs) to oversee the collection, auditing and publication of information. The governments of host countries agree to enforce transparency on companies working in their territory and to be transparent themselves about contracts and receipts.

The original focus of the effort was similar to the idea behind the Association for the Empowerment of Workers and Peasants (MKSS) social audit in India. If the government states what it says it spent and the recipients can confirm that the money has been used appropriately, there is limited room for fraud. In theory, if the companies publish what they pay the government and the government says what it received from the contract, there is less room for companies to pay less than they should and to bribe officials to look the other way.

How effective is the EITI

There is some evidence that it has an impact. Joining EITI is associated with a fall in perceptions of corruption, as measured by Transparency International's Corruption Perception Index, which surveys the public on their experience of and views about corruption.[1] The Nigerian EITI (NEITI) has shown that, in the period after joining the initiative, the proportion of oil revenues going to government rose from a low of 56% to a high of 74%.[2] But how much these changes can be ascribed to transparency is always hard to tell.

The EITI points out that there are significant benefits from engaging in the process of transparency beyond the immediate measurable improvements in revenues. The establishment of multi-stakeholder groups provides an opportunity for local communities to communicate directly with companies and government about the impact of mining and how the revenues from contracts are used. EITI establishes an environment that has some degree of accountability beyond national borders and national governments; one which can allow the negotiation of ever greater levels of transparency between powerful interest groups.

This takes time. Audits comparing discrepancies between payments by the company and money reaching the government coffers have identified only relatively small discrepancies. The first audit by the Nigerian EITI found a difference of only $16 million,[3] a trivial sum compared to the estimates of the real level of corruption. More recently, it has helped recover over $2 billion of lost revenues. But these figures are still some way short of the tens of billions allegedly misappropriated.

We should not be surprised that initiatives such as the EITI take time – it is often working against outright criminal activity which, by its nature, is expert at evading legal requirements for transparency. Trials in the US have shown how the distribution of

---

[1]   Liz David-Barrett and Ken Okamura, Working Paper No 38, European Research Centre for Anti-Corruption and State-Building, Said Business School, University of Oxford, November 2013, https://eiti.org/files/ The-Transparency-Paradox.-Why-do-Corrupt-Countries-Join-EITI1.pdf

[2]   *10 Years of Neiti Reports – What Have We Learnt?*, NEITI, 2014, www.neiti. org.ng/sites/default/files/publications/uploads/ten-years-neiti-reports.pdf

[3]   Nigeria Extractive Industries Transparency Initiative, *Financial Audit 1999–2004. Report on Financial Flows*, Hart Group, 2006, https://eiti.org/ files/Nigeria%201999-%202004%20EITI%20Report.pdf

illegal bribes for Nigerian oil concessions now works.[4] Payments are made by intermediaries from accounts unconnected to the businesses concerned. Money is deposited in secret Swiss bank accounts or holdalls stuffed with cash are handed over in hotel lobbies. The EITI audit process will not capture activity of this sort.

As with all forms of transparency, we can expect those subjected to it to make use of every avenue to avoid the auditors. For example, the NEITI has voiced its concerns at the lack of any accurate mechanism for measuring how much oil is being taken out of the ground.[5] If you can't tell how much oil the company is taking and you can't see how much money they are putting in Swiss bank accounts, it is open to question how far the scheme limits scope for corruption.

A 2009 Organisation for Economic Co-operation and Development (OECD) report on EITI said: 'the information, if it is designed to have an effect, needs to be of a certain quality'.[6] It then lists a number of weaknesses. For example, the EITI audit process checks that the amounts the company says it paid match the amounts the government says it received but not whether either figure is correct – that is, to what extent the right tax has been paid on the right amount of oil extraction, or the correct royalties on licences. Also, reports often fail to disaggregate figures, 'meaning that it is impossible for an outsider to judge how much the government received from each company'.

Others have made the point that the audit only tells you how much money went into government.[7] It doesn't say what then happened to it. If there is no transparency around public finances

4   www.justice.gov/opa/pr/uk-solicitor-pleads-guilty-role-bribing-nigerian-government-officials-part-kbr-joint-venture

5   Ejiofor Alike, 'Nigeria: DPR has no system for measuring crude oil production, says Neiti', *This Day*, 8 July 2014, http://allafrica.com/stories/201407080443.html

6   Dilan Ölcer, *Extracting the Maximum from the EITI*, OECD Development Centre Working Paper No 276, February 2009.

7   Ivar Kolstad and Arne Wiig, 'Is transparency the key to reducing corruption in resource-rich countries?', *World Development* Vol 37, No 3 (2009), 521–532.

then, again, the scope to misuse funds is only marginally affected by adopting the EITI.

In 2013, in response to these criticisms, the EITI significantly increased the scope of its information requirements and strengthened the rules around compliance in areas such as disclosure of beneficial owners. But by its nature, the EITI process involves engaging people in a level of transparency they can live with and then using that engagement to gradually ratchet up the requirements. It is notable that some of the same companies that have welcomed the EITI have strongly resisted US and EU attempts to establish stronger legislative requirements around disclosure of payments. The US requirements that were included in the Dodd–Frank Act have been successfully fought off by industry legal challenges for many years.

There is an exponential relationship between the quality of data and its usefulness. Very high quality data is very useful data. But if the quality degrades by 10% the usefulness degrades much more quickly and rapidly drops towards zero. Allowing the creation of relatively low quality data can be used to create the appearance of transparency with little risk of being held to account or constrained from illegal or undesirable activity.

The EITI is very aware of the risk that corrupt governments might use it to try to give a false signal of their level of transparency. In 2015, Clare Short, chair of the EITI International Board, said in a blog post:

> implementing the EITI is not a measure that all is well … we must remind ourselves that EITI compliance does not mean that a country is free of corruption or exhibits full openness or respect for civil liberties. Just because Nigeria is compliant with the EITI Requirements, does not mean that USD 20 billion has not gone missing through the subsidy system.[8]

She said EITI was not a 'seal of approval' but rather 'a reflection of a political commitment to reform'.

---

[8]   https://eiti.org/blog/eiti-not-seal-approval-sign-change

Jonas Moberg, the organisation's director, says: 'Can we, in figures, show that transparency works? That's a tough one. Our approach is to push this bit by bit, start with small things'.[9]

The aim is that the process will start to build the civil society organisations, the accounting systems and the public expectations that can in the longer term shut down opportunities for corruption. EITI has greatly improved the transparency around payments between companies and governments, raising standards of auditing in the process, and is now a powerful voice calling for improvements in monitoring of oil outputs.

The value of international initiatives is twofold. Firstly, they are the only mechanism by which any degree of external or top-down pressure can be brought to bear on corruption within national governments. But, perhaps most importantly, they provide a framework for the establishment of international standards for the capture and recording of information and for the legal and constitutional arrangements that prevent governments corrupting information flows.

FUNDAR

Mexico has made a number of commitments to increase transparency in the mining and oil industries, including joining the Extractive Industries Transparency Initiative (EITI), an international collaboration to set standards for transparency around financial flows in mining and oil.

Peréz Garrido describes how companies can take advantage of the poverty and ignorance of indigenous people by offering them paltry sums of money, which seem large to them, in return for surrendering rights over their territory. The impact on communities in terms of health and the environment can be devastating, she says. She believes the difficulty in bringing transparency to this area is that the government and the mining companies are in collusion.

There has been good progress in bringing more transparency to many parts of life in Mexico such as education. But these are areas where the state and those calling for transparency share an interest in effecting

---

[9]   Author interview.

change. When it comes to getting in the way of mining projects and supporting indigenous people, the government is not, Peréz Garrido reckons, on her side.

The information she is seeking is not complicated. She wants to know where mining concessions have been granted to companies and where companies have requested future mining concessions. She wants to know the terms of the contract and to see what obligations there are on the companies.

Fundar has created a map of Mexico which shows indigenous territories overlaid with mining concessions they know about as well as population statistics about health and income. It is the only public picture of what is going on across the country. She says this is a political project. She worries that a lot of transparency projects are funded by international donors or central government but do not really connect with people on the ground. They do not have a clear political agenda.

Peréz Garrido has a two-pronged strategy. First, detailed research into the impact of mining on communities and the actions of the mining industry is used to lobby people with influence at a senior level. Second, the same information is used to inform and support indigenous communities.

Transparency and information makes up just one of many tools, she argues, and on its own it cannot achieve much. It is information together with political action that makes a difference. The organisation uses the courts. In Sierra Norte it has successfully held off mining projects for 30 years. It uses social organisation. 'We run workshops with the communities. We explain to them the interests of the companies and the government, we tell them about their consultation rights and help them with the organisational process of developing a defence strategy.'Transparency is important – but means little if the process is not fair. Peréz Garrido says consultations processes are a 'simulation'. They are not independent and, even if people say no, the consultation still comes out with a yes. She wants truly independent consultations that are binding on the government.

The problem with bringing greater transparency to the mining and oil industries, she says, is that it really matters. It gets to the heart of corruption in the Mexican state. 'With the other commitments, it is simple to comply', she says. It is easy for government departments to find some data they are happy to publish. There are two commitments, according to Peréz Garrido, where the government is dragging its heels: extractive industries and security. The reason is simple, she says. It is because these are the ones that matter most – 'the relevant, significant important commitments'. These are the ones that really challenge the power structures in Mexico.

However, things do change. Since interviewing Haydee, the Mexican government has released a large amount of data with detailed geographic information about mining concessions.

12

Open data and forced disclosure

'Open data' refers to data that is routinely published and that can be used by the public. Ideally such data is published under open data licences that allow reuse in any circumstances. However, for our purposes, we are interested in any data that is publicly accessible and can be used. The data used by the Romanian Coalition for a Clean Parliament was not available under such licences but was used to powerful effect nonetheless (see case study below).

Forced disclosure refers to statutory or regulatory requirements on a particular organisation – whether state or private – to put certain specified information in the public domain. Common examples are requirements for companies to publish accounts and names of directors and shareholders; registries of land or other assets; and requirements for politicians to declare gifts.

Qualitatively, there is nothing essentially different about information made available as part of a social audit or public reporting programme as opposed to an open data or forced disclosure programme. The latter are generally more granular and tend to be delivered in the form of databases for analysis rather than as reports to be consumed.

The important difference is the philosophy behind such schemes. Forced disclosure programmes work on the basis that if the information was made available to the customer, it is then their responsibility to use it and their self-interest should give them an incentive to do so. Open Data programmes are posited on the belief that people will pick up on such information and make use of it. They are based on the idea that information on its own *is* enough – or rather that in the right circumstances it *can* be enough.

This optimism is in large part based on the potential for technological innovation to change the relationship between citizens, government and data. The combination of cheap and widespread access to computing power to interpret and analyse data, as well as the existence of web or internet-based communications systems to turn such analysis into information for specific audiences, has certainly made previously inconceivable forms of citizen-driven data activism possible. The hope is that there will be a market opportunity for information businesses to take public information that might be too complex for most people to deal with and turn it into actionable advice on what to buy or who to vote for.

Open data policies aim to make data available in standard machine-readable formats such as downloadable CSV (comma separated value) files or through application programming interfaces (APIs), with the aim of drawing private investment capital into the development of technologies that make use of the data. The idea is that data + technology + venture capital/engaged citizens could result in a more effective form of transparency.

These policies have been most effective in areas that are not directly relevant to our discussion and relate to disputes over the economic control of information – situations in which government agencies either earn revenues from a monopoly right to resell the data or simply wish to retain a monopoly on the processing of that information. The economic benefit of making such information open is a big driver for government programmes to release meteorological data, hydrographic data and geographic data.

The data sets that are standardly released in this way tend to have few implications for individual privacy, making release of granular data relatively straightforward. But, equally, they have few implications for the fairness of government policy. Consequently the release of such data has given rise to some extremely effective businesses that have improved the efficiency of various industries[1] but have had limited relevance to the questions of fairness that underpin our concept of transparency. Mexico found it relatively easy to publish hydrographic information (see Chapter 8) but much harder to publish information about disappeared citizens (see below).

Open data and corruption

The Sunlight Foundation in the US is collating a directory of open data initiatives globally as part of an effort to assess their impact. This is needed, it says, because 'proof on the social and political impact of open data initiatives is incredibly scarce'.

The organisation's database of over 100 projects lists the three most common areas for open data. Top of the list is information about political finances – the expenses of politicians, donations to political parties, the assets of officials and so on. The second category is public budgets. The third is business – information such as directorships and ownership of companies.

There are some good individual instances of such data being used to combat corruption. The Coalition for a Clean Parliament in Romania (see below) is a particularly strong example in which extremely imaginative use of publicly available data was used to measure something that might be thought immeasurable: the degree to which politicians were corrupt.

There are a handful of corruption cases in the US which came to light through careful examination of open data – most notably the successful prosecution of Duke Cunningham, which saw the largest ever financial penalty for corruption set at $1.8 million. A journalist working through land registry information on property ownership was able to uncover details of transactions revealing that Cunningham had been on the take from arms companies. A Federal Bureau of Investsigation (FBI) officer said at the time that it was the first case he was aware of where public revelations in a news story had led to a prosecution. All the others relied on tip-offs and traditional police action including covert surveillance.

Public data about political donations is widely used in the US to highlight where politicians have received money from

---

[1] See for example Joel Gurin, *Open Data Now*, McGraw-Hill, 2014.

groups with an interest in legislation and to identify the degree to which people vote in line with the interests of these donors. Websites such as MapLight.org provide a clear presentation of where politicians get their financial support and how they vote. It is a useful resource. However, it is based on the premise that money is corrupting politics. As with all corruption, evidence is hard to find. Studies attempting to show a significant connection between the voting patterns of legislators and their donors' interests have failed to convincingly demonstrate an association.[2] This may in part be because of disclosure requirements and websites like MapLight. It may be because money can buy influence in more subtle ways. And it may be because politicians are less corrupt than some imagine.

Open budgeting has been successful in allowing citizen engagement in debates about public policy. In the UK the complete treasury model of economic growth and projected borrowing is made public, allowing civil society organisations such as the Institute of Fiscal Studies (IFS) to present analyses of UK budget impacts that are as authoritative as those coming from the treasury itself. Along with the more recently created governmental budget oversight (the Office for Budget Responsibilities) there are, within the UK, two organisations with varying degrees of independence from government that are able to comment with authority on fiscal policy. The green budget from the IFS has become a national institution, providing alternative narratives around each annual budget which the media use to inform their presentation of the issues and their questioning of ministers.

However, as with social audit, the ability of these techniques to combat corruption is limited to the degree that government agencies in control of the relevant information are willing and able to allow citizen groups with grievances or those who would question the official account access to sufficiently useful information.

In the case of the Greek budget crisis, large numbers of people across government were complicit in the deception and,

---

[2]   Thomas Stratmann, 'Some talk: money in politics. A (partial) review of the literature', *Public Choice* Vol 124 (2005), 135–156.

indeed, it could be argued that the Greek people had little to complain of while they lived under the false assurance that the government could afford the money it was spending on them. The budgetary deception was achieved by failing to record expenditures such as capital injections into public corporations. This was disguised in the accounts by misclassifying items as revenues and reporting high-level aggregates of income and outgoings to make irregularities harder to identify.[3]

The simplest way to prevent open data from having any impact on the fairness of allocation is to fail to record the necessary detail in the relevant datasets. A striking example of this was the campaign for budget transparency by the Dalits in India – a campaign for justice that rested on forcing government to record data correctly.[4]

The Dalits or 'untouchables' is a community not recognised in the traditional caste system and as a result Dalits are excluded from mainstream society. They make up 16% of the population and are among the most disadvantaged; 60% are illiterate and have had no formal education. The Constitution of India provides guarantees against discrimination and subsequent government plans have confirmed that budget allocations should be made for all Indian communities on the basis of their size. If the Dalits constitute 16% of the population, they should therefore receive 16% of the national budget. In reality they receive a far lower allocation.

In 2007 to 2008, only 6.1% of development funds were channelled through the SCSP (scheduled caste sub-plan) mechanism, instead of the targeted 16.2% that should have been allocated. By 2011/12 the allocation had reached just 8.84% of the total outlay. These figures are only non-binding allocations – promises rather than actions. Trying to find out where the

---

[3]   European Commission, *On Greek Government Deficit and Debt Statistics*, January 2010.

[4]   Vimala Ramachandran and Sapna Goel, *Tracking Funds for India's Most Deprived: The Story of the National Campaign for Dalit Human Rights' 'Campaign 789'*, International Budget Partnership Study No 6, August 2011, www.internationalbudget.org/wp-content/uploads/LP-case-study-NCDHR.pdf

money had actually gone was impossible as the budget code (789) used to identify spending under SCSP was largely unused.

The implementation of code 789 became central to the National Campaign for Dalit Human Rights (NCDHR). Having discovered it could not get hold of the information about the disbursement of SCSP money, the NCDHR filed a right to information (RTI) application as to why the correct coding was not being used and then appealed when the application received no answer. The organisation even organised public rallies on the issue – raising awareness that fair treatment of Dalits hung on the correct recording of government budget codes.

The Commonwealth Games provided the breakthrough. Allegations of corrupt contracting in the preparations for the 2010 Commonwealth Games attracted significant media attention. Evidence emerged that money was being diverted from SCSP funds to pay for the games. By this time, the NCDHR had enough data and skills to be able to investigate and confirm that this was occurring. It published a report. A further RTI petition was put in which revealed the full extent to which funds had been diverted (7.44 billion rupees). The government agreed to return the money.

Open budget information is of value only to the degree that it is granular and correctly coded to programmes that are intelligible to the outside world and at some level verifiable. The fight against corruption is often less to do with the use of that information than ensuring such information exists. It is the creation of such accounting systems that is an essential part of any anti-corruption strategy.

This is an area where international efforts to lay down standards have been of great value. Warren Krafchik is head of the International Budget Partnership, a non-governmental organisation working in over 100 countries on budget accountability that helped support the HCDHR and promotes transparency of national budgets. He has worked to establish mechanisms to ensure that budget information is recorded and disseminated in formats that are relevant to the concerns and issues of citizens and community groups.

Budget information is well suited to an open data approach since it is possible to get to a high level of granularity without infringing personal privacy. To fully trace the use of public money, it would be necessary to track it down to the individual bank accounts and, in some cases, anti-corruption policies have required public servants to declare their personal assets in full. But there is a great deal that can be achieved without going so far. Information that tracks money down to individual programmes and institutions – for example the amount of money spent on teachers' salaries in an individual school – can be enormously powerful without taking the final step of revealing each teacher's pay.

Open data and privacy

The biggest limitation to the use of open data is the openness of it. Because such data is available to anyone, it precludes any information that might identify somebody. And in many areas, such as health, education, return to work programmes or community safety, data at an aggregate level which avoids any possibility of identifying an individual also makes it largely useless for the purposes of assessing the fairness of allocation systems.

This is a problem for Ana Cristina Ruelas who works for Article 19, the human rights group dedicated to protecting freedom of expression. Article 19 has been documenting the frequent murder of journalists in Mexico to suppress voices challenging corruption and criminal cartels.

Ruelas is a lawyer who has always wanted to work in human rights. Her first job, as a trainee, was in a prison in Chiapas where both men and women were held and rape and violence were common. She is now working as the liaison with the Mexican government on their commitment to increased transparency around human rights.

The crisis of the 'disappeared' in Mexico has become a central political concern. The tally of the disappeared now runs into the tens of thousands – more than in the disappearances in Argentina or Chile during the 1970s and 1980s. This is happening in a country that has one of the strongest anticorruption laws in the world, one of the strongest RTI laws and a government that has made transparency and combating corruption a central part of its political programme. The Right To Information law included a clause saying there could be no exceptions for information relating to gross violations of human rights. All such information must be made public.

Despite the strong wording, the new law failed to have the hoped for impact. The requirement to release any information relating to gross human rights violations was sidestepped. When, in 2010, 72 migrants were killed in the first San Fernando massacre, no one with the necessary authority felt able to determine that this act constituted a human rights violation. El Instituto Federal de Acceso a la Información Pública (IFAI), the national body with responsibility for enforcing the RTI law, said that without this it could not invoke the right to information. The files remained secret.

Article 19 took IFAI to court, and won. The law was reformed and a new national body, the Instituto Nacional de Transparencia, Acceso a la Información y Protección de Datos (INAI), was established with wider, stronger powers. Legal appeals from the government continued but INAI was able to release some relevant files.[5] The information revealed that it almost certainly did count as a gross human rights violation. Gang members involved testified that the police had acted as lookouts while the cartel members carried out the killing.

Opening up information about human rights abuses is perhaps the most sensitive and difficult area for transparency in Mexico. Many arguments and tactics are used to prevent transparency, one of which is to invoke people's rights to privacy.

In 2000, when the Partido Revolucionario Institucional (PRI) party lost power after 70 years in charge, one of the first acts of the new government was to open up all the files in the national archive relating to the dirty war in the 1960s and 1970s, during which the Mexican army and police were responsible for thousands of extrajudicial killings. People were able to go to Gallery 1 in the national archives and look up the files on relatives who had disappeared and discover what had happened to them.

In 2014, the government reversed the decision because of concerns that the policy conflicted with other laws that protected

---

[5] https://migrationdeclassified.wordpress.com/2014/12/23/san-fernando-massacre-case-file-details-charges-against-police/

personal privacy. It was decided that the files could only be viewed, on request, with all names removed. After a wave of public protest and disquiet, INAI held a meeting at which it was agreed that the law on privacy was being interpreted too strictly and the decision was reversed.

Ruelas is currently working with the government to help it implement two commitments that it gave as part of its open government programme – to open up access to the national databases of disappeared people and detained people. These are not the archive records but the current data on individuals who are either in police custody or who have been reported missing. The issue was first raised by the Inter-American Court of Human Rights in the case of Montiel and Cabrera.[6] The court endorsed the view of the United Nations Subcommittee on Prevention of Torture which had recommended that

> The office of the Attorney General develop a system for documenting the chain of custody of detainees, with a standardized record for logging, immediately and completely, the essential information about the deprivation of liberty of an individual and about the personnel responsible for that individual at all times.

The person concerned and responsible officials should have access to this. All records should be signed and countersigned.

The court supported this recommendation and added that the system should be continuously updated and interconnected with other databases, to allow people to be quickly located and to ensure it meets requirements of access to information and privacy.

When Mexico joined the Open Government Partnership, the government chose to implement this through two commitments it has given as part of its open government partnership Action Plan programme – to open up access to the national database

---

[6] www.corteidh.or.cr/docs/casos/articulos/seriec_220_esp.pdf or www.corteidh.or.cr/docs/casos/articulos/seriec_220_ing.pdf

of disappeared[7] and create a transparent system of public information about detained people.[8]

Ruelas is currently working with the government on this and is excited by what it could mean. 'This could show ... everything', she explains. With complete records of all cases of the disappeared and detained it would be possible to start to fully understand what is happening.

'It will show if there is a generalization of crimes against humanity such as torture, arbitrary detention or forced disappearances', she explains. This is important. To take a case to the International Criminal Court, where individuals can be prosecuted under international law, you need to show that rights violations were not one-off events but systematic over time – in other words, it wasn't just a few bad apples, it was a deliberate coordinated policy.

The idea that it might now be possible to start to assess the extent to which this was happening was, for Ruelas, one of the key objectives for opening up access to the government databases. However, its implementation risks making that impossible.

The public websites have been designed to protect the privacy of citizens. On the database of the disappeared you can look up individuals by name and get back a minimal amount of data, if there is a match on the database, with a date and broad location of where the disappearance occurred. This aims to allow relatives to check if someone is on the database without disclosing private information about individuals.

This is of some help for families who often have no idea if their case has been registered. But it falls short of the Inter-American Court of Human Rights requirement that the information be linked to a database of all detainees to allow cross-checking. The database of detainees will also be opened up in a similar way. But the information will not be real time, meaning that once someone goes missing it will not be possible to establish immediately whether they have in fact been detained. This is troubling, as mistreatment of the detained often happens within the first few hours.

---

[7]   https://rnped.segob.gob.mx/
[8]   https://consultadetenidos.pgr.gob.mx

For Ruelas, a vital component of this work is the extent to which it allows her and others to hold government to account and to build a case against those responsible. She needs to be able to look across all the data and identify patterns. But that might mean her having access to private information about citizens.

The government has said it will publish statistics about the disappeared and about detainees. But it will only publish at a high level – not at the level that Ruelas needs. It will not publish details of the authority that detained them and the proportions arrested with and without a warrant. 'This is information that is necessary to determine the effectiveness of security policy', Ana says. Furthermore, she has no way of knowing the methodology used to produce the data. An initial review of the data on the disappeared produced 80,000 records. After cleaning and de-duplicating it fell to 22,000. But no one outside the ministry knows the methodology by which this was done.

There is great potential for the opening up of the databases to provide evidence against those responsible for the disappeared. If nothing else, as with the Kenyans tortured by the British, it may hold out the prospect of justice in the future. Ruelas wants to be able to link up the government data with the information that lawyers and victims have gathered. However, the way that the project is being implemented is making this hard to do.

At the heart of the difficulty there is the fact that, if the fairness of government policy is your concern, you need information about people. Whether it is the criminal justice system, community safety, the allocation of public monies or the provision of healthcare and education, the most powerful verifiable information is the data about what happened to individuals. To make any sense of that information, you need to have the full details. The publication of aggregated tables of data robs the data of the majority of its content. The way in which such tables are designed also gives the publishing organisation a great deal of control over the types of narrative that it is possible to construct from the information.

Nations vary greatly in what they regard as private information. In some Nordic countries, for example, an individual tax record is a public document, but in most countries it is considered private information. In the UK the electronic record of births and deaths is government data that is only accessible under strictly controlled licence. In the US death records are public information and in Mexico the full data on births was published as part of their initiative to reduce maternal mortality.

The degree to which information about an individual is considered public or private is something for each society to determine. But, even it is regarded as private, it has an essential value to others in enabling them to determine if they are being treated fairly or whether the institutions of their society are corrupt. To the degree that open data conflicts with privacy it creates a fundamental obstacle to making information useful as a mechanism for transparency. The reluctance to deal with that conflict produces government data portals populated with thousands of data spreadsheets, none of which hold the answer to the question that any specific individual wants answered.

COALITION FOR A CLEAN PARLIAMENT: POLITICAL CORRUPTION IN ROMANIA

In 2004 Romanian civil society activists organised effectively to expose corrupt members of parliament (MPs) and to oust almost 100 from parliament. The Coalition for a Clean Parliament (CCP) brought together academics and activists to execute a carefully targeted campaign against corrupt politicians from all political parties. They were motivated by frustration at the government's failure to take effective action and decided to take matters into their own hands.

This was primarily an information campaign driven by the imaginative use of data to press for change. Corruption by its nature is secret, so the first problem is how to identify corrupt politicians. The CCP used 'indicators' – data that was not in itself proof of corruption but which was likely to correlate with being corrupt. Six indicators likely to reflect corruption were identified, which were discussed and refined with all of the political parties. All except one (the Greater Romania Party) accepted the CCP's approach to trying to identify corruption as legitimate. The six indicators were:

1. Repeatedly shifting from one political party to another – behaviour that is more likely to reflect efforts to seek personal enrichment for support rather than endlessly shifting political beliefs.
2. Having been accused of corruption on the basis of published and verifiable evidence – on the grounds that those accused are more likely to be guilty.
3. Known former agent of the Securitate, the communist secret service – an organisation that had consistently abused human rights.
4. Owning a private firm with significant unpaid tax – suggesting a corrupt relationship with the tax authorities.
5. Officially stated assets that cannot be reconciled with known income – suggesting corrupt sources of financial remuneration.
6. Any known action where the holding of public position was relevant and which yielded a personal profit – actions which, even if legal, might be considered corrupt or ethically questionable by definition.

Having agreed the methodology, the CCP used press reports and official websites reporting financial information about MPs and company financial records and scored each of the candidates. It was determined that any candidate meeting one or more criteria should be blacklisted and labelled as unfit to hold a seat in the future parliament.

The next move was not to go to the press but to go back to the parties, to show them the information and ask if they would withdraw any of the candidates blacklisted. The CCP offered to do further research and analysis if individuals contested the findings. Some candidates did appeal successfully and were removed from the blacklist. Many of the candidates were withdrawn by the parties at this stage. But many remained.

The CCP then printed up the blacklist of remaining 'corrupt' candidates and distributed 2 million flyers with the information across the country. Flyers were used because newspapers are not widely read (less than 10% of the population follow political media). The campaign was funded by Balkan Trust, Romanian Soros Foundation and Freedom House.

The ruling social democratic party (PSD) party found it was disproportionately represented on the blacklist and at this point decided to withdraw its support. It denounced the campaign and recommended that MPs sue the CCP and seek a court injunction on the flyers. The members of the CCP were labelled 'civic terrorists' and 'a bunch of criminals'. Both the courts and the electoral authorities ruled in favour of the CCP.

Some parties published copycat flyers – with the names of the blacklisted candidates changed to opposition candidates to sow confusion. But the campaign received widespread support from international media and over 2000 volunteer activists.

Of 202 candidates blacklisted, 98 lost their seats (either withdrawn or defeated) and 104 were re-elected. With a disproportionate number of ruling party candidates on the list, the SDP fell from power and a new government came into office.

Five people, including two former ministers, issued lawsuits for defamation. Alina Mungiu-Pippidi comments: 'If Oscar Wilde is right that one should be judged by the quality of one's enemies, then Romanian civil society has made enormous strides with its Coalition for a Clean Parliament.'[9]

---

[9] Alina Mungiu-Pippidi, 'Fighting political corruption in postcommunist Europe'. Introductory essay in *Romanian Coalition for a Clean Parliament: a Quest for Political Integrity European Research Centre for Anti-Corruption and State-Building*, Working Paper No. 1, http://www.againstcorruption.eu/wp-content/uploads/2012/09/WP-1-Romanian-CCP-new.pdf

13

Editorial control

In the previous five chapters we have described the triumphs and frustrations of a wide range of different individuals and organisations in their attempts to use information as a tool to combat corruption and improve public service outcomes. They are sometimes confronted by the fact that, even if they have the information, there is nothing they can do. But equally, they are often halted by the fact that, while in theory information is open to them, the specific information they require to evidence the narrative they wish to present is unavailable.

Our contention is that this is, in large part, due to the extent to which the organisations being subjected to transparency are able to manipulate the information environment in which they work and the nature of information that is made public through the various mechanisms described.

For instance, if we take the Extractive Industries Transparency Initiative (EITI) example, the fear is that my government is handing out contracts in return for bribes and misusing the funds generated. If I look at how the scheme operates and the information it produces and ask the question 'will it generate the information that can determine whether this is happening or not?', the answer, all too often, is no.

Professor Susan Rose-Ackerman has pointed out that bureaucracy may unconsciously design systems that create opportunities for bribery by allowing unaccountable monopolistic control of particular parts of a bureaucratic process. Such controls make life easier for bureaucrats, regardless of whether they exploit them for personal financial gain or whether they use these powers to limit oversight and give themselves control over their working lives.[1]

We can see that similar incentives might be expected to cause organisations which are implementing transparency systems to lean, whether deliberately or unconsciously, towards systems that minimise the degree to which information is available in formats that allow them to be held accountable.

The central issue of concern here is the degree to which the organisation subject to transparency can retain a degree of editorial control over information flow. To return to Klitgaard,[2] if an organisation has unaccountable monopoly control over any part of the flow of information – from the design of the content, through to the way it is recorded, analysed and presented – we can expect this to be exploited to reduce accountability and increase opportunities for corruption.

Methods of editorial control

The techniques used to maintain control of information are not limited to the ability to prevent people accessing information. More often subtler techniques of editorial control over information are used. This includes the power to determine:

- what is and what is not recorded
- the format, definitions and descriptions of what is recorded
- which other parties information is shared with
- the content of what is shared with other parties, including powers of redaction for deliberative privacy, personal privacy, commercial confidentiality and national security
- the format of information that is shared with other parties
- the terms on which information is shared with other parties.

---

[1] Susan Rose-Ackerman, *Corruption: A Study in Political Economy,* Academic Press, 1978.

[2] Kiltgaard's definition of corruption as discussed in chapter 6 taken from Robert E Klitgaard, *Controlling Corruption,* University of California Press 1988

Professor Alasdair Roberts has catalogued the wide range of methods used to control information when subject to access to information (ATI) legislation.[3]

First there is the power to change recordkeeping and to alter what is recorded. A British cabinet minister interviewed by Robert Hazell about the impact of the freedom of information (FOI) law said that if cabinet minutes were made subject to FOI he would simply cease to record minutes. Equally effective is simply not speaking your mind in official communications. Canadian government officials who had been on the sharp end of FOI requests said that they had become much more careful about how they worded official memos.[4]

Even if a record has come into existence, it is possible to destroy it subsequently. In Canada in the 1980s, records of meetings held to discuss blood supplies contaminated with HIV (human immunodeficiency virus) were destroyed after an ATI request; and in the 1990s defence officials destroyed information relating to Canadian forces in Somalia. The US National Security Agency famously destroyed video recordings of suspects undergoing 'harsh interrogation techniques', in the face of advice from their lawyers not to do so.

Creating an 'oral culture' in which people know not to write things down is another effective technique. Roberts quotes Canadian officials describing how they agreed to keep 'minimum records' in relation to activities likely to be subject to ATI. The Butler Review into the intelligence failings in the UK in the run-up to the invasion of Iraq expressed concern at the unaccountability that resulted from a 'sofa culture' within government where important discussions took place informally.[5]

This use of private communications channels is a particular concern. Had Kwame Kilpatrick used a personal mobile phone his text messages might never have come to light. George W.

---

[3]   Alasdair Roberts, 'Dashed expectations: governmental adaption to transparency rules', in *Transparency: The Key to Better Governance?*, ed Christopher Hood and David Heald, The British Academy, 2006.

[4]   Alasdair Roberts, 'The Insider', *Saturday Night Magazine*, October 2005.

[5]   *Review of Intelligence on Weapons of Mass Destruction,* Report of a Committee of Privy Counsellors chaired by The Rt Hon The Lord Butler of Brockwell, TSO, 2004.

Bush chose, on becoming president, to stop using email and instead to rely on verbal communication – which by its nature is not disclosable. President Obama insisted on being able to retain a personal Blackberry, promising that all official-related communications would be handed over. Hillary Clinton, when secretary of state, conducted all her emails through a personal email account run from a personally controlled server housed on her personal property. She has been clear that all official-related communication will be made available under FOI rules; however, this is a process over which she has significant control – a problem that has led to considerable public disquiet.

In Canada there have been legislative remedies in the form of a 'duty to document' and criminal sanctions for the destruction of official information. But Roberts says it is not clear that such measures can provide an effective counter to the powers of the executive to control how decisions are taken and how such events are recorded.

Those subject to FOI also have significant powers to withhold information under the various legislated exceptions. We cannot know whether the House of Commons felt that publishing members of parliament's (MPs') home addresses really was a matter of privacy or whether they were aware of the potentially sensitive nature of the information. But there is an unavoidable conflict of interest where executive authorities that determine the appropriate use of such exemptions are aware of the degree of embarrassment they are likely to experience.

A range of other techniques can also be used. For example, deciding to publish information but doing so in ways that make it relatively hard to find or make sense of – such as burying it in impenetrable 'data portals', or publishing it electronically for only brief periods of time and then removing it, or moving it to another location.

Table 13.1 sets out the key mechanisms by which executive powers are able to manage the impact of public rights to information. None of these powers, in itself, is catastrophic to the intent of right to information (RTI) legislation. But collectively they are sufficient to make it extremely difficult to use such legislation to build a case against the executive. More

Table 13.1 Table of editorial control mechanisms and countermeasures

Mechanism	Description	Examples	Data issues	Legal counters
Private channels/ scope of what is recorded	The power to control what is communicated via informal channels in which no official record is created	Private email accounts used by public officials	Deciding the scope of what information is recorded (for example, Indian education data)	Requirements to conduct official business in official channels
Format of record keeping	The power to determine what is documented and the format of records	How much detail is in minutes, budgets or rationales	Which fields are recorded in official data sets – for example, ethnicity	Duties to document to specific standards
Accuracy of record keeping	The power to determine investment in record keeping and standards to which they are maintained	Poor record keeping and misfiling	Data accuracy degrades rapidly without implementation of standards	Stronger information standards and auditing functions
The application of exclusions	The power to determine whether data should be excluded from disclosure requirements	The decision to exclude MPs' addresses from UK expenses records as personal information. The increasing use of deliberative privilege in the US	Privacy exclusion can justify the refusal to share meaningful data	Some exclusions – for example, national security – are by their nature in the control of the executive. Others can have independent powers to overrule
Timing of release	The power to determine which claims will be delayed through contest and which will be pre-released	Through fighting FOI claims to delay release (for example, EDA). By leaking information to selectively pre-release	Official data sets take time to prepare. Often they are only available years after the events recorded (for example, Indian education data)	Stronger penalties for delay, and incorrect refusals
The format in which information is shared	The power to share information in a format that makes it hard to interpret	The Croatian government putting up contract information for short periods and in formats that made aggregation hard	Releasing data in non-machine readable formats such as PDFs. Changing data formats to make time series analysis impossible	Requirements to publish data in specific formats

likely, at best, you will get some documentation to help support your narrative.

Tightening the rules and developing ever more precise regulations will help to lessen some of these issues, but some of them are unavoidable. It is neither reasonable nor possible to insist that all communication by public officials be public information – and for as long as they are able to use private channels of communication, those are the channels that will be used for nefarious purposes. Transparency will never replace the need for search warrants and wiretapping.

However, some forms of data are less susceptible to editorial control, in particular verifiable data about events rather than records of decision-making procedures. Also some forms of narrative are easier to evidence than others.

The newer generation of initiatives has attempted to get round this by focusing more on data than on FOI. This focus on data has the potential to get round many of the problems encountered with FOI. It is possible to specify in advance what data should be available, to specify the content of information in a way that reduces the editorial control of the subjects of transparency, and to provide it in formats that allow the recipient to use it to support whatever argument they wish to put forward.

Where documents provide evidence of processes or outcomes for the individual, data can provide evidence of outcomes across whole populations or systems. It lends itself naturally to reinterpretation and verification.

In India, the MKSS (Association for the Empowerment of Workers and Peasants) demonstrated that simply having the official record of what had been spent – hard data – and comparing that to the visible evidence provided an immediate way of challenging the official story and creating a more credible alternative narrative. It may have proved hard to leverage that narrative in the courts and through the political system, but it served to expose what had been concealed.

However, here again, editorial control over the data process can be just as devastating as editorial control of the FOI process itself – with small amounts of control being used to powerful effect.

The internet activist Aaron Swartz argued that transparency was ineffective in combatting corruption because it was too easy to evade:

> When you have time to prepare, it's pretty easy to disguise the data. And this is exactly the pattern we've seen. It's always been investigative journalism, not data mining, that's revealed the big scandals about politicians. I, more than anyone, would love to believe that the next great Watergate is just lying in plain sight to be uncovered by a swashbuckling econometrician, but the sad fact is, it simply isn't so.[6]

Returning to our four types of unfairness, we can see that transparency to evidence whether an individual allocation was done correctly, according to the rules, is perhaps the easiest type of narrative to evade through editorial control of information. Using transparency to demonstrate that correct procedures have not been followed will more often reveal a lack of evidence than evidence of a failure.

In contrast, if the narrative is that the outcome of an individual decision is insupportable, the information required to support or oppose is likely to be less subject to editorial control. The decision itself is public information and information about its effects or likely effects is often as much in the hands of the people affected by the decision. They have all they need to make a public appeal about the injustice of their situation.

Individual narratives are more powerful if they are evidence of systemic unfairness in allocations. But the best evidence for this often requires data about outcomes and processes across populations. To the degree that organisations are allowed to control the creation of that data and the degree to which they can restrict publication to high-level summary data, the less likely it is that transparency will be of any use in evidencing

---

[6] Aaron Swartz, 'A database of folly' first posted on Crooked Timber, July 3, 2012, http://crookedtimber.org/2012/07/03/a-database-of-folly/ and reprinted in *The Boy Who Could Change the World: The Writings of Aaron Swartz*, The New Press, 5 Jan 2016

such unfairness. Equally, it is less likely that such data can help an individual determine whether their own circumstances are to be expected, or rather the result of biased or inaccurate allocation mechanisms.

The greater degree that data is derived from independent verifiable sources and shared in granular preferably raw and unedited formats, the more likely it is that transparency will yield the information necessary to evidence a particular narrative.

- *Verifiable data.* The data used by MKSS in India (Chapter 10) was of value to the workers whose rights they were representing because they could verify it. In effect, they collected an additional parallel data set from the community, bypassing the administration, and tallied one set of data against the other. In the next chapter we will look at further examples of the use of independently generated data.
- *Granular data.* Budget projections – the sort of data the East Devon Alliance (EDA) was looking for (Chapter 9) – is an area where editorial control can be greatly reduced by defining structured formats in which the data can be released, thereby allowing independent review. The work of the International Budget Partnership and other bodies are making this possible. For this to result in full transparency, independent authority should be established over the form in which budgetary information is published and shared. At a national level, the UK is not far off this position with the creation of the Office for Budget Responsibility and the publication of the Combined Online Information System (COINS) database that includes very detailed information on budgets and budget projections. But most other government organisations, in the UK and elsewhere, allow sufficient executive editorial control over the form in which budgets are presented to greatly limit their value to transparency.

In the case of Pro-Vida (see Chapter 6), Fundar could provide a comprehensive account of where the money had gone because it had the underlying receipts. If the organisation had simply been handed a set of carefully collated accounts in the first place, it would quite likely have been impossible to get to the bottom of what had happened.

Aggregation and granularity

Information, like sugar, comes in more or less granular forms. Granularity refers to the degree to which the particular data items in a data set are created by aggregating more specific information. So, for example, a data set telling you the sex and height of everyone in a class is much more granular than a data set that tells you the number of boys and girls in a class and the average height of each group. The first data set has more data points and more information. The second has aggregated those data into just four data points and has consequently discarded much of the information in the original.

Aggregate data is of use only to the degree that it happens to provide you with the particular aggregation you needed. If you want to know whether, in that class, boys are on average taller than girls, it would inform you of this. However, if you wanted to know, for example, how many girls were taller than the average boy, it would not.

The aggregation of data – and the resulting loss of information – makes it possible to tell only particular narratives, with the result that we can easily be misled. It is a phenomenon often encountered as the 'tyranny of averages'.

For example, there is some evidence that boys are, on average, better at performing certain mathematical tasks than girls – a finding that sometimes gets simplified to 'boys are better at maths than girls'.

This analysis, however, tells you nothing about the distribution – that there are very good mathematicians and very poor mathematicians among both boys and girls. The variation amongst girls and amongst boys is much greater than the rather small difference between the average of each group. This means that a very large percentage of girls are better at maths than the average boy. But if the numbers get simplified to 'boys are better than girls', there is a risk that many girls may wrongly underestimate their own abilities and potential as mathematicians.

The tyranny of averages can have significant consequences for policy makers. UK education policy has been influenced in the past by analyses of educational attainment which showed worse outcomes for children from poor families compared to wealthier families. It also found that results were worse for students from black and minority ethnic (BME) communities compared to children from the white population. This made sense: BME communities were disproportionately more likely to be poor. Consequently, large efforts were made to focus educational efforts on such communities.

However, this narrative was determined by the way in which the averages had been calculated – focusing on large disparate groups such as 'poor people' and 'minority ethnic' people. When more granular analysis was done, the narrative changed. First, it emerged that there was huge diversity in the levels of educational attainment within BME communities, with some experiencing better than average outcomes and some significantly worse. Second, it became clear that when looking at ethnicity and poverty *together*, the group that had the worst outcomes from education were poor white children.[7] On average white children did better than black children. And on average rich children did better than poor children. But because white children are more likely to be rich, the figures disguised the fact that white children from deprived homes were the least advantaged.

Our ability to understand the world around us depends on our ability to avoid making such false generalisations. Transparency policies frequently refer to the need to make data available in granular formats to prevent this loss of information and to allow data to be used to support many different narratives and purposes. But the authors have never seen a policy that attempts to distinguish between data that is sufficiently granular and data that is too aggregate. One result of this is the phenomenon of the 'data portal' – something that has become very popular among governments in recent years – which is a website containing

---

[7]   *Unseen Children: Access and Achievement 20 Years On*, Ofsted, June 2013, www.gov.uk/government/publications/unseen-children-access-and-achievement-20-years-on

thousands of different tabulations of data at varying levels of aggregation and granularity.

The experience of using a data portal can be extremely frustrating. It involves hours sifting through different tabulations in the hope that you will find one that might, by good fortune, have captured the very analysis you are looking for. It is our experience that, more often than not, you cannot find the data you would ideally want.

The degree to which data is sufficiently granular depends on whether or not it is able to answer the specific question you have. If you want to know about the experience of poor, white children, the average for poor children and the average for white children will most likely not answer your question.

The lowest level of granularity for any data set is a record of a specific event – a payment into a bank account, a sale or purchase of goods, an individual enrolling at a college or being appointed to a job, a train stopping at a station at a particular time, the recording of a blood pressure reading from a monitoring device, the recording of a kilowatt of power through an electricity meter or the passing of a signal between your mobile phone to a phone mast at a particular location.

Most of the data we encounter in life is aggregate information that has been created by applying particular rules, definitions and calculations to create a particular piece of information. The degree to which that matters depends on the context.

In national accounting, for example, having disaggregated information down to, say, particular government programmes can be helpful for democratic accountability. But on the issue of criminal accountability for theft or fraud, going down to the level of individual payment transactions is the more useful level of information.

In areas concerning outcomes for people, the most relevant level of granularity is the level of the individual. Data aggregated above this level will have already involved certain decisions about the types of individuals that the data can describe and the degree to which it is possible to understand the associations between allocation systems and outcomes for these individuals.

Calls for government to publish open data have provided many useful data sets. These have, often through the creativity of individuals, been used effectively to support particular narratives, such as the evidencing of which politicians in Romania were most likely to be corrupt. But such data has, in the main, been published at a level of aggregation that is not designed to support the creation of new narratives or the discovery of new knowledge about allocation outcomes for individuals.

The result can be arguments between government agencies, or corporates, with more complete information and the external bodies calling for transparency that have to use proxy data or averages to try to evidence their concern.

For example, in the UK the current government has recently introduced reforms to welfare payments for those too ill to work. Such people have been required to attend 'work capability assessments' where they are asked to perform a number of tasks in order to ascertain whether they are in fact fit for work. The aim is to try to make it harder for people to remain out of work for a long time. This has been informed by evidence that long-term unemployment is harmful for people – for example that it is associated with a significant increase in the risk of depression and suicide.[8]

The first complaints about the new system came in the form of individual outcomes that seemed insupportable – people in the final stages of cancer being declared fit to return to work. Their public appeals that the system must be unfair prompted public protest and questions in parliament.

The government responded by appointing an independent investigator to assess the quality of the service and to publish their findings. Five such reports have now been produced which have done a good deal of useful work, including testing alternative approaches to assessment and identifying weaknesses in the way the process categorised abilities. For example, people who were only intermittently able to perform a task and people who were always able to do it were categorised as the same.

Despite this, complaints that the process is harmful and unfair have persisted. In 2015, researchers in Liverpool and Oxford

---

[8] Milner A, Page A, and LaMontagne AD, 'Long-term unemployment and suicide: a systematic review and meta-analysis', *PLoS ONE*, Vol 8, No 1 (2013): e51333. DOI:10.1371/journal.pone.0051333

published a paper which showed a correlation between taking the tests and committing suicide.[9] However, in doing this they had not been able to look at the information about the people who had taken a test. Instead, within each local area of the country, they had to look at the average number of tests and compare it to the average level of suicide. Those areas that had seen an increase in tests had also seen an increase in the number of suicides. While the analysis had attempted to rule out alternative explanations – other than that the tests themselves were responsible for the suicides – the data could not determine if the suicides were among the people taking the tests.

An argument ensued in which the government indicated that the report was 'misleading' and the researchers defended their work. The peculiarity of this situation is that the government holds the data that would enable the researchers to test whether the government's objections were fair or not. But it did not offer to let them analyse this information.

The appointment of regulators, inspectors and independent assessors is the most common response to concerns that allocation mechanisms are unfair. These organisations are expected to be transparent and to publish their findings. Such policies are an important part of creating fair societies. But, as the story of work capability assessments illustrates, this is not a substitute for being open about data and transparent about the outcomes of allocation systems.

[9]   B. Barr, D. Taylor-Robinson, D. Stuckler, R. Loopstra, A. Reeves and M. Whitehead, '"First, do no harm": are disability assessments associated with adverse trends in mental health? A longitudinal ecological study', *Journal of Epidemiology and Community Health*. Vol 70, No 4, 339–345. DOI:10.1136/jech-2015-206209

FIGHTING FOR INFORMATION

Sidmouth is a small regency town on the South Coast of Devon, England. It is home to the East Devon District Council – a local elected authority with power over the granting of permission to develop land in the area. This power is valuable. The region is a designated 'area of outstanding natural beauty' and a popular holiday and retirement destination. If you get permission to build a house anywhere in the area you stand to make a great deal of money. The authority to dispense this largesse is vested in a small elected authority which has had one party consistently elected to govern for most of the last half century.

Concerns about the propriety with which the council was acting led a number of local campaigners, journalist and activists to start to raise concerns about conflicts of interest. In 2012, the *Telegraph* newspaper carried out a sting on one local councillor, Graham Brown. Graham Brown was an elected councillor. He had also been given the job of running the Local Planning Forum through which the council sought advice on which land could be developed. He also had a business providing consultancy on how to get planning permission to develop property. When secretly videoed by the *Telegraph* he explained his approach as follows: 'if I turned a green field into a housing estate and I'm earning a developer two or three million, then I ain't doing it for peanuts'. He was later forced to resign while denying that there was anything improper about his behaviour.

The East Devon Alliance (EDA) is a group of local citizens campaigning to end what they regard as corruption in the local council. They are trying to use freedom of information to assist with this. They have met strong resistance from the council.

One of the most valuable properties in the area is the site of the council building itself. Knowle, built in 1810 under the supervision of Sir John Soane, stands at the top of a broad park with mature trees sloping down into the town. When the council announced it planned to relocate and sell off part of the site for redevelopment, 4000 people marched through the town to protest.

One of the campaigners, Jeremy Woodward, filed a Freedom of Information request on 14 February 2013 to see the minutes of committee meetings and any reports relating to the decision. The council rejected the request on the grounds of deliberative freedom. These were internal documents. It took over two years of legal argument with appeals first to the information commissioner and then to an Information Tribunal; the final appeal allowed some information to be released.

It came with a damning judgement from the tribunal into the way the council had handled the request, which stated: 'Correspondence on behalf of the Council, rather than ensuring the Tribunal was assisted in its function, was at times discourteous and unhelpful including the statement that we had the most legible copies possible – a statement which was clearly inaccurate as subsequently, we have been provided with perfectly legible documents.' These tactics had significantly delayed the decision.

Paul Freeman of the East Devon Alliance then put in a second FOI asking for a copy of the business case supporting the decision. This was rejected on the grounds that the council did not have a document entitled 'business case' or any single document comprising information that one might expect to see in a business case. It said it could not respond to the request because 'the phrase "business case" could potentially be interpreted broadly'. The council's response included providing references to links to information on its website which it then altered so that they no longer worked.

The decision once again went to appeal, prompting further negative comments about the evasive tactics of the council. The information commissioner was unimpressed and described the council's approach as 'regrettable'. But while it may be regrettable, these tactics have enabled the council to hold requests for information at bay for years.

The East Devon Alliance is everything that politicians hoped for from FOI. Shortly after the bill became law Lord Falconer complained that it was being used by journalists rather than citizens. In East Devon it is most definitely the citizens using FOI to further their cause but they have been faced with defiant resistance from the council.

FOI has been of value to the EDA – but more by exposing the approach of the council to transparency than by actually releasing information. They have managed to secure two strongly worded condemnations against the council and raised questions about the way in which it operates. The council's delaying tactics were sufficient to ensure that these did not come out until too late to have an impact on the most recent local elections. Nonetheless, EDA managed to win a quarter of the seats on the local authority. The council's evasive behaviour in response to FOI has helped them build their case.

14

Regulation and transparency

Until now we have looked at 'negative' forms of editorial control over information released under transparency initiatives. These include the ability to determine what is recorded; how it is stored, transmitted and deleted; the accuracy and detail of recording; as well as the use of redaction and control over the timing of release. These are all mechanisms that can be used to limit available information.

There is one type of editorial control that takes a different form – the ability to actively use the released information to manage the political narrative. This is most commonly encountered when governments use selective leaking to manage the media, in dispensing 'scoops' by way of patronage. In both the US and the UK, the increase in people being prosecuted by the government for unofficial leaks stands in marked contrast to the lack of action on the pervasive use of leaks by the executive branch of government. This has now become a noted abuse of power.[1] In a similar way, public debate can be shaped through the proactive publication of information by government and

---

[1]   For the US see for example Mary-Rose Papandrea, 'Leaker traitor whistleblower spy: national security leaks and the First Amendment', *Boston University Law Review* Vol 94, No 2 (2014), 449-544; or for UK see Tenth Report of Session 2008-09 from the Public Administration Select Committee: Leaks and Whistleblowing in Whitehall. The response from the Labour administration is also notable. Having demonstrated an unprecedented mastery of the use of the political leak, government's official response to the committee declared: 'Unauthorised disclosure of official information [by ministers] can never be sanctioned and the corrosive effect of such disclosures cannot be underestimated'. Such abject disingenuity by government is, if anything, even more corrosive.

regulators. This can allow a significant degree of editorial control over such debate by setting the parameters by which public policy is deemed successful or otherwise.

In particular, the publication of performance information about regulated services such as utilities, police services, schools and healthcare has become an important tool in the hands of central government and regulatory agencies in shaping these services and our perception of them.

The publication of this information is cited as an example of increasing transparency. It is often justified on the grounds that such information empowers people by enabling them to choose better performing services or to express their views more effectively as to how services could be improved; or by exposing poorly performing organisations to public shame and condemnation, which then incentivises them to do better.

In Chapter 10 we looked at the degree to which 'social audit' – in which the public and media respond to performance information – has been effective in improving standards. However, by our definition of transparency, the publication of regulatory performance information is not necessarily something that evens the playing field between those providing services and those receiving them. Indeed, it could be used to achieve the opposite effect.

Publication of performance information will only increase someone's ability to assess whether they are being well served if the published information coincides sufficiently with the issues they are concerned about. It will only enable them to make better choices if the information helps them identify preferred services.

For citizens concerned that they are being treated unfairly by a regulated organisation and who call for greater transparency, the publication of information by the regulator will often only add to their woes because it will fail to address the issue that they regard as being important. All it does is change the focus of their demands from greater transparency about regulated organisations to greater transparency about the way the regulator operates.

This potential risk is exacerbated by conflicts of interest that can incentivise regulators to misrepresent public interest in order to make the regulatory task more achievable – to define regulatory success in a way that is easier to deliver, even if it less accurately reflects success in terms of public benefit. Regulatory organisations will often have conflicting obligations written into their founding objectives – for example, the duty to identify failings in regulated organisations and the duty to maintain public confidence in the regulated industry. Doing the first often undermines the latter.

Indeed, just as countries in receipt of international aid can benefit by using false signals of transparency to attract donors, governments can use transparency and publication of regulatory information for political purposes, such as weakening political standing of industries or professions or creating false reassurance in the mind of the electorate about standards.

Regulatory failure and transparency

In the chapter on social audit, we presented widespread evidence that the publication of performance information – including regulatory assessments – has, in the main, delivered significant public benefits. Our aim here is not to question the value of regulation or of public reporting. It is to describe the mechanisms by which its impact is eroded and the role that transparency can play in fixing this problem.

The main points we want to argue are that:

1. *The publication of regulatory assessments helps to enforce regulatory standards but does little to empower the public.* Publication of regulatory assessments is a very powerful tool in enforcing regulatory standards. Naming and shaming has been shown to have a strong effect, most notably on poorly performing organisations. Such information has also been used on occasion in informing public campaigns. However, this information is rarely useful to the public in making choices about the products or services they use.

2. *Transparency around regulation should enable the assessment of outcome of regulation – that is, the net social benefit from such activity. The publication of regulatory assessments is not a reliable means to achieve this.* Publication of assessments – in the form of performance data, survey data and regulatory opinion - is an important part of making the process of

regulation transparent. It enables a clear understanding of how organisations are being regulated. But it provides no reliable information on the degree to which regulation has led to improvement. This is because the process of regulation necessarily distorts assessment data to such a degree as to make it unreliable as an indicator of the beneficial impact of regulation. While it can provide a measure of the degree to which standards have been complied with, it is unreliable as an indicator of the consequent real-world benefit.

3. *Regulators face significant conflicts of interest in the design of assessment. The publication of regulatory assessments can increase that conflict.* Regulators are often conflicted between a desire to improve public wellbeing and a desire not to be seen to have failed. Publication of regulatory assessments is used in the first order as a measure of the performance of the regulated organisations and in the second order to measure the performance of the regulator. If such assessments do not improve over time the regulator has failed. In the second order role, regulators become conflicted about the type of information that should be made public.

We believe that these three problems drive a significant amount of regulatory failure. Our contention is that all of these concerns are best addressed by implementing transparency policies based on data sharing. This will make the primary job of assessing standards easier, as greater openness will allow greater insight into what is driving performance against regulatory standards. It may also open up the possibility of more effective public empowerment by allowing more tailored use of information to address individual concerns. Perhaps most importantly, it will allow the outcomes of the regulatory process to be more clearly visible by seeing how improvements in regulatory assessments relate to changes in broader measurements of welfare.

We will argue that a central role of regulation should be not simply the assessment of standards but the construction of information systems that allow the relationship between regulatory assessment and wider real-world outcomes to be as transparent as possible. As with all other allocation systems, we will argue that transparency of regulation must mean making not just the process transparent but making the outcomes of such activity as visible as possible.

These issues can be detailed as follows.

i. The publication of regulatory assessments helps to enforce regulatory standards but does little or nothing to empower the public

This issue has been looked at in some detail by Archon Fung and colleagues,[2] who compared a number of US programmes that have forced disclosure of information to the public to better inform their decisions. One example they find compelling is the display of information about hygiene standards on stickers in the windows of food outlets. This information, they argue, is 'embedded' in the decision-making processes of the public as they will often size up options on the street by examining different establishments and, at that moment, are provided with this additional piece of information that would otherwise not be visible to them.

When Volvo wanted to tell people its cars performed well on safety tests, they did not publish the statistics. They published pictures of their cars with lifebelts instead of wheels. They turned the data into a narrative.

Consumer Reports in the US and similar organisations around the world perform a comparable task when they collect detailed technical information about products and then boil it down to identify a few 'best buys'. The technical information is there for those who want it, but it has been helpfully collated into a simple recommendation for those who do not.

The difficulty faced by public sector organisations with regulatory responsibility is that there is a tension between presenting information for regulatory purposes and presenting it for consumer purposes. Table 14.1 sets out the differences.

These issues help explain why the publication of regulatory information in public services has had less impact on patient choice than expected. The decisions are complex and, without

---

2   Archon Fung, Mary Graham and David Weil, *Full Disclosure The Perils and Promise of Transparency*, Cambridge University Press, July 2008.

a clear narrative that links the choice of a provider to the individual's particular circumstances, most people find it an impossible task to try to make decisions based on abstract technical information.

Table 14.1: Information for choice vs information for regulation

	Choice	Regulation
Statistical significance of performance data	Any significance where the corresponding benefit is of greater value than the inconvenience of accessing the service. So, for example, if I have two bank accounts to choose from and nothing to separate them, evidence that one is superior, even with low levels of statistical significance is useful	Needs to be high. Regulatory action tends to have much greater impact than individual choice and therefore needs to be reserved and only acted on where there is a significantly higher significance/probability of difference in performance
Specificity of information	The individual wants an analysis that identifies differences in performance that are most relevant to their specific circumstances. So, for example, a bank might have a poor reputation for service among high value clients but a good reputation among small deposit holders. The average is of no interest to either group	Regulators need to focus on preventing the most widespread and serious harms so they want information at the highest relevant level of aggregation and about the most egregious failings, neither of which may be relevant to a particular individual
Relevant comparator group	Where only a limited subset of providers is relevant to a particular individual for, say, geographical reasons, they are only interested in comparison among that group	Regulators are interested in comparison against industry norms and are charged with establishing standards across the whole market not identifying performance within sub-markets
Narrative format	Needs to be woven into a market narrative that recognises the emotional context of individual decisions	Technical presentation to inform actions of professional regulators will work

In view of these differences, claims by regulatory organisations that they publish – or force the publication of – information in order to inform public choice should be taken with a large pinch of salt. Claims that such information can be taken by intermediaries and turned into more compelling narratives for the public have some degree of truth. But, in the main, to create the necessary narrative, intermediaries need information that is structured differently to that provided by regulators. They need access to the raw data in order to be able to construct the most relevant measures and narratives. Working with data from regulators to create narratives for consumers results in rather crude kludges that have limited effectiveness.

Furthermore, attempts by regulators to directly interpose information into people's natural decision-making processes have had limited effect. Forced disclosure of terms and conditions or complex disclosure information on pharmaceutical packaging has been shown to be of very limited effect.[3] Similarly, there is evidence that requiring salespeople to declare commissions can have the opposite effect to that intended. For example, studies have shown how salespeople are able to use commission disclosure to their advantage. They could use it as evidence of their superior trustworthiness or to make the customer feel that rejecting their advice might appear to be an attack on their honesty. This enables them to sell worse deals to the customer than comparable salespeople who were not required to declare commissions.[4]

ii. Data from regulatory assessments are not a reliable means to assess the impact of regulation and do not constitute outcome transparency for regulatory processes

The outcome of regulation is the level of social benefit achieved for the cost. This sum is normally calculated in terms of the cost to regulated organisations of complying with regulations along

---

[3] O. Ben-Shahar and B. Schneider, *More Than You Wanted to Know: The Failure of Mandated Disclosure,* Princeton University Press, 2016.

[4] Daylian M. Cain, George Loewenstein and Don A. Moore, 'The dirt on coming clean: perverse effects of disclosing conflicts of interest', *Journal of Legal Studies* Vol 34, No 1 (January 2005), 1–25; Daylian M. Cain, George Loewenstein and Don A. Moore, 'When sunlight fails to disinfect: understanding the perverse effects of disclosing conflicts of interest', *Journal of Consumer Research* Vol 37, No 5, (2011), 836–857; George Loewenstein, Daylian M. Cain and Sunita Sah, 'The limits of transparency: pitfalls and potential of disclosing conflicts of interest', *American Economic Review* Vol 101 (2011), 423–428.

with the regulator's own budget. Measuring the net social benefit of regulation (i.e. public gain versus cost) is hard and much research has gone into trying to identify the cost to the economy of regulatory activity. However, in many cases regulation is only introduced where serious harms have been identified and the ability to limit these is widely regarded as of high value. In these circumstances the bigger concern is less the cost of regulation and rather the effectiveness of it – that is, the degree to which it limits the harm identified. Ineffectiveness takes many forms, a selection of which are illustrated below.

Displacement, tunnel vision, balloon effects, unintended consequences

Numerous terms have been developed in different industries to reflect the problem whereby attempts to target and limit a particular harm can in fact cause other harms to increase, as attention moves from one area of concern to another. So, for example, if regulators target rollovers as a risk in cars, that risk will be reduced but savings will be made elsewhere in the construction of vehicles. These can then lead to small increases in a myriad other risks that are not captured in the data.

It is quite possible for such effects to have an overall negative impact. For example, some researchers have concluded that tightened security at airports following 9/11 caused an increase in road traffic that contributed to an estimated 500 deaths per year over the subsequent decade[5] – quite possibly more than the deaths prevented by the security measures. Because deaths in terrorist incidents are attributed to government failure and are prominent in public debate, they get greater regulatory focus while road deaths are categorised as events over which

---

[5] Garrick Blalock, Vrinda Kadiyali, and Daniel H. Simon (2007) 'The impact of post-9/11 airport security measures on the demand for air travel', *Journal of Law and Economics*, Vol 50, No 4, November, 731–755.
Garrick Blalock, Vrinda Kadiyali, and Daniel H. Simon (2009) 'Driving Fatalities after 9/11: A Hidden Cost of Terrorism', *Applied Economics* Vol 41, No 14, 1717–1729.
Michael Sivak and Michael J. Flannagan (2004) 'Consequences for road traffic fatalities of the reduction in flying following September 11, 2001', *Transportation Research Part F: Traffic Psychology and Behavior*, Vol 7 No 4.

government has less control and where the blame lies more with the individuals.

A striking example of this effect comes from Bangladesh where concern about arsenic poisoning led to a public health campaign to persuade people to switch from backyard wells to surface water sources. While the latter were less likely to be contaminated by arsenic, the toxin of concern, they were *more* likely to be contaminated with bacteria. Bacteria, however, were not the salient concern. Research found that where people switched from backyard wells, infant mortality rates rose by 27%.[6] There is no way to know how one source of harm would have compared to the other if behaviour had differed. But it is likely that, with full information, people might have preferred to accept the risk of arsenic contamination.

One of the most serious scandals to hit the National Health Service (NHS) in recent years was a catalogue of failures in care at Stafford hospital, run by the Mid Staffordshire NHS Foundation Trust. This was tunnel vision on a grand scale. The hospital put all its efforts into achieving the necessary performance on a handful of key metrics tracked by regulators – the majority of which related to waiting times and financial balance. In the process, basic standards of nursing and medicine that were not subject to the same degree of scrutiny were allowed to collapse, leading to avoidable deaths and injury to patients.

Gaming, minimal compliance, cheating

Regulated organisations develop ways to comply with the assessment while delivering none of the intended benefit. The terms 'minimal compliance', 'gaming' and 'cheating' are used to describe such activity depending on the degree of dishonesty attributed to the regulated organisations. However, they are perhaps all best viewed as the inevitable consequences of regulatory activity.

---

[6] Erica Field, Rachel Glennerster and Reshmaan Hussam, *Throwing the Baby out with the Drinking Water: Unintended Consequences of Arsenic Mitigation Efforts in Bangladesh*, Working Paper, Cambridge, MA: Harvard University and M.I.T, 2011.

There is a conflict here between the requirement that transparency in regulation or assessment meets basic standards of justice – you have to know what you are going to be measured on or assessed against – and the desire to prevent gaming and compliance. This is recognised in that policing activity is not required to be transparent – for example, a freedom of information (FOI) request in the UK for complete details of the processes used by local authorities to identify potential benefit cheats was refused for valid reasons. But, equally, the more detailed the information and the more mechanistic the process by which a regulated body is assessed, the easier it will be to identify techniques for minimal compliance.

Another example, from law enforcement, occurs when measures of crime reduction result in attention being focused on solving minor crimes that can be easily resolved and ignoring more difficult cases. It is almost impossible to design measures of process (for example, measures of the amount of activity done or the time taken to do it) that do not provide opportunities for cherry picking, top-slicing or 'creaming and parking' in which activity that is easier to deliver within set targets gets prioritised inappropriately. For example, in healthcare, waiting time targets result in less urgent patients being treated ahead of more urgent patients.

At the extreme, cherry-picking involves a refusal to provide services to people where there is a risk the provider will miss regulatory targets as a result. For example, the police can cherry-pick to some extent in their ability to persuade victims whether or not to report crimes. In the UK, police were found to be underreporting rape by 26%, by using their discretion to classify reports as 'no-crime'.

Sometimes the changes are subtle. In education teachers being monitored on the performance of their pupils in exams have responded by influencing children to take exams that they believe will be easier to pass, even if the qualification is of less use to the child in later life.

Sometimes changes are alarmingly blatant. For example, US hospitals that are measured on 30-day post-operative mortality rates were found to have developed a practice of switching off life support machines on the 31st day after a procedure.

Often, the organisations or people involved are not even aware of how their behaviour is changing in response to assessment. A study of the management of infection rates in UK hospitals – something that is closely monitored by regulators – looked at how doctors categorised infections. Central line-associated bloodstream infections (CLABSIs) are a particularly strong focus of regulation because they are serious and regarded as avoidable. However, deciding whether an infection should be classified as 'central line-associated' is a matter of judgement. The researchers found that simply knowing that the information was being collected caused doctors and nurses to err more towards not classifying infections as CLABSIs, without any intention to game the system.[7]

Where the loopholes are big enough, the ability to game the system can instantly deprive regulation of any impact. For example, when the UK Labour party imposed its own rules requiring political donations to be published, they switched from taking donations to accepting long-term interest-free loans with no fixed repayment date. These 'loans' did not qualify as donations. Until the loophole was closed, the new rules did nothing except provide false reassurance.

Industries have proved themselves remarkably inventive in designing ways to shake off regulatory constraints. The tobacco industry has been accused of designing the holes on the filters of low tar cigarettes in such a way that they will yield low levels of tar when smoked by a standard testing machine used for regulation but yield high levels of tar when smoked by a person. The holes are positioned in such a way that the machine does not cover them but the fingers and lips of people do.

Volkswagen (VW) is currently under investigation for installing 'defeat devices' into its cars that would reset the engine to emit lower emissions when the pattern of driving matched Environmental Protection Agency (EPA) emissions testing routines. While VW's behaviour is undoubtedly in breach of

---

[7]   M. Dixon-Woods, M. Leslie, J.F. Bion and C. Tarrant, 'What counts? An ethnographic study of infection data reported to a patient safety program', *Milbank Quarterly* Vol 90 (2012), 548-591, http://onlinelibrary.wiley.com/ doi/10.1111/j.1468-0009.2012.00674.x/abstract

regulations, efforts by other manufactures to simply optimise engines around testing thresholds can also do much to limit the impact of regulation without breaching the rules.

More often, all that is required to dodge assessments is to change the way information is captured. In response to regulatory measurement of waiting times for cancer, some UK hospitals decided to classify patients as receiving 'watch and wait' as a treatment even if different treatment was intended. This then took them off the waiting list. A hospital that refused to do this might then appear to be performing worse on this indicator while, in reality, delivering surgery to patients in a more timely fashion[8]

If you are looking for information about the impact of regulatory assessments, changes in the performance of organisations against regulatory assessment is one source that is most likely to misrepresent the real-world reduction in harm. If this is the only information we have about the real-world harm, we are unable to take an informed view about the degree to which regulation is having the desired effect. Despite the wealth of evidence of this effect, there is still the temptation to treat improvement in assessment data as evidence of improvement in the real world.

Over time, even the best constructed regulatory structures should be expected to degrade as organisations develop mechanisms to appear compliant at minimal effort. It is not possible to determine from regulatory information how far it has degraded or to assess the degree to which it is still yielding a net benefit. Transparency in the form of data sharing about regulated activities provides a mechanism by which this can be assessed in a pluralistic and democratic manner.

---

[8] *Uses and Abuses of Performance Data in Healthcare*. A report of the Dr Foster Ethics Committee, April 2015, www.drfoster.com/wp-content/uploads/2015/04/Uses-and-abuses-of-performance-data-April-2015-FINAL-DIGITAL-with-cover1.pdf

iii. Regulators face significant conflicts of interest in the design of assessments and the publication of regulatory assessments can increase this conflict

Regulators are often responsible both for assessing standards and demonstrating improvement. This creates a conflict of interest.

First it creates an incentive to assess against standards where improvements are more likely to be delivered. This favours process measures over outcomes.

Second, the success of the regulator depends on it being able to show improvement. This creates an incentive to ignore gaming or compliant behaviour. As evidence grows that regulatory assessments may not adequately capture real-world risks, regulators can become trapped in an attempt to defend their practices and assessments and to restrict information that might question their account.

In one of the most comprehensive and compelling descriptions of this type of failure, Ben Goldacre has examined in detail failures in the regulation of the pharmaceutical industry and the way in which the regulators have contributed to the problem by concealing these failures.[9] The pharmaceutical industry apparently faces a highly elaborate 'gold standard' level of regulation in which the efficacy of products must be demonstrated in randomised controlled trials. It is a testament to the power of gaming that the industry has been able to run rings around this system through selective publication of results (every so often even the worst drug comes up positive), manipulation of the testing environment (by restricting the range of patients drugs are tested on) and manipulation of the evidence (by, for example, collecting data on lots of possible benefits and selecting the one that matters in retrospect).

The result is summed up by the observation from the Food and Drug Administration (FDA) that the best day any drug ever enjoys is the day it is launched. Its track record from then on declines rapidly as we gradually discover the various things that are wrong with it when used in the real world.

To give just one example, Goldacre tells the story of rosiglitazone, launched in 1999 as a new drug for diabetes that

---

[9]   Ben Goldacre, *Bad Pharma,* Faber and Faber, 2013.

might safely control blood sugar levels and protect people from heart attack and death. Almost immediately, concerns about increased risk of heart problems were raised by US academics but were attacked by GlaxoSmithKline (GSK), the drug company. The World Health Organization raised the same issue with GSK in 2003. It then took until 2005/6 before GSK conducted an internal analysis that confirmed these findings, which were then shared with the FDA. It then took a further two years before the FDA published the findings – something it did only after Steve Nissen, a cardiologist, published his own a meta-analysis in 2007 showing a 43% increase in the risk of heart problems in patients on rosiglitazone.

In other words, for more than a decade, information showing that there were significant risks attached to the drug were kept hidden, not just by the company selling the drug but by the agency responsible for regulating that company. In 2010 the drug was either taken off the market or restricted, all around the world.

It is an open question whether it was right to ban the drug or not – a higher risk of heart disease may nonetheless be offset by other benefits. The problem, as Goldacre puts it, was that 'these discussions happened with the data locked behind closed doors, visible only to regulators'.[10]

Often the truth only came out because of action by the courts. In 2004 GSK, the company selling rosiglitazone, had been found to be withholding data showing evidence of serious side effects from the antidepressant paroxetine in children. This prompted an investigation in the UK and a court case in the US alleging fraud. The settlement required GSK to commit to post its clinical trial results on a public website and this gave Professor Nissen enough data to identify the signs of increased risk of heart disease (from rosiglitazone).

Goldacre points out many similar instances of pharmaceutical companies and regulators working together to withhold information. There are also regulatory efforts at 'transparency' which fail to achieve the level of transparency necessary to allow external observers to assess in any way whether the regulator or the pharma industry are acting in our interests.

---

[10] ibid., Chapter 1: 'Missing data'.

He is clear that the answer must involve data sharing at the level of the individual patient. He calls for all trial results to be made public but adds that:

> we should work towards all triallists having an obligation to share patient level data wherever possible, with convenient online data warehouses and streamlined systems whereby legitimate senior researchers can make requests for access in order to conduct pooled analyses and double check the results reported in published trials.

The necessity for this is illustrated by the example of Vioxx, an anti-inflammatory that turned out to cause an increased risk of heart attack. The published trial results showed no increased risk of heart attack. But the published results failed to make clear that the cut-off point for looking for heart attacks had been set earlier than the cut-off point for looking at some other outcomes such as stomach problems. In other words, they ignored heart attacks happening after an arbitrary date – a date which effectively concealed the true impact of the drug. This was not obvious in the published data. Vioxx was withdrawn in 2004 but by then millions of people had been prescribed the drug, leading to tens of thousands of people suffering serious consequences in terms of heart disease.

It would of course be possible to bring in new regulations to address the particular problem with the way that the data about Vioxx was presented. But the problem should be seen not as a limited set of undesirable behaviours that need to be policed. Instead, the natural tendency of all such systems is to prompt creative and ingenious ways to evade the limitations imposed by rules. Every time one ruse is eliminated another will be invented. The more effective response is for regulators to put in place appropriate data-sharing arrangements.

Data sharing and regulation

The response to these issues is not to create ever more rules but instead to focus on the management and control of data.

Regulatory structures should be designed to allow the maximum possible transparency around the outcome of regulation. Some of the techniques that can help achieve this can be described as follows:

1.   Regulation must be informed by assessments of real-world data as well as test data (see the story of crash statistics below).
2.   A broader range of data is collected than the specific areas under assessment, in order to understand the relationship between performance against assessment and performance in unassessed areas. With real-world data, for instance, a much wider range of contextual information should be collected along with information that relates directly to regulated standards. With test data, random measures should be included as well as regulated measures. So, for example, if collecting data on car emissions for a *standard* driving pattern as part of a regulatory intervention, it would be wise to collect data on other patterns at the same time. These might be randomly selected and changed periodically to provide a reference check against regulatory data.
3.   The raw data that informs both real-world assessment and test assessment must be shared with independent experts able to assess the true impact of regulation.

Regulators are not always happy to share data. The European Medicines Agency has supported attempts to restrict access to medical data on the grounds that it is commercially confidential to the organisations they are regulating. They have also questioned the dangers of wider access, because researchers and journalists will produce misleading or sensationalist results. Using the same argument that Milton put forward in *Areopagitica*, Goldacre rightly answers: 'let them, because these foolish analyses should be conducted and then rubbished in public'.

The other issue that arises is privacy. Access to the underlying data, even with the patient's name and identifiers removed, nonetheless risks identification of patient information.

It is this issue that perpetually bedevils efforts to access the underlying records of what government and companies are doing – whether it is dashcam footage from the police, the records of which farmers received payments from the EU, details of the location and circumstances of the disappeared in Mexico or information about the efficacy of drugs.

This issue is examined in its many contexts in the next section, but with regulation, as in any other area of transparency, the public faces a choice between our collective ability to assess the fairness of the most fundamental allocation systems in society and our desire to limit access to information about our lives.

NHTSA AND THE STORY OF THE FORD PINTO: WHAT'S A SAFE CAR?

The Ford Pinto has gone down in history as one of the most dangerous cars ever built. The story of the Pinto is usually told as an ignominious example of corporate greed and secrecy allowing dangerous products onto the market. It helped change car regulation in the US for the better. And because of those changes we now know that the story was wrong.

It all started in 1977, with an article in *Mother Jones*, which estimated that several thousand people had been killed by the car. It is not clear where the figure comes from. But the thing which made this case notorious was the allegation that Ford had hidden the truth about its product and chose to allow people to burn to death in their vehicles rather than spend $11 per car.

When Ford launched the Pinto in 1971, the regulator, the National Highways and Transportation Safety Agency, was proposing new safety regulations that would test how cars performed in rear-end collisions up to 30mph. These were opposed by Ford, amongst others in the industry, in part with the knowledge that their new Pinto would perform poorly in such a test. The Pinto had a fuel tank in the rear of the car with little protection which meant it was liable to explode in such collisions.

In 1972 Lilly Gray and 13-year-old Richard Grimshaw were in a Pinto when another car, travelling at 30 miles an hour, hit it from behind. The petrol tank burst and the car ignited; Gray died and her passenger was left with appalling injuries. Grimshaw took Ford to court and, in February 1978, he was awarded $2.5 million damages. In an act that caught everyone's attention, the jury also awarded punitive damages against Ford of $125 million. This was reduced on appeal to $3.5 million.

The case of *Grimshaw v Ford Motor Co* meant that the media took close interest when in Indiana, in August 1978, three teenagers died in a burning Pinto after a van hit the back of their car, which was parked by the side of the road. The state of Indiana could have prosecuted the driver of the van: they found marijuana and alcohol in the vehicle. They could have prosecuted the highways agency: the crash site had already been identified as risky. Instead they decided to prosecute Ford for reckless homicide. It was during this trial that a memo came to light showing Ford's calculations that it would cost $11 per car to correct the problem with the fuel tank. The memo goes on to show that this, in total, would be more than the cost of compensating victims who burnt to death in their cars and that therefore no action should be taken. The case has attracted a huge amount of attention.[11] In particular, there was public horror that Ford had known of this fault in the car and kept the information secret.

In 1979, in response to public concern, the National Highway Traffic Safety Administration (NHTSA) instituted the new car assessment programme to evaluate, publish and share information about car safety. Since then the NHTSA has been criticised for many things, including for making decisions which protect the US industry and for failing to tackle the US anti-interventionist attitude to road safety that has led to significantly higher deaths than elsewhere. However, one area where it has won considerable praise is in its approach to the use of information, being named by the General Accounting Office (GAO) as one of three agencies possessing 'a commitment to self-examination, data quality,

---

[11] The cost–benefit analysis conducted by Ford was done in line with the approach recommended by the car regulator. Liability law recognises that people cannot be expected to guard against all possible events. If an event is expected to be rare and the cost of protecting against it is high, if you do nothing about it you are not being negligent. The calculations that Ford did were in line with standards that the regulator and the industry had adopted as a rule of thumb as to when failure to correct a problem is negligent. This is an example of the tensions created by tragic allocation decisions. There is nothing wrong with selling a car that you know will be involved in more fatal accidents than another car. It happens every day. But quantifying that knowledge forces us to confront the price we put on life.

analytic expertise, and collaborative partnerships'. It is an example of how data transparency in regulation can work without undermining the authority of the regulator.

The NHTSA carries out standard crash tests on all cars. It then analyses the data and awards cars between one and five stars according to how they perform. This data is then published. However, in addition, all of the underlying data is also publicly accessible and can be used for reanalysis.

The NHTSA carries out a range of crash tests on the makes of car, simulating different types of collision and collecting information about the damage done to the car.

The NHTSA, as regulators tend to be, is cautious in its interpretation of the data with a focus on ensuring minimum standards. As a result it identifies only a small number of cars as being average or below average in safety. The vast majority – over 90% – get four or five star ratings. From the regulatory point of view, this represents the opinion that most cars on the roads are pretty safe.

That is the point of view we would expect a regulator to take. But the NHTSA, recognising that others may come at the question from a different angle, does not simply publish its ratings. It makes all the underlying data available.

Jack Gillis used to work at the NHTSA. The conservative ratings irked him because they made it impossible to distinguish the very safest cars from the rest. He took the data and devised a different presentation which identified the cars that, according to his analysis, were the safest. The car industry was not amused and, according to Gillis, pressurised the NHTSA to withdraw publication. It did. But as the data was transparent, Gillis was free to pursue his project. He left the NHTSA, found a new publisher, and now publishes *The Car Book* each year with his more discriminating ratings.

Others have done similar things. Consumer Reports and US News both publish their own ratings of cars which include safety data. Forbes publish an analysis of which cars it regards as the least safe based not on crash test ratings but on the death rates.

The NHTSA has done more than simply publish its test data. It has also gone out and collected real-world data. The Fatal Accident Reporting System (FARS) collects information on about 6 million road traffic collisions each year, with details of the make and model of car, the type of collision and the resulting fatalities. All this data is then made available to anyone who wishes to understand the relative safety of vehicles.

Interpreting it is far from straightforward. How, for example, do you take into account the fact that some cars will appeal more to dangerous drivers? Attempts to adjust for things such as the age and sex of the driver can help to make sense of the information. But like all real-world data, interpretation is complex.

As described above, however, such information is essential to understanding the degree to which standard test data is failing to capture real-world conditions and to inform the testing regime. When a number of accidents involving Sports Utility Vehicles (SUVs) rolling over were reported, a congressional committee looked into the issue and introduced new standard rollover tests.

After the rollover scandal, there has been continued media focus on the question of whether SUVs are safer or more dangerous than other cars. That might appear to be a relatively simple question. But the subsequent debate proves that even apparently straightforward questions can prompt a of myriad apparently conflicting answers – all of them correct.

When in 2007 the NHTSA and the Insurance Institute for Highway Safety (IIHS) published analysis of crash statistics, CBS reported the findings as showing that 'cars were safer than SUVs' while others reported that the data conclusively showed 'SUVs safer than cars'. If cars of equal weight were compared, then cars were safer than SUVs. But if you simply compared all SUVs with all cars, the driver was less likely to die in an SUV. In other words, bigger cars are safer, SUVs tend to be bigger, but for any given size, a SUV is less safe than its car equivalent.

Then there is the question of whose death you care about. Most ratings look at the likelihood of the driver of the vehicle dying – which is perhaps the question of most concern to the car buyer. But some cars are more likely to inflict mortal injuries on others. The likelihood of being involved in the death of another driver or pedestrian is surely something that many car buyers would also want to consider. The design of SUVs has been criticised for protecting the driver at the cost of the safety of other road users.

Such debates sometimes prompt complaints that it is all too confusing and the public need to be given one source of information that they can rely on. But which of the above pieces of information do you then select? And who gets to decide? Transparency, like democracy, is working when the public are offered conflicting narratives representing different interpretations of the facts.

This level of transparency has had an impact in improving the safety of vehicles and enabling consumers to protect themselves with information. The NHTSA first started publishing data in the 1970s. In the 40 years since, the share of the car market held by US manufacturers has dropped steadily. While many possible explanations have been mooted, the evidence suggests that the reason is the simplest – that cars from Japan and Europe offered better value – lower prices for safer, more reliable vehicles, information that was available to the people buying cars.

But to return to the story of the Ford Pinto, the FARS data, which goes back to 1975, made it possible, some time after the media furore had abated, to carry out a retrospective analysis of the impact of the car's fuel tank design. In *The Myth of the Ford Pinto Case*,[12] the late Gary T. Schwartz, law professor at University of California, Los Angeles (UCLA), examined the data to see what it could tell us. The first thing he observes is rather obvious. It is that only 4% of fatalities occur in fire crashes and that only 15% of these are due to rear-end collisions. In other words, over 99% of all car accident fatalities happen for other reasons. So the design problem in the Pinto could not have caused thousands of deaths and was not the most important safety consideration when comparing cars.

The data did confirm that the Ford Pinto had a higher than average risk of fatalities from rear-end collisions that caused a fire. But it also found

---

[12]   Gary T. Schwartz, 'The Myth of the Ford Pinto Case', *Rutgers Law Review*, Vol 43, No1), Summer 1991: 1013-1068.

that it was not the worst. The Vega saw more drivers die in this way. In both cases the total number of such deaths was low and in single digits.

Finally, Schwartz found that the overall fatality rate per million vehicles on the road was lower for the Pinto than for many more highly regarded competitors such as the VW Beetle or the Toyota Corolla. The Pinto's rate was about average. In other words, the allegation that the Pinto was in some way a uniquely dangerous car was untrue and may well have persuaded people to purchase cars that were more dangerous.

Part Two
Transparency 2.0

Transparency 2.0 refers to transparency policies that attempt to get round the problem of editorial control and recognise that transparency must aim to create multiple competing narratives which present different views as to the impact, effectiveness and fairness of public policies and markets.

While we use this term to describe a range of related initiatives, the key feature they have in common is the aim of enabling independent assessment of the fairness of allocation systems. These systems use a number of techniques including the generation of data independently of executive authorities and the sharing of data in raw, granular uninterpreted formats with the intention that the recipient – rather than the person giving the information – will determine how the information is to be used.

We can divide these initiatives into two quite distinct groups:

- Individual data sharing – in which citizens are given direct access to the information and data about them in a format that allows them to use it for their own purposes, including verifying the way in which that information has been used to categorise and allocate things to that person.
- Population data sharing – in which data about whole populations is shared with non-governmental organisations to enable those organisations to develop their own narrative interpretations of the data.

Chapter 15 looks at mechanisms to make information creation more independent of allocation systems.

Chapter 16 looks at efforts to share population data.

Chapter 17 looks at programmes to share data at an individual level with citizens.

Chapter 18 looks at the management of privacy and surveillance that occur when population data is shared.

15

Ceding control of the data

In 1993 Madhav Chavan was teaching chemistry at Mumbai University. He had gone to college in the US and then returned to India to teach. But he also had a passion for social causes and a desire to work to improve the conditions of the poor. After some time spent working to improve rural sanitation, he turned his attention to improving literacy rates.

In the same year, Unicef announced that it would put up a small sum of money - about £1000 – to fund the establishment of a school in the slums of Mumbai. The children there are still likely to end up illiterate.[1] Chavan gave up his job and began working among the poorest children, trying to find ways to help them develop skills that would give them a better chance in life. He founded a charitable organisation, called Pratham, to help them. In time, Pratham developed an educational approach to improving literacy that started to show real results. It then encountered an unanticipated barrier. It turned out that having a solution to the problem was not enough. Solutions are only useful to people who think they have a problem.

Within the ministry of education, there was a view that Pratham was tackling a problem that was already being fixed. India had signed up to a millennium goal to increase enrolment in primary schools. The plan was to get all children enrolled in primary school by 2015. It was going well. The numbers rose strongly and by 2010 India could claim it was making good progress towards the goal. According to the World Bank report,

---

[1]   Literacy rates in Mumbai slums are estimated at 60%.

the proportion of primary school-aged children with a school place had increased over the decade from 81% to 94%.

That sounds like a successful response to the problem of literacy. Putting more kids in school must surely help solve the problem. Unfortunately, that turns out not to be true and it is Pratham we have to thank for discovering this. Since 2005, Pratham has produced the *Annual Status of Education Report* (ASER) which has become the most influential source of data about education in India. It is produced wholly independently of the government.

The problem with measuring enrolment is that you can be enrolled at a school and learn nothing. There are many reasons for this. High rates of teacher absenteeism are part of the problem. Poor quality of teacher training is another. Cultural factors are also important, such as low expectations. If teachers expect children from poorer backgrounds to learn little, they will direct their teaching to other children and their predictions become self-fulfilling.

Pratham decided it needed to find out exactly what pupils were learning, partly to show that there was a need for the type of work it was doing on literacy and partly to be able to show that its approach worked.

The Indian government, like most governments, collected data on educational attainment using standardised tests. But the tests were infrequent and irregular; they changed each time they were done so there was no reliable way to measure progress; and the results were kept secret – no one outside the ministry knew what they contained.

Pratham decided to get right to the heart of the matter and started going house to house, knocking on doors and asking parents if they would let the organisation test their children. The tests were rigorously designed but simple to administer. Conducted one to one, they enabled a reliable assessment of each child's literacy.

The results surprised even the people at Pratham. What the ASER showed was that the rise in enrolment was not causing an improvement in educational attainment. Between 2005 and 2010 data from both the Indian government and the World

Bank showed enrolment rates rising strongly.[2] But the ASER data showed that on its measure of attainment, there was no improvement. The data showed that half the children should be at Std V (equivalent to fifth grade) could not read a Std II text. More importantly, it was not improving. Between 2005 and 2010 it remained flat, with about 50% of children in Std V able to read a Std II text, before falling to less than 50% in 2011.

These were figures not just for children in schools but for all children. In other words, putting more children in school was having no impact on their chances of learning to read. If anything it was actually having a negative impact.

Writing about Pratham's first report, Abhijit Banerjee and Esther Duflo, the development economists, describe the finding that only 30% of children could do basic division 'stunning', adding that 'all over the Third World, little boys and girls who help their parents in their family stall or store do much more complicated calculations all the time with the help of pen and paper. Are schools actually making them unlearn?'[3]

Subsequent analyses highlighted the discrepancy between official National Assessment Survey (NAS) figures and ASER figures. In 2013, a working paper for the UN Secretary-General's Global Initiative on Education observed that while: 'The National Assessment Survey (NAS) ... finds that learning levels are increasing slightly over time', the ASER survey 'finds that learning levels are decreasing'.[4] The apparent contradiction prompted government officials to dismiss the ASER survey as amateurish and cursory, prompting a sharp response from Lant

---

[2]   Indian government figures show gross enrolment rising from 108% to 116% between 2005 and 2010 while the World Bank shows net enrolment rising from 86% (2003) to 94% (2010). Gross enrolment is the number of children enrolled in primary school as a percentage of the children of the relevant age band. It can be higher if, for example, some children are enrolled in primary school outside of those age bands. Net enrolment is the percentage of children within the primary school age band who are enrolled in primary school.

[3]   Abhijit Banerjee and Esther Duflo, 'Poor economics: a radical rethinking of the way to fight global poverty', *Public Affairs*, 2011, p 75

[4]   *Accelerating Progress to 2015 India*, The Good Planet Foundation, 2013. http://educationenvoy.org/wp-content/uploads/2013/07/INDIA-UNSE-FINAL.pdf

Pritchett, Professor of the Practice of International Development at the Harvard Kennedy School who was quoted in the *New York Times* saying: 'Only in India could a survey covering 500,000 children be dismissed as cursory. ... It is meant to be simple enough so an illiterate mother or father can understand what a child can and cannot do – simplicity is one of its virtues. I think the government deliberately conflates – as if 'cursory' means it's inaccurate at what it measures. I think it is super accurate at what it measures.'[5]

One reason to question the NAS figures was that they did not test all children, they only tested the children who came to school on the day of the test. As a result, teachers were able to influence which children took the test by encouraging some and discouraging others.

Officials at the ministry were not pleased at what Pratham was doing – not least because the survey included children in both state and private education systems and the comparison was not flattering to the state provision.[6]

In addition, the ASER data was about what was happening now. The internal government data took so long to collect and process it could only tell you what was happening three years previously. If that's the only available data, having a long delay provides a useful loophole. If it identifies problems, it is always possible to rebut concerns by arguing that these issues have now been fixed.

The problems facing the education systems in developing countries tend to be more serious than those in developed countries. High rates of teacher absenteeism and misappropriation of school funds do not occur in the same way in the UK. However, one thing education systems around the world share is the temptation faced by education ministries not to publish

---

[5] Tina Rosenberg, 'In India, revealing the children left behind', *New York Times*, October 23, 2014. http://opinionator.blogs.nytimes.com/2014/10/23/in-india-revealing-the-children-left-behind/?_r=0

[6] Pritchett L, Aiyar, Y *Value subtraction in public sector production: accounting versus economic const of primary schooling in India*, Working Paper 391 Centre for Global Development (2014) combines data on the lower cost of private education in India compared to state education with ASER data showing better outcomes from private education.

data which enables others to challenge official accounts of improved outcomes.

When the Blair government came to power in the UK in 1997, it argued for a big increase in spending on schools. The prime minister was asked what were the three top priorities for his administration, and he replied: 'Education, education, education'. British economic growth depends on the effective education of a skilled workforce that can compete in global markets.

A series of reforms were introduced which included building new schools, giving schools greater managerial and financial independence from local government, and setting a new national curriculum. Two other sets of reforms were introduced at the same time – a reform of the exams and qualifications system and a drive to use 'transparency' about school performance to improve standards.

School league tables had been introduced under the previous Conservative administration, in the face of protest from teachers who argued that measuring the quality of education was reductionist. Blair expanded the range of information published about schools and encouraged the idea of parents and children choosing schools.

At first glance the results of these policies looked impressive. Between 1967 and 1987, the number of children at 16 achieving a pass mark in at least five subjects had improved modestly from 22% to 26%. Margaret Thatcher then declared that having three-quarters of pupils reach school-leaving age without a pass in literacy and maths was unacceptable. School inspections and league tables were introduced. Ten years later the rate of students passing had risen to 45% (an improvement of nearly 75%).[7]

This was widely credited as an achievement. The opposition did not question the results so much as express concern that they had only been achieved through a drastic narrowing of the curriculum to focus on reading, writing and arithmetic and that the loss to children was not captured anywhere in the data.

---

[7] House of Commons Library Education: Historical Statistics, Standard Note: SN/SG/4252. Last updated: 27 November 2012. Author: Paul Bolton, Social & General Statistics.

Blair bought into the approach in 1997 but with some modifications. He wanted to continue testing and publishing league tables and keep the focus on the fundamentals of maths and literacy. But at the same time he wanted there to be more flexibility in the exam system to allow children greater freedom in terms of what and how they learned. Exams became more modular, with more project work and more teacher assessment. And schools were given greater freedom to opt for more vocational forms of examination – in future these too would be counted in the league tables.

The policy appeared to be successful. The rate of improvement began accelerating. By 2012, 82% of children had achieved a pass mark in at least five subjects.

However, this improvement in attainment jarred with increasing evidence that employers were encountering school-leavers with poor literacy skills and were having to retrain them. But official data seemed to show that today's children were four times more capable than the generation that was now complaining about their employability.

Subsequent analysis has been unable to agree how much of the gain was real and how much of it was simply due to 'grade inflation' and the devaluation of qualifications.[8] However, the rapid rise in General Certificate of Secondry Education (GCSE) performance is in marked contrast to independent measures of performance such as the Trends in International Mathematics and Science Study (TIMSS) survey. This survey is not used to measure schools but to compare across countries. Between 1995 and 2011 the performance of year 9 (13-14-year-olds) in the UK in maths and science showed no major improvement.

As with the NAS tests in India, this did not come about because of any deliberate intention to corrupt information. It is what we should expect to occur when information systems are managed by organisations which are judged on that same information. The problem is a simple imbalance of incentives.

---

[8]   Jo-Anne Baird, Ayesha Ahmed, Therese Hopfenbeck, Carol Brown and Victoria Elliott (2013), *Research Evidence Relating to Proposals for Reform of the GCSE*, Oxford University Centre for Educational Assessment Report OUCEA/13/1.

Any data collection system has imperfections and weaknesses. When that data system is used to judge organisations, the latter will be expected to respond promptly to problems that are brought to light. To the degree that these problems have been identified incorrectly because of inaccuracies in the underlying information, such inaccuracies will be righted. In contrast, any errors in the data system that incorrectly identify *success* will not prompt the same degree of scrutiny. Over time, this results in a gradual but incessant corruption of the information available to the administration, making it ever more biased against identifying problems.

This process can act at many different levels simultaneously. For example, there is a tension between equity and the types of skills an exam can measure. Children of more educated parents tend to do better in academic exams. If tests are made more modular, with clearer rules about what is required, it reduces the gap between the children of less or more educated parents. But, at the same time, it is easier to teach to the test and, consequently, it may provide a less reliable indication of broader skills. During the period of grade inflation in the UK, the move towards more modular exams may have contributed to this process.

The increased use of teacher assessment may also have played a part. Using more teacher assessment rather than invigilated exams allows a wider range of skills to be tested, including a child's ability to work on longer-term projects. But it also gives the teacher the unenviable task of deciding their own pupil's marks. In situations where children are borderline, a teacher is naturally inclined to err in the child's favour. It is the behaviour we would expect of teachers who care about the future of their pupils. But what might seem right to each individual teacher can become a powerful corrosive force when, year on year, the standard children are expected to achieve is slowly driven down.

Methods for improving reliability of data

These are just two examples of a phenomenon in which public authorities are seemingly incentivised to allow the development of information systems that are generous in measuring their own performance. It does not require any intention to deceive for this to occur – just the natural biases of the information systems.

The same incentives exist in health systems recording the outcomes of health services, or police services recording the data by which crime clear-up rates are measured. Such systems must allow a degree of discretion in recording of information – for example determining the diagnosis of a patient or determining whether a reported incident should be recorded as a crime. Small shifts within the many areas of discretion in data recording can accumulate to create results that do not reflect the reality.

In the last chapter we described how regulatory pressures can contribute to this phenomenon and argued that the information set needs to be wider than the areas of immediate focus in order to be able to assess the relationship between activities that are under close scrutiny and those that are not.

In this chapter we want to look at mechanisms that can help to improve the robustness of the underlying capture of data. The most popular is audit, but this is expensive. We want to argue for three ways in which data sharing can help to address the problem.

The first two are ideas that are core to the idea of data sharing. Giving individuals greater control over the data held about them and allowing them to share this data as they choose with others provides a mechanism by which the accuracy of this data can be checked (see Chapter 16). For example, you can see if the prescriptions recorded about you by healthcare organisations are correct. Or if the incident you reported to the police is not recorded as a crime, you are made aware of that.

Secondly, sharing of granular population-level data sets allows pattern analysis that can identify implausible patterns of data recording. This has been used to identify, for example, cheating in exams when too many children in a particular class have consistent answers to exam papers, or when unfeasibly large numbers of patients are recorded as needing unusual and expensive operations.

The third mechanism relates to the way in which data is collected at source. The more that information can be gathered in ways that are outside the control of any organisation that will be held to account on the basis of the data, the more confident we can be in the reliability of the information.

The most common technique of this sort today is the collection of survey data about outcomes and experiences of customers or users of the service. It is important to try to make the process as independent as possible. For example, in the US, universities are expected to collect data about the earnings of their graduates and publish this information. However, some have been accused of deliberately skewing the sample they survey in order to improve their results.[9]

Collecting data directly from machines and devices also helps. Dashboard camera footage, location and movement data from phones or wearable devices or medical test data taken directly from monitoring machines are all sources that it is hard to influence.

Lastly there is the growing use of open platforms that allow individuals to create their own records about their experiences or complaints about products, services or any other aspect of life.

Open Data Platforms

The potential for substituting administrative data collection with open platforms has been demonstrated by the adoption of 311 feedback services in US cities. City administrators have an interest and often a responsibility to collect information on the standards of the services they provide. This has, traditionally, been done through administrative reporting systems, such as asking ambulances to record and report response times or hiring engineers to survey the quality of the roads. The internet has provided an alternative approach: the real-time reporting by citizens of their direct experience of the services they receive.

311 started in Baltimore in 1996 – at a time when the city was trying to reverse nearly half a century of decline. Urban flight had led to lower civic revenues and greater needs among the remaining population. It was set up as a new general enquiries and complaints telephone number for its citizens – and was intended to encourage public feedback on local services. Are the roads in good repair? Is refuse collected on time? Are streets well-lit at night? The original intention was to reduce demand for

---

[9] http://nymag.com/news/features/law-schools-2012-3/

overwhelmed emergency 911 services. Up until this point, 311 had been reserved on many North American phone networks as a test number. It had also enjoyed a celebrated film and television career, appearing as the fictional area code for phone numbers including those of the Bionic Woman and Ghostbusters. A study of 311 published in the *Public Administration Review* in 2013 describes the impact as follows:

> Baltimore saw immediate and substantial positive results through lower crime rates and cost savings totalling $100 million in the first three years ... In light of Baltimore's success, the Clinton administration promoted 311 to improve government performance at the local level. Boston mayor Thomas M. Menino viewed 311 systems as a way to achieve the core value of local government – 'helping people' – which could be accomplished by paying 'attention to basic quality of life issues ... such as filling potholes, removing graffiti, and ensuring that the city streets are clean, safe, and well-lit'.

Baltimore was followed by Chicago in 1999 and New York City in 2003. By the mid-2000s, 311 had spread across North America into Canada and had started to become a multichannel service offering citizens the opportunity to give real-time feedback on municipal services including waste collection, road quality, environmental pollution and dead animals.

Stephen Johnson describes how 311 transformed public service delivery in New York and how it changed the dynamics of the relationship between residents and the city:

> After US Airways flight 1549 crash-landed on the Hudson, a few callers dialled 311 asking what they should do with hand luggage they'd retrieved from the river. The city had extensive plans for its response to an urban plane crash but dealing with floating luggage was not one of them. Within minutes they had established a procedure for New Yorkers who wanted to turn in debris they'd recovered from the

river. This is the beauty of 311. It thrives on the quotidian, the predictable: the school closing queries and pothole complaints. But it also plays well with black swans.[10]

In more humdrum ways, 311 has proved to be a tool of communal intelligence that has enabled effective public service improvement. Johnson tells the story of the 'maple syrup' events that were first reported by the *New York Times* in 2005 – strange sweet odours in different parts of the city. People feared initially some kind of chemical attack, but the odours were proved harmless. They persisted for several years until somebody analysed the 311 calls and initiated a mapping project with citizens to source their direction and intensity and finally to locate the source in a manufacturing plant in New Jersey that processed fenugreek for use in cheap maple syrup substitutes.

In Chicago, one of the early pioneers, city officials used a sophisticated analysis of 311 data to identify 31 predictive variables that preceded calls reporting rat infestation. When they mapped these against the actual operations of the Department of Streets and Sanitation rodent control unit, they discovered a correlation of around 80% – that is, that the rat catchers were mounting successful operations in most cases. But they then ran a programme, in partnership with computer scientists from Carnegie Mellon University, to see if better use of this predictive 311 data (for example, calls asking for replacement black dustbins seemed to indicate rat infestation) could help improve the efficiency of the sanitation team. In the first week the team was directed by the analytics to a house that hadn't yet been the subject of a rat infestation call and it had the largest infestation ever seen in the city.[11]

311 now generates vast amounts of real-time data on civic services. In New York, more than 80,000 people a day provide feedback to 311 – by tweet, text, phone call, email or automatically via an array of open source apps – on more than

---

[10]   Stephen Johnson, *Future Perfect,* Riverhead Books, 2012.
[11]   Stephen Goldsmith and Susan Crawford, *The Responsive City*, Jossey-Bass, 2014.

3000 public services. The service has translators for more than 180 languages.

The *Public Administration Review* study concluded: 'citizens can and do play a complementary role in identifying and reporting needs for services in combination with the local government'.[12] In this way, they reduce the monetary and human capital costs required to determine where services are needed in the co-production of government services. As demonstrated by the Boston example, more is asked of citizens than Borins (2008, 56) sees as 'the minimum level of social cooperation'; that is, that 'they refrain from violence'. Co-production in Boston and in many other cities using 311 systems has transformed citizens into 'sensors', 'detectors' or 'reporters' of the problems facing the city. It showed that lower-income residents as well as young, college-aged individuals were more likely to use the Open311-enabled smartphone app than the traditional phone number or website.

By 2010, the White House announced a new Open311 standard which has been adopted by most US cities. It enables third-party analysis of the raw data, as well as the development of apps and digital tools to support citizens in providing feedback. The feedback is reported in real time on maps on the internet so that hotspots can be identified.

311 has allowed crowdsourcing to become a key component of the performance management of local services. In Boston, for example, the city authority set up New Urban Mechanics to develop new approaches to technology innovation in supporting service improvement. In 2010 this group developed an app called Street Bump,[13] which uses a smartphone's sensors to allow subscribers to map the surface height of local roads and automatically report potholes to the municipal authority. More than 1250 sunken manhole covers have been fixed.

Open311 describes itself as 'a rich ecosystem of cities, technology platforms, and forward thinking initiatives around

---

[12] Benjamin Y. Clark, Jeffrey L. Brudney and Sung-Gheel Jang, 'Coproduction of government services and the new information technology: investigating the distributional biases', *Public Administration Review*, Vol. 73, No 5, pp 687–701. © 2013 by The American Society for Public Administration. DOI: 10.1111/puar.12092.

[13] http://newurbanmechanics.org/project/streetbump/

the world that are building common infrastructure for people to better engage with their government and get connected to their community'.[14] Johnson comments: 'Open311 is designed to be a true "read–write" platform: anyone can use the system to contribute new data, and anyone can extract data as well. That means outside parties can develop new interfaces both reporting problems and visualizing those that have already been reported'.[15]

He argues that Open311 is already offering opportunities for local communal revitalisation. In Helsinki an app called Brickstarter enables citizens to fund ideas for civic improvement directly. In London, FixMyStreet enables the public to report graffiti, broken paving slabs and other environmental problems so that transparency promotes action by local authorities.

311 has demonstrated the power of citizen- or user-generated data as part of ensuring standards of public services in cities. Partly because of the success of 311 and other online initiatives like Trip Advisor, in April 2013 the National Health Service (NHS) in England embarked on a similar experiment – to offer patients and the public the chance to rate local services and to provide free text feedback on their experience. The initiative, called the Friends and Family Test, is a method derived from the Net Promoter Score, a tool commonly used in business to evaluate quality of customer satisfaction. By the end of 2015, more than 12 million people had taken the opportunity to rate their hospital and the majority had also offered feedback on local services.

Healthcare is now seeing the development of independent platforms in which people can record their experiences and share them. An initiative called Patients Like Me was launched in 2005 with the goal of connecting patients with one another, improving their outcomes and enabling research. It was inspired by the life experiences of Stephen Heywood, diagnosed in 1998 at the age of 29 with amyotrophic lateral sclerosis (ALS), or Lou Gehrig's disease. The company was founded in 2004 by his brothers Jamie and Ben Heywood and long-time family friend Jeff Cole.

---

[14] www.Open311.org
[15] Johnson, *Future Perfect*, p 71.

Through a health profile made up of structured and quantitative clinical reporting tools, members of Patients Like Me are able to monitor their health between doctor or hospital visits, document the severity of their symptoms, identify triggers, note how they are responding to new treatments, and track side effects. They have the opportunity to learn from the aggregated data of others with the same disease and see how they are doing in comparison.

This patient-reported data – much more comprehensive than the conventional medical record, for example accounting for the emotional state of a person at a given point in treatment – are opening up new possibilities for research into treatment and medicines. The Food and Drug Administration in the US recently agreed a collaboration with Patients Like Me to explore how patient-reported data can give new insights into drug safety. In this way, person-centred outcome measurement underscores the potential for Transparency 2.0 to improve accountability, service quality, efficiency and also unlock innovation and economic growth, particularly in new knowledge industries.

It may be that these kind of measures – the simple user rating and free text user comments, together with more structured patient-centred outcome measurement – will also have more currency over time in promoting patient choice in healthcare because they are inherently easier to understand and visualise than the more complex statistical measures that are derived from the administrative clinical record. This has often been the experience in other industries.

The growth of wearable technology capable of monitoring medical information will create a further independent source of information about health. Studies have already shown that it is possible to use information about patterns of use of mobile phones as an indicator of risk of depression. In the not too distant future we may get to the point where the patient arrives at the consultation with the doctor holding far more information about their health already digitally recorded than the doctor can access from medical records or by performing standard tests.

Building information systems that rely on the individual as a direct source of data depends on the trust that the individual has in the system. The failure of the Maji Matone project to encourange open reporting of water suppy failures in Tanzania failed, in part, due to lack of trust in the sytem (See Chapter 10).

On a more positive note, this approach enables the rapid and cheap collection of data in situations where it would previously have been impossible. The use of the Ushahidi platform to collect information in disaster scenarios is one example (see below). The other advantage of these systems is that they can be constructed such that the entire data set generated can be shared and used by different people and different organisations to reach conclusions quickly about how best to respond to problems and to assess the impact of such responses. The ability to share entire data sets to allow the independent assessment of needs and outcomes is the subject of the next chapter.

USHAHIDI: CITIZEN FEEDBACK AND DISASTER RELIEF

In 2010, in management of the response to an earthquake in Haiti which devastated Port au Prince and cost around 200,000 lives, a group of virtual volunteers started to post text or social media messages from survivors on a simple online digital map, helping relief workers find victims. The digital platform they used had been developed for a different purpose: to map human rights abuses by the Kenyan government against those suspected of opposition. The platform – called Ushahidi, which means 'testimony' or 'witness' in Swahili – was started in the aftermath of Kenya's disputed 2007 presidential election that collected eyewitness reports of violence reported by email and text message and placed them on a Google map.

The organisation uses the concept of crowdsourcing for social activism and public accountability, serving as an initial model for what has been termed 'activist mapping' – the combination of social activism, citizen journalism and geospatial information. Ushahidi now offers products that enable local observers to submit reports using their mobile phones or the internet, while simultaneously creating a temporal and geospatial archive of events.

In 2010, thousands of online volunteers and Creole interpreters based in more than 40 countries – all coordinated first from a dorm room at Tufts University in Boston and then from the basement of the Fletcher School of Law and Diplomacy – translated and mapped more than 40,000 messages in the first few days of the disaster and were able to advise US and local Haitian search and rescue efforts. Digicel, the largest telecommunications company in Haiti, launched a free SMS (Short Message Service) number to allow anyone to text urgent updates to the inbox of the Haiti crisis map.

Patrick Meier, the initiator of the Haiti Crisis Map, notes in his subsequent book, *Digital Humanitarians*,[16] that there are now 40 distinct social media channels available everywhere that internet connections are available. This, he says, is the 'nervous system' of the planet. Given that in many countries there are more mobile phone subscribers than citizens, the exploitation of user-generated content is a vital new asset for humanitarian response.

Four months after the Haitian earthquake, on 20 April 2010, BP's offshore Deepwater Horizon oil rig exploded killing 11 workers and precipitating the largest accidental offshore oil spill in the history of the petroleum industry. On 3 May the Louisiana Bucket Brigade (LABB) publicly released the Oil Spill Crisis Map, the first application of the Ushahidi platform in a humanitarian response in the United States.

In the years since the BP oil spill, LABB has continued to use the map (now the iWitness Pollution Map) as a repository of eyewitness reports and photos documenting the impacts of petrochemical pollution on human health and the environment. Reports to the map come from cities all over Louisiana, including Baton Rouge, St. Rose and Chalmette. Since 2010 LABB has collected over 14,000 reports, making it one of the longest running deployment of an Ushahidi instance.[17]

---

[16]   Patrick Meier, *Digital Humanitarians*, CRC Press, 2015.
[17]   https://www.ushahidi.com/blog/2013/04/22/mapping-our-environment

16

Independent narratives

Sir Brian Jarman, emeritus professor at the faculty of medicine at Imperial College London, came to medicine late in life. His PhD was in seismology and he had an early career prospecting for oil in Libya before deciding to retrain as a doctor.

By the 1980s, Jarman was working as a trainee doctor at Beth Israel Hospital in Boston along with Howard Hiatt, a co-author of the Harvard Medical Practice Study, which is one of the most influential academic papers ever published on safety in healthcare. In 1991 the *New England Journal of Medicine* published the first results from the study. This was 'not the first study to examine adverse events in healthcare organizations, but it established the standard by which adverse events are measured and laid the groundwork for policy discussions on patient safety in several countries'.[1]

The researchers had taken over 30,000 randomly selected records from 51 New York State hospitals in 1984 and reviewed them to identify adverse events – unintended incidents that had occurred in the course of treatment and which had harmed the patients. They then calculated average rates of such harm. The results came as a shock. They estimated that of the 2.7 million patients discharged from these hospitals in 1984 nearly 100,000 had experienced an adverse event. One-third of these could be

---

[1]   T.A. Brennan, L.L. Leape, N.M. Laird, L. Hebert, A.R. Localio, A.G. Lawthers, J.P. Newhouse, P.C. Weiler, H.H. Hiatt, 'Incidence of adverse events and negligence in hospitalized patients: results of the Harvard Medical Practice Study I', *New England Journal of Medicine*, 1991, Vol 324, pages 370–376. DOI: 10.1056/NEJM199102073240604

considered negligent; more than one in 10 had resulted in the death of the patient.

The study influenced thinking about medicine around the world and led to a succession of studies that have confirmed the high rates of medical error. One New Zealand study identified medical errors as one of the biggest threats to public health alongside road traffic accidents.

It also had a profound effect on Brian Jarman, who returned to the UK and became professor in the Department of Primary Care at Imperial College. Jarman wanted to know what the comparable rates of medical error were in the UK. But rather than going through the notes of individual patients, he realised that the National Health Service (NHS) held data on every patient across the country which could be used to investigate the same issue. Having worked as a hospital doctor he had a strong sense that some hospitals were safer than others. If the rate of mortality from medical errors was of the level indicated by the Harvard Medical Practice Study, it ought to reveal itself in higher death rates among patients in less safe hospitals.

Jarman applied to the Department of Health (DH) for the data. To his surprise he was given permission but on one condition: he had to sign the Official Secrets Act. The government was prepared to let him do research, but if he published anything without permission he could be committing a criminal offence. This was frustrating. But not nearly as irksome as what happened when he completed his research. He published a paper in the *British Medical Journal*, outlining his method of identifying hospitals with higher than expected mortality rates which he proposed as a way to help reveal problems with safety of care. But when he asked the DH if he could identify the hospitals with higher rates, the secretary of state said no.

We can only speculate as to why. But there is no doubt that there are serious political ramifications to allowing publication of information indicating that certain NHS hospitals may be providing care that is substandard. At that time, no such information existed about any hospital.

However, in 2000 the chief medical officer published a report estimating that there were 850,000 'adverse incidents' in the NHS each year, which cost in excess of £2 billion. At the same time the Nuffield Trust, an independent policy think tank, published a report called *Dying to Know*. It assessed the benefits, or otherwise, of releasing information about quality in healthcare to the general public.[2]

In its report, the Nuffield Trust stated: 'We would expect a new movement to emerge. The movement involves public disclosure of information about quality at the level of a named doctor, a named hospital, primary care organisation or a named health authority' (p 10). It concluded: 'We have established that where you go or whom you see affects quality far more than who you are' (p 9). In other words, not telling people about variations in quality of care was costing lives.

Jarman's figures indicated that the same person with the same condition could be sent unknowingly into one hospital and find that he or she has a more than 50% greater risk of dying during the course of treatment than in another hospital. Some hospitals, it emerged, have six times as many doctors per bed as others. The existence of this lottery is well known in the health business, though it has never before been quantified.

Then a scandal occurred. A public inquiry found that at a hospital in Bristol heart surgeons without sufficient skill had been carrying out surgery on infants, resulting in excessively high death rates. Brian Jarman, who had been one of the four panel members for the inquiry into events at Bristol, went back to the DH with the authors of this book to again request permission to publish the evidence of high mortality rates in certain hospitals.

At this point – in 2001 – Alan Milburn was the newly appointed secretary of state for health. He was outspoken in his advocacy for a NHS that was transparent and accountable to patients. In one interview, he told the BBC that the NHS had to stop being a 'secret society'. His frustration – shared by the then prime minister Tony Blair – was with the absence of authoritative data on the comparative performance of different parts of the health service and its relative efficiency in allocation of public resources.

---

[2] Martin Marshall, Paul Shekelle, Robert Brook and Sheila Leatherman, *Dying to Know: Public Release of Information about Quality in Health Care*, Nuffield Trust and RAND, 2000.

He was prepared to give transparency the kind of political sponsorship that is critical to its success and recognised that it would be more effective if implemented by an independent organisation than by the government itself.

The result was a deal that at the time was unique. Permission was granted to Jarman's team at Imperial College to hold the NHS data set in exactly the same form as it existed within the DH. Each month McKesson, the company that had the contract for compiling the data, would send one copy to the DH and a second copy to Imperial College. The college had a licence to publish whatever it chose, without the need to refer to the ministry of health.

Jarman developed a partnership with Dr Foster, an organisation set up by the authors of this book, to create the *Good Hospital Guide* and offer accessible analysis of healthcare outcomes for patients, the public and professionals. The project was founded on the legal basis that this would serve the public interest – as, by law, permission to use the data would only be granted if this could be shown to be the case. Central to the whole idea, therefore, was that the organisation would serve the interests of the public and not the interests of the ministry or the NHS. This was substantiated by creating an independent committee to oversee the work of the company and with rights to curtail its activities if these were found to be counter to the public interest.

Dr Foster was able to negotiate with media companies, including the leading national newspapers, to agree the terms for publishing information about variations in quality of care. The first Dr Foster Hospital Guide appeared in the *Sunday Times* in 2001 to considerable controversy. There was strong support from people such as Sir Donald Irvine, president of the General Medical Council, and Dr Jack Tinker, dean of the Royal Society of Medicine, and strong opposition from others in the NHS.

Many regarded it as a clear contradiction in terms to suggest that an independently produced assessment of clinical standards could serve the public interest. The NHS's accountability was to the ministry and to parliament and not to some self-appointed group of ex-journalists. One doctor likened it to an act of terrorism – an illegal act designed to undermine the proper constitutional sources of authority.

The benefits of independent narratives

Dr Foster has had a significant impact on the debate about quality in healthcare in the UK. In more than one instance, hospitals identified as sub-standard have been subsequently investigated; the approach to outcome measurement has become a standard feature of quality monitoring in the NHS; and its publications have raised public awareness of issues such as higher mortality rates at weekends. Prompted by concerns of poor care, the public inquiry into the scandal at Stafford hospital concluded: 'There is no doubt that, without the work of the Dr Foster Unit and Dr Foster Intelligence, comparative mortality statistics would not have been published as quickly, or as fully, as they now are.'[3]

Granting Dr Foster such independence did at times create headaches for the government. For example, in 2009 a Dr Foster report calling into question standards of safety at a number of hospitals was not welcomed within government, perhaps in part as there was a forthcoming general election. It prompted extensive media coverage and a slew of questions in parliament about the state of the health service.

Just as when IMCO (Instituto Mexicano para la Competitividad) published its information on schools and caused a media uproar in Mexico, the publication of evidence of poor quality care in hospitals was a headache for the UK government. It could have brought Dr Foster to a stop relatively quickly by closing down its access to data. This was how the Tanzanian government initially responded to Haki Elimu collecting data about schools.

But the issue is not whether you agree or disagree with the information that Dr Foster published – and there were many who disagreed – the question is whether you support its right to exist. Whether, on balance, the risks were worth the benefits.

There were certain advantages. For Milburn, there was an underlying ideological commitment to the idea that loosening control of the narrative that could be told with public data was a restoration of control to where it should be – in civil society and away from the offices of the minister.

---

[3] Report of the Mid-Staffordshire Foundation Trust Public Inquiry, Executive Summary, Vol 1 paragraph 5.237.

But there were also more immediate political advantages as well. Allowing an independent assessment of quality of care gave rise to a more nuanced response to uncertain information. Complex social outcomes cannot be captured in a single number or a single measure and attempts to do so will tend to result in gaming. Dr Foster allowed that argument to take place while the government observed at some distance, before ultimately coming down in favour of such measurement and developing an additional methodological approach.

Also, for some people, information produced independently of government had greater credibility. Attempts by the Department of Health to give hospitals star ratings had been mired in controversy over the degree of political interference involved and scepticism about the reliability of the information. In a review of ratings systems, the Nuffield Trust cited interviewees who 'gave examples of direct political interference in the star rating of trusts'.

The government's control of clinical performance assessment also created suspicion amongst professionals. In his report on failings at Stafford Hospital, Robert Francis QC commented as follows on the rating system run by the healthcare regulator:

> While there was a consultation period and the manner of assessing compliance was left to the HC [Healthcare Commission], the fact is that the standards were formulated and handed down by the DH. This must have contributed to the impression that the process was government controlled and thereby reinforced the disengagement of front-line clinicians from a concept, which if it was to work, demanded their involvement and endorsement.[4]

This is not to say that there was professional consensus around the Dr Foster ratings. Indeed, their value derived from the fact that they inspired debate about an issue where there was evidence of major harm to the public but where, for obvious political

---

[4]   Report of the Mid-Staffordshire Foundation Trust Public Inquiry, Executive Summary, Paragraph 1.60

reasons, there was little or no consensus about either the scale of the problem or the best way to identify it. The Dr Foster approach was supported by some clinicians and fiercely criticised by others. But because they were not 'official', it was easier to speak up against them, thereby allowing a more open discussion. By bringing forward evidence of these failings, the government benefited from being able to create a more nuanced demand for improvement in an area where lack of consensus around the measurement of outcomes made official action difficult. The downside was the risk of being politically ambushed – being portrayed as the cause of the problem, not the solution.

On what terms should population data be shared?

A key part of making data sharing work is striking the right deal with government. The terms under which Dr Foster operated were in some ways more restrictive than a traditional university department or newspaper. For example, unlike an academic department, Dr Foster agreed to give several days' advance notice of any publication, allowing those within government time to decide whether to support or disagree with the contents. This prevented the information being used to set up political ambushes. Often government ministers would come out in support of reports. At other times they strongly disagreed with the findings.

Unlike newspapers, Dr Foster was committed to academic standards of transparency. Methodologies were published in academic papers, allowing approaches to analysis to be peer reviewed.

Data sharing means giving up much of the mechanisms of editorial control described in Chapters 13 and 14. It means enabling others to directly contradict official accounts. Ceding control over data sets and allowing others equal access is never politically easy.

Any country wanting to embark on this journey faces significant political challenge. In Tanzania, President Kikwete has made transparency a key commitment of his government and he has signed up his country to be part of the Open Government Partnership.

January Makamba is a politician emotionally and intellectually committed to the idea of transparency. He is Tanzania's deputy minister for communications, science and technology, a job he took after five years as aide to President Kikwete. At 41, he is one of the youngest senior politicians in Tanzania's ruling Chama Cha Mapinduzi (CCM) party and he has a strong interest in technology and transparency, and the potential of both to alleviate poverty.

In his home constituency of Bumbuli, in the rural highlands, few people have access to computers, but mobile phones are widespread. Makamba set up a Short Message Service (SMS) platform that allowed anyone to text him with their concerns. He says he cannot fix everyone's problems, but the fact that he listens and does what he can builds support among his voters. He wants government and public services to do the same.

He sees a connection between lack of transparency and poverty in his home area, saying: 'Media access is low, educational attainment is very low, illiteracy is high, respect for authority – or reluctance to ask questions – tends to be high.'[5] These things are self-reinforcing. Lack of education and deference conspire to prevent people from exercising effective pressure, either politically or individually, to change their circumstances.

For Makamba, one of the biggest obstacles to greater transparency is the oppositional stance of the media and many in civil society. He believes that greater transparency and sharing of information will allow issues of corruption, inefficiency and inequity to be identified and reduced. He also knows that there is a risk that every problem is presented as evidence of the government's failure. 'There ought to be better ways to work together', says Makamba.

'You have some CSOs [civil society organisations] that are interested in the limelight, in quick press releases and sensationalism', he says.

> They tend to see themselves as protagonists of government. There is a lot of hunger for credibility by criticising anything the government does. Everyone

---

[5]   Author interview.

is at fault here. Government needs to be more open and accommodating. Civil society is also at fault for sometimes feeling that their credibility depends on the viciousness of their rhetoric.

There is a lack of clarity and transparency around the standards to which NGOs (non-governmental organisations) operate – both in terms of what they are currently and what they ought to be. This presents an obstacle to transparency.

We are proposing that transparency requires that information in its most granular form should be accessible where the public interest requires it, to third party organisations. The hard question is what sort of data organisations can play that role. Open data activists have argued that data should be available to all who want it, for whatever purposes they choose. This is problematic partly because it limits the data that can be used in this way to information that is stripped of any link to individual people. The other problem is that it makes no effort to try to prevent the illegitimate, deceptive or unfair use of such information.

There are two ways to look at this question: first, in terms of the rules under which data organisations operate and, second, the structure that such organisations should take.

Based on our experiences at Dr Foster, we would propose a number of rules.

i. A transparency rule

This means that the organisation needs to not only publish its methods but also to share underlying data used in its calculations, to allow others to replicate and either verify or challenge interpretations. In the case of Dr Foster that meant there could be no attempt to create intellectual property in statistical methodologies or to use commercial confidentiality to conceal how results were achieved. This rule will be challenging for commercial organisations that wish to use data in this way.

Equally important is that organisations are transparent about their sources of funding. The sort of analysis of public data we are describing is currently undertaken by three types of organisations – NGOs that aim to represent a particular interest or community on a non-profit basis funded by grants or memberships; universities that carry out research independently of any particular interest group and usually with state funding; and companies that earn revenues from the provision of information either to the public or to organisations managing or providing services.

ii. A no-ambush rule

This means reaching some form of agreement about how information is released and how prior notification is managed. In situations where governments are repressive, the leaking of information and clandestine techniques are necessary. But there is also a need for a space in which data is shared under agreed rules as to how the results of analysis will be promulgated. We are arguing that there is a public benefit, where the political conditions are right, in having organisations that operate on a more consensual basis, to agreed rules, concerning how information moves into the public domain.

It is essential that such arrangements do not give any person rights of veto of publication or rights to restrict the areas that data can be used to examine. This is simply advocating that any organisation affected by publication of information has the opportunity to consider the evidence and respond appropriately.

iii. An independent review rule

This means that any organisations involved in data sharing should be subject to some form of competent technical oversight, allowing complaints about misinterpretation or misrepresentation of data to be lodged. In the case of Dr Foster, an oversight committee was established to rule on a public interest test- that all information published had to further the public interest and contribute to better healthcare. Known as the Dr Foster Ethics Committee, it had an independent secretariat, its minutes were published and none of its members were paid. In a more developed data-sharing economy, a regulator such as the information commissioner might take on this role.

Structure of data organisations

There are many bodies which currently play the role of data organisations to different degrees. Universities do so to an increasing extent. For some time academic organisations including both publishers and universities have been making moves to encourage greater sharing of research data sets. At the same time there is growing academic recognition of the value of using real-world data as opposed to specially collected survey data. However, in the main, academic organisations seek legitimacy and credibility through the respect of peer organisations and through publication. Commercialisation of research results is also of significant value. Representation of different interest groups in society, however, is not something that academic institutions naturally lean towards.

As data organisations, universities provide an interesting model. They often survive on large amounts of public funding, but their culture and way of operating mean that their credibility as independent organisations is not undermined. This is helped by the fact that much of the public funding comes in the form of subsidies for teaching rather than direct funding of research.

Private companies are a second type of organisation that have established themselves as potential data organisations. Some businesses build a strategy explicitly around the task of data management. These range from specialised infomediary organisations such as citizen.me, which will act as secure data stores, to particular services such as Microsoft healthvault – a secure store for personal health information.

Also in this category we might include businesses which aim to generate value through insight into customer needs, in exactly the way that Amazon or Google do, but which are operating in spaces where there are large amounts of relevant public data assets or data held in other organisations. In healthcare, one example would be Patients Like Me (see Chapter 15), which gets patients to pool data about issues such as drug side effects, or Your.MD, which is aiming to use artificial intelligence to derive better diagnoses by asking patients to enter symptom details. Similar organisations are now aiming to provide people with better information about education, too.

These organisations are all focused on how they can provide better individual-level advice – better diagnostics than your doctor can offer, better drug information than pharma companies provide or better advice on where to seek treatment. They are attempting to correct the 'market' aspect of allocation systems rather than the adjudicatory element.

The business model for such companies derives value by striking a better bargain with companies selling products and services, either by trading the data for a better price or by more accurate identification of the person's needs. Their competitive advantage is the promise of giving the individual greater control over how their information is used. In economic terms, by limiting the degree to which they can lock customers in, the company is pre-committing to ensuring it delivers better value to the customer. However, to the degree that such services are offered for free, with the company making a return on enabling access to data or serving up offers to its customers, conflicts of interest still abound. This is why many in this space are established as not-for-profit entities, although the evidence from other areas, such as mutually owned financial companies, would suggest that this offers relatively little protection from exploitation.

A third category of organisation consists of a range of donor-funded bodies such as development NGOs in developing countries, or charities representing different groups of citizens such as Diabetes UK or the Consumers Association in the UK or the National Association for the Advancement of Colored People (NAACP) or American Association of Retired Persons (AARP) in the US. NGOs in developing countries are, in some cases, extremely data literate and push for access to more information. In contrast, representative organisations in the developed world tend to be more focused on working for their user base in more traditional ways and have been slower to see the potential for accessing data either directly from their members or from public data assets.

In contrast, the types of organisation that have shown most interest in using data to evidence the fairness or otherwise of allocation systems have tended to rely on donor funding, often from governments. The question then arises as to who they really represent. This is as true of funding from domestic governments as foreign donor funding. *Sock Puppets: How the Government Lobbies Itself and Why*, published in 2012 by the Institute of Economic Affairs, argued that the UK government's funding of civil society organisations was a subversion of democracy since the government was using public money to control the public debate on policy. The same argument could be made about funding of academic research in areas of social policy.

CSOs lie halfway between universities and companies, in that while they do have a direct interest in helping individuals make better decisions, they are equally interested in informing the debate with regard to how allocation systems could be improved by changing the rules. Unlike universities, however, they advocate explicitly from the point of view of a particular interest group.

It would be foolhardy to try to predict exactly how the organisational infrastructure of data sharing will develop in future decades. We are confident that it must develop because without it we will cease to be able to operate as democratic societies. But the relative roles of academia, commerce and representative organisations are impossible to gauge. It is likely that organisations will develop out of all of these routes. However, it is also likely that in their mature forms they will look very different from the organisations we have today.

One element that is absent from all of the above is the degree to which data organisations might receive public funding in proportion to the degree to which they attract public support or are used by the public as a source of information. Much as political parties are funded according to votes in some countries – or GPs (general practitioners) in the UK are funded according to the number of patients using their services – the provision of data services might be something that is state funded but provided privately within a market.

SIKIKA: MALARIA STOCK OUTS IN TANZANIA

Malaria is a treatable illness that causes in the region of a million deaths a year. Huge efforts to reduce this over the last 20 years have seen death rates from Malaria halve. The work has involved prevention programmes such as the use of mosquito nets together with work to increase the availability of anti-malarial drugs.

Stock-outs, where health clinics run out of medicine, cause death. David Mwakyusa, the minister for health and social welfare in Tanzania in 2010 put it simply: 'If there are no malaria treatments, someone will die. It is very likely to be a child. Reducing stock-outs saves lives.'

In 2010, Tanzania put in place an innovative system to reduce stock-outs. 'SMS for life' was a system through which health clinics regularly sent information by text through a secure reporting website about their drug stock levels.[6] Access to the website was controlled through a unique user ID and password and granted to medical officers and those tasked with maintaining supplies of medicines.

Piloted in 2009, the results were impressive. The proportion of health facilities with no stock of one or more antimalarial medicine fell from 78% at the start of the project to 26% by the end of the pilot phase. In one district, stock-outs were eliminated by week 8 of the pilot. During the study, Artemether/Lumefantrine (AL) stocks increased by 64% and quinine stocks increased 36% across the three districts;[7] 888,000 people in the three pilot districts had access to all malaria treatments at the close of the pilot, versus 264,000 people at the start.

Following this success the programme was rolled out across the country. As part of its work with Open Government Partnership, Tanzania committed to making the data on the system public. This has not yet happened. But as the system was rolled out and became routine, the performance started to drop.

Concerned by what was happening, someone with access to the data chose to share it with the NGO Sikika, which started to track the data. In February 2013, Sikika issued a report highlighting chronic shortages

---

[6]   http://healthmarketinnovations.org/program/sms-life

[7]   Jim Barrington, Olympia Wereko-Brobby, Peter Ward, Winfred Mwafongo and Seif Kungulwe, 'SMS for Life: a pilot project to improve anti-malarial drug supply management in rural Tanzania using standard technology', *Malaria Journal* Vol 9 (2010), 298, www.malariajournal.com/content/9/1/298

of drugs in many clinics, with some districts reporting stock-outs in over 80% of clinics.[8]

Sikika's reason for publishing the SMS for life data was that the system stopped working when people were not looking. Irenei Kiria, executive director, of Sikika said in a statement that the programme was not producing the 'required progressive permanent improvements'. Instead, he said 'we have only noticed momentary improvements often correlated to public outcries or media coverage'.[9]

Sikika was motivated by immediate concern about stock-outs. But it recognises that such tactical actions, however necessary, can affect long-term effective relationships with government. Partly this is a question of finding the right tone of voice. Florian Schweitzer from Sikika says: 'It is important to see the government, if not as a partner, then as people who have dignity and self-esteem.'[10] This means avoiding strident rhetoric for cheap effect. It means recognising that if data identifies a problem, it does not necessarily identify a lack of effort on the part of those responsible to correct it. He adds:

> People in government want to be treated fairly, that the data is accurate, that there is information about the output and the process that led to that output. Authorities have different capacities, some might have been created six months ago and have barely any managers. So when it comes to accountability, you need to appreciate the local circumstances.

[8]   http://sikika.or.tz/wp-content/uploads/2013/09/publication300.pdf

[9]   Press Statement from Sikika, 'Statement on chronic shortages and stock outs of antimalarial drugs', Tuesday, 29 January 2013, http://wavuti.weebly. com/uploads/3/0/7/6/3076464/alu_press_release_29_jan_2013_english1. docx

[10] Author interview.

17

Getting my own data

Founded in 2011 in the US, the Icahn Institute for Genomics and Multiscale Biology at Mount Sinai is planning to fund the collection of information on up to 1 million people. 'Multiscale biology' refers to their plan to bring together data at every level – DNA and gene expression, protein and phenotypic information, together with metabolites and clinical tests, plus information about a patient's environment. The idea is to attempt to understand the interrelationship between these different elements in the progression of illness. The Resilience Project aims to use the information to find out why some people with genes that are associated with particular illnesses nonetheless remain healthy.

The Icahn Institute is run by Eric Schadt, a computational mathematician who is pioneering some of the most advanced applications of machine learning in modern medicine. Among the members of Schadt's team is Jonathan Karr who recently published a paper in *Cell* which described how, for the first time, science has developed a software algorithm which can mimic an entire life form (in this case a simple organism) and learn to make behavioural decisions based on its environmental, digestive and neural encounters.[1] Schadt freely acknowledges that the team can't predict the decisions this software will make and agrees strongly that society needs to work out a framework for the transparency of these algorithms. The institute works on the basis that all the intellectual property it develops will be made freely available for reuse by third party researchers.

---

[1]   Author interview.

Using these software design skills, Schadt and his team are also pioneering the effective clinical interpretation of complex genomic, phenotypic and molecular data from Mount Sinai Hospital to develop personalised treatment protocols. He has focused on a number of cancers where genomics offers the earliest opportunity of improving clinical outcomes. Cancer tumours are made up of different DNA to their host humans – they are literally alien – and they can have multiple DNA personalities, which makes it hard to collect DNA sequences. However, if the DNA can be sequenced and annotated, i.e. turned into clinically comprehensible information, it can inform precise pharmaceutical interventions – determining whether a drug will work and in what quantity. This can often be, particularly for people in the early stages of a disease, the difference between a good or a bad outcome.

There are other teams working to bring together the new data-processing sciences in medicine with the developments in machine learning in order to start making sense of human molecular interactions. Patrick Soon-Shiong, a cancer surgeon who was born in South Africa and now lives in California, has invested more than $1 billion in developing an infrastructure that can analyse 'omic' data (for example, genomic, proteomic and metabolomic data) from multiple sources and feed back to clinicians.

Soon-Shiong, who made an estimated $8 billion from the sale of a cancer drug he developed, has been described as the richest doctor 'in the history of the world'. *Forbes* magazine, in a cover story, described his vision for transforming the treatment of cancer through genomic and molecular analysis as 'the closest thing that Earth has ever had to Star Trek's fabled tricorder' – the hand-held devices that can instantly scan almost any object, collect data and analyse it.[2]

Soon-Shiong says he can sequence DNA from a cancer tumour in 47 seconds. Some of the biggest employers in the US, like Bank of America, are putting their faith in Soon-Shiong improving the management of cancer and are contracting with

---

2   Matthew Herper, 'Can Patrick Soon-Shiong, The World's Richest Doctor, Fix Health Care?', *Forbes*, Sep 10 2014

him to reduce absence through illness and improve survival rates of their staff.

Soon-Shiong is in good company in pursuing the potential of the large volumes of data that we can now collect about an individual. Google is getting involved. Its original office building outside of Palo Alto has now been given over to a new initiative – Google Life Sciences – now named Verily – which set itself the task, as only Google could, of mapping every molecule in the human body. This requires the processing of unimaginably large amounts of data.

Governments worldwide are investing in programmes to start to unlock the colossal data sets that gene sequencing and molecular biology can produce about individuals. In both Japan and Korea national programmes to map illness down to the molecular level are being driven not just by the economic potential of exploiting such knowledge but equally by their recent history. More than other countries, Japan and Korea have experienced in a remarkably short timeframe the impact of hugely extended lifespans. It is seen not as a medical miracle but rather as one of the worst crises in their post-war history. *Kodokushi* means 'lonely death' in Japanese and describes the phenomenon, first identified in the 1980s, of elderly people who have outlived their families dying alone at home and not being discovered for a long period afterwards. Nobody knows how many elderly people are victims but the numbers are rising: one estimate suggests that more than 32,000 people are dying in these circumstances each year. In South Korea, President Park Geun-hye has decreed that happiness is the country's first political priority – by this she specifically means a reduction in the gap between onset of morbid illness in old age and death.

The UK is also investing in genomics. In 2012, Prime Minister David Cameron launched the 100,000 genome challenge: a programme led jointly by NHS England and a new body, Genomics England, to make the UK the first country in the world to sequence 100,000 whole human genomes. The first whole human genome – the full 'conversation' stored on our DNA – was sequenced in 2003 and cost $3 billion to complete. Today, the price for sequencing a whole human genome is under $1000. Since Cameron announced the UK project, other countries, including the United Arab Emirates, have launched similar initiatives.

Even more data will come from analysing in huge detail our bio-chemical processes. In a large purpose-built room at the Hammersmith Hospital campus in west London, there is a suite of machines producing thousands of data points on the products of our metabolism based on biological samples like blood and urine. They are old-fashioned in a way, with wires and tubes in careful array stretching around the ceiling. These first made their appearance at the 2012 London Olympics where they were used to test athletes' urine for banned substances. They are the most advanced mass spectrometers in the world and are able to analyse the biochemical signatures of small molecules – and their first job is to analyse what is in our blood and urine.

Before the Imperial College team started their work, the conventional view was that urine was, relatively speaking, uncomplicated. Using both NMR spectroscopy as well as mass spectrometry, they have subsequently been analysing thousands of molecular signatures in blood and urine, and analysing these with respect to disease states and metabolic disorders such as obesity, raised blood pressure and atherosclerosis. These analyses are detecting many molecular signatures that have previously been unidentified.

These machines are reminiscent of the old IBM mainframe computers – huge rooms full of spooling discs. Moore's law forecasts that these spectrometers will be the size of a laptop within a few years and be a fraction of their current cost. Molecular diagnostics will be a routine conversation between us, our bodies, our environment and our clinicians – one that will largely be conducted by us and our 'machine advisers'.

These new sciences mean that we will have a set of new tools to prevent and treat human illness. We will know our risks of illness (and in some cases the certainty that we will suffer from them) because we will know the detail of our genetic design; we will have insight into the behaviour of all the molecules in our body – and particularly the trillion or so bacteria that inhabit our guts and determine much about our wellbeing and susceptibility to diseases such as cancer; we may start to know how our genes and our molecules interact with our environment.

Medicine is an allocation system and, despite its scientific ambitions, it uses some very rough and ready categorisations to decide what to do with patients. Work with genomic and biomedical data sets is starting to reveal just how rough and ready many diagnoses are. Researchers can already see that terms such as 'breast cancer' or 'diabetes' capture a number of quite different situations. The increase in the volume of information about individuals will allow the creation of much more precise categorisations. Furthermore the set of categories and labels that are applied to you will very likely put you in a class of one. Personalised medicine will mean tailoring your treatments to the vast amount that is known about your specific circumstances. Deciding whether a drug is right for you will not depend on your diagnosis but on a much deeper appreciation of your genetic and molecular makeup. But before we can begin to make this possible we need to put in place systems to manage the way in which these data are created, controlled and used.

Sir John Burn, a leading British clinical geneticist, has opposed offering genetic tests to all people because the data management systems are not yet in place to ensure this is handled securely. If simply added to people's medical records, it would mean 'hundreds or thousands of healthcare workers could have access to the data'. According to Burn, 'the security issue will introduce enough hot air for [universal gene sequencing] not to happen'.[3]

He is, however, concerned at potential obstacles to the use of this data for research. 'There needs to be a sense of urgency with genomics; we're on the cusp of generating unbelievable quantities of data which we've absolutely no idea what to do with. It's potentially going to cost us a fortune and we'll miss really useful clinical data because we can't see the wood for the trees.'

Burn points out that we do not have a consent system fit for an age of big data. Our system is designed to cope with people agreeing to take part in individual drug trials or agreeing to an operation. It is wholly unfit when we want to carry out big

---

[3]   Dr Rebecca Hill, 'Crystal ball gazing: an interview with Professor Sir John Burn on genetics in 2012', *BioNews*, 648, March 12, 2012 http://www.bionews.org.uk/page_133126.asp

data analytics using the information to explore endless possible hypotheses.

In an interview for *Bionews* he said:

> It doesn't really fit when you're trying to work out how a million variants match up to 100,000 phenotypes in any combination – we simply don't have the resources to keep asking people if it's OK for us to use the information for this purpose or that purpose. People are bemused by these constant requests. They normally just ask 'Where do you want me to sign?' We want to put approved researchers in a position where they can harvest all the available data, analyse and cross reference it, and say 'We think this marker is predictive of this disease'. For that, we need a generic consent system that says it's OK to use samples taken within the context of the NHS for health research, as long they're anonymous and it won't hurt the person in question. I think we're pushing an open door there, we just need to present it in the right way.[4]

Personal data stores

Burn is right. This is not sustainable in the longer term. Citizens need to be able to give broad consents in terms of the issues that matter to them. And they need to be able to trust the organisations to which they are granting consent.

The first way of making the complexity of this situation manageable is by ending the position where multiple organisations own different pieces of data about individuals. Regardless of the ethics, purely to make the situation manageable, data about a person held by governments, public services and companies should be automatically and routinely transferred to the

---

[4] Rebecca Hill, 'Crystal ball gazing: an interview with Sir John Burn on genetics in 2012', *Bionews*, 12 March 2012, www.bionews.org.uk/page_133126.asp

individual and held on their behalf by an organisation of their choice that meets the necessary standards of security.

Such organisations would monitor how data is accessed, keep an ongoing log of all access and create the interfaces whereby consent is given for research uses. Covert access for national security purposes would not, of course, be reported to the individual but would be logged independently as a matter of record and could be accessed by, for example, the courts with appropriate legal authority.

The necessary infrastructure needs to extend beyond any one service or source of data. The needs of medical research make clear that we will not be able to draw some hard and fast distinction between data which is medically relevant and that which is not. For example, my mobile phone may record the tremor of my hand (as is already being used to indicate Parkinson's), my level of sociability (using the length and frequency of calls as a proxy) or my state of mind (using analysis of speech patterns). None of this would currently form part of any medical record. Crucially, as we start to get to grips with the overwhelming quantities of data, we will realise that information previously thought irrelevant was important. Only by maintaining personal data stores can I control the way that historical data about me is preserved and potentially made available as I would choose.

If we then add in information from wearable sensors about sleep patterns or heart rate along with the types of genetic and phenotypic information described above, what I have is not a medical record but a record that I can use to inform not just what healthcare I might need but my diet, my sleep habits, my social life and my daily routines.

It is exactly this information that researchers need, too, but I am not going to allow such a record to be the possession of my local hospital. It is mine. I may happily lend them access for research purposes, but I will not cede control.

Giving individuals control over data will allow more democratic systems for guiding where research efforts are focused. Researchers tend to be interested in exploring the big medical questions like cancer because this attracts attention and grant funding. That, you might say, is a good thing, since cancer affects so many people. The problem occurs, however, if everybody works on the same big questions and no one takes an interest in rare illnesses that are poorly understood.

Dr Jimmy Lin set up the Rare Genomics Institute to address exactly this issue after an encounter with a mother who had brought her child to the Johns Hopkins hospital with unexplained symptoms. After running every test that modern medicine could devise the doctors came up with nothing. Witnessing the hopelessness of that child's situation, Lin created an internet platform that allows patients with rare conditions to raise funds to have their genes sequenced and to then make that information available to researchers in the hope of identifying the cause of their illness. The development of services like Patients Like Me provides a platform where people can collectively identify areas for which they would be happy to volunteer their information for research.

In order to fairly exploit the potential of our greater understanding of human biology and genetics for our collective benefit, we believe there needs to be a wholesale shift in the way in which data is both physically held and legally controlled.

Technology companies are increasingly in the business of providing space in which you can hold information. There are many new businesses aiming to develop personal data stores or personal information management services. Some are on one area, for example, Umotif and Patients Know Best (health), Bill Monitor (utilities) or Money Dashboard (finance). Others such as Personal.com or Mydex have a more general remit.

OpenPDS[5] (open personal data store) is an open source project to build a personal data store with strong privacy protections which is explicitly designed to reduce the privacy risks of surveillance. Instead of extracting data and using it to run an algorithm, the PDS runs the algorithm for you and sends the answer back.

For most of us, personal data stores are going to require stronger laws and much more effective enforcement of our rights. The reasons for moving to an information infrastructure built around personal data stores are, first, because it will be impossible to know if data-driven systems are fair without it

---

[5]   http://openpds.media.mit.edu/#philosophy

and, second, more pragmatically, it will be extremely difficult to enable properly consented research and surveillance systems without doing this.

Individual rights over data

Laws guaranteeing individual access to personal records are now common in developed democratic countries. However there is often a significant gap between the law and the reality. Malte Spitz became a hero to many after tirelessly fighting his telecoms operator to access the data they held about him and then revealing exactly how much they had collected.[6] Bruce Schneier has similarly detailed the degree to which companies hold huge amounts of information about people.[7]

Laws that grant rights to data access provide powers to the individual to review data and to object to incorrect information or incompatible uses of data. But as the Ashley Madison leak in 2015 highlighted the degree to which individuals can enforce their desire to have data removed is often impossible to verify.

More importantly, data protection laws are ineffective at enforcing data portability – giving people the power to take their data in an intelligible format and pass it on to another service provider. The fact that my online grocer may allow me to see all my shopping for the past year does not mean that they will enable me to take that data and share it with a competitor.

Lack of data portability is a powerful barrier to competition. Efforts to increase competitiveness have begun to focus on this. In the UK, enabling people to directly transfer the data about their standing payments from one bank to another made switching accounts much easier. In the US, there have been efforts to limit 'data blocking' in healthcare which prevents patient information following the individual from one healthcare institution to another. Both the IT (information technology) companies that build information systems and the providers of products and services that use these systems share an interest in

---

[6] www.ted.com/talks/malte_spitz_your_phone_company_is_watching
[7] Bruce Schneier, *Data and Goliath: The Hidden Battles to Collect Your Data and Control Your World*, W.W. Norton, 2015.

making it harder for the individual to take their data along with their custom elsewhere.

In the UK the Midata programme is a government-sponsored initiative to get companies to allow customers the right to take copies of their data in electronic machine-readable formats and to have such data recorded as far as possible in standard formats.

The potential for such programmes to improve the transparency of markets is significant and a growing industry of infomediaries has developed, with venture capital backing, to exploit the opportunity.

The Midata programme has attempted to apply this to markets which, despite consumer freedom to switch, are still considered oligopolistic. The theory is that the hassle and cost of switching suppliers is high, while the benefits of switching lack salience. The banking sector and the utility companies are prime targets.

The 'cheap energy club' in the UK now has 1 million people taking part. They are able to get data about their energy use from their energy supplier which they pass to an online infomediary. This then works out whether an alternative supplier would offer them a better price. A similar scheme was launched in April 2015 whereby the six largest high street banks added a Midata button to their online banking services. This button allows you to download a CSV (comma separated values) file to your computer which you can then share with a website called GoCompare. com. This has built an engine to calculate which bank would offer you a better current account deal.

The need for data portability becomes ever greater as more and more of the services we use depend on access to our data to deliver what we want efficiently and effectively. My tendency to buy things from Amazon, for example, is driven in large part by the fact that not only do they already know where to send stuff and how to bill me but because they are increasingly good at knowing what it is I am likely to want.

The more that data is used to provide effective, efficient services – whether these are video recommendations or diagnoses – the more the barriers to data portability create a problem. Healthcare is an area where this could soon become critical. Right now, it is aggravating that I cannot ensure my electronic records will be transferred from one doctor to another whenever

I choose. But at least I am capable of going to see a new doctor and explaining my symptoms. She may have to repeat some tests unnecessarily, but the process is manageable. In the not too distant future, personalised medicine may require that someone looking after my health is able to access my genomic profile. This is not information that I can explain to the doctor, nor do I want it being repeatedly collected by different healthcare organisations, nor do I want it to be anybody else's business to control who I share it with.

To have control over their own electronic data, the individual needs to have a complete and up-to-date copy of the relevant data and to be free to do with it as they please. However, it is important to recognise that some information is necessarily under a degree of dual control. This occurs when the only value in data comes from its external validation. So, for example, information about my diagnosis which is known to have come from a licensed doctor is quite different from information about my diagnosis which I have determined for myself. Validated information about my earnings has a different value in negotiating a loan than self-declared information.

Most personal data today arises out of an interaction between an individual and a service or product they are using. This gives the supplier of the product or service some claim to rights in that information. Currently, the law is crude in the distinctions it draws between things that the supplier can insist on being allowed to do with this data as a condition of service. Some uses of personal data, such as marketing, require explicit consent. Others, including the provision of direct medical care, are areas where consent can be required as a condition of the service and can be presumed. At the extreme, the state, as supplier of citizenship, can insist on use of information for security, tax collection and public health purposes.

However, outside of policing activities, there need be no barriers to providing details of how data has been used – that is, a real-time log of all uses of this data. This is not information that most of us would ever want to look at in detail. But I do want it to be possible for a trusted organisation to manage this for me. We would also argue that it requires transparency of population-level data, to ensure that such organisations are not misusing this information.

A particular issue that needs addressing is the way personal data is defined in different ways in specific areas of life. As we have described, data are used to categorise people – to identify the likelihood that they will respond to a particular drug or a particular advert, the likelihood that they will attack a government office or pay their taxes. This involves pooling direct attribute data about individuals and looking for associations across populations – for example, your age and a raised blood pressure reading indicate a given risk of stroke; your gender and a tendency to buy aluminium-free deodorant indicate a likelihood of being pregnant and so on.

In some cases, these derived attributes are regarded as personal information – for instance, the assigning of a diagnosis to a person creates a piece of information about that individual. However, in other cases it does not. For example, running an algorithm of your personal attributes to ascertain whether you are an impulsive gambler does not necessarily create a new disclosable piece of data about you – even if that algorithm is used to determine the content of the web page you are looking at.

Laws on the personal control of data need to give people rights to see not only what data is held about them but the specific algorithms that have been run on this data and the conclusions that are then reached. Current rights to know how your data has been processed do not achieve this.

This is a very high level of transparency which has implications for commercial confidentiality. It also implies legal rights of access to very high volumes of data that no individual could make sense of without a significant support infrastructure in the form of infomediaries. However, it is by establishing such legal rights that we might start to see a market develop in which more effective solutions are found to the issue of enabling people to take more control over their information.

Such control opens up new possibilities. Most importantly, it enables the creation of new rich, linked data assets. For example, a person with diabetes may decide to take a copy of their medical record and upload it to an online app that will help them manage their food shopping in line with their condition, as well as linking it to real-time data from the wearable device recording their heart rate, blood sugar level and other biometrics. This data, when combined, could provide their clinician with important additional insights in caring for their patient, as well as researchers with valuable longitudinal data in evaluation of the efficacy of the medication being prescribed.

Government programmes to create linked records have faced protest at the risk of invasion of privacy. Commercial organisations have worked around the problem in a different way by pooling data through other mechanisms such as non-obvious identifiers (such as cookies) or by sharing information about the statistical associations between different personal attributes and likelihood of, say, having diabetes.

Neither solution is satisfactory. The better approach is to allow the individual to hold data about all aspects of their relationships with different organisations and to control the way in which data about them is linked and used to inform decisions affecting them.

Digital inclusion

Arguing that giving individuals greater control over information about them is essential to the creation of a fair and transparent society creates a problem. Some people are better able to make use of such rights than others.

In the UK, three-quarters of the population go online. But there are over 12 million people who lack the basic digital skills to send and receive an email or browse the internet, and more than 6 million who have never been online. Over 10 million do not have access to broadband at home, largely because they cannot afford it. This puts them at a life disadvantage in many different ways – more than 50% of these people are of working age but because they do not have access to internet services where most jobs are advertised they are less likely to be in employment.

Those with the most health and social care needs are often the least likely to be online. Older people, in particular, often lack computer confidence but have high health and social care needs, and 33% of those with registered disabilities have never used the internet. For this reason, the British government is committed to providing free Wi-Fi access across NHS sites so that individuals who cannot access digital services – or their own data – at home can do so at their local GP surgery or in any other NHS facility they are attending.

Martha Lane Fox, a leading government adviser on digital inclusion, commented in a newspaper article that:

> Universal free access to broadband, with the skills to use it, has the potential to be one of the great public health advances of the 21st century. Those who lack access to the public utility of the internet will, like those who lacked access to the public utility of clean water and sanitation in the 19th century, be at risk of increasing inequality and poorer health status. We need to take action now to harness the power of the network age for all to transform the NHS, and the health of our nation.[8]

Public authorities committed to the benefits of transparency will in time have to invest in providing free internet access to members of the public as a basic utility.

NHS DATA ACCESS PROGRAMME

The National Health Service (NHS) in England has promoted a programme allowing individuals online access to medical records and other related digital transactions. In 2015, all general practitioners (GPs) had to enable their patients to have access to certain services (only a handful had been doing so up to this point, as part of a pilot). By the end of that year, 97% of practices had switched on the necessary digital infrastructure, and more than 8 million people had registered either to have access to health records, to order a repeat prescription or to book an appointment. The public demand for this is real – 55% have said they want online access to these kinds of services.

From 2016, all GPs are required to proactively offer these services to their registered patients so that more than 10% in each practice are actively

---

8   Martha Lane Fox and Tim Kelsey, 'A digital NHS for everyone', *Daily Telegraph*, 8 Dec 2015.

engaged with them. The NHS – and the government, which strongly supports this initiative – believes that greater patient engagement with digital services will improve access, reduce cost and improve people's propensity to self-care when they have long-term conditions.

The clinical community has, for the most part, been supportive of these online initiatives – but some have been concerned. The British Medical Association, the trade union representing 170,000 doctors in the UK, has so far resisted providing patients with access to historical records, and certain parts of their record, including the 'free text' field which is traditionally regarded as the preserve of the doctor. They say that providing these records would impose an undue administrative burden on their members, but it seems unlikely that the public will be willing to accept the absence of such data from their review for much longer. As medical records become more open, doctors who have previously used them to communicate privately with other doctors will need an alternative means to do this where appropriate.

Other concerns have been raised around the ethical governance of online record access and appropriate consent. Before the NHS launched its programme of encouraging patients online, it commissioned the Royal College of General Practitioners to produce guidance for professionals on its implementation. This clearly confirmed that there were circumstances in which a person could legitimately be denied access to their own record – notably, when it could, in the view of their doctor, cause them harm.

Access to records in machine-readable formats is the only way to realise the main benefits of personal data sharing. Digital records can be shared with different analytic intermediaries – including mobile applications – and the value of the data in the record extracted and enhanced by linking it to other data. In England, the US and Australia, the governments are encouraging app developers and entrepreneurs to construct new digital services that will enable patients and citizens to get most value from their records – including improving self-care. The US administration is promoting a digital standard for personal record access, called 'BlueButton', while in England app developers are being offered access to a series of open APIs (application programming interfaces) on the personal data assets hosted by NHS organisations. In Australia, commonwealth has launched the My Health Record programme to support people obtain access to their personal data and third party digital services that can add value to it.

A key obstacle to wider global adoption of personal record access is the financial and opportunity cost of implementing digital record-keeping systems in huge existing bureaucratic infrastructures. In England, the government has backed NHS leaders in prioritising investment in the digital modernisation of all NHS services, not just those in general practice, so that citizens and the health professionals who serve them can access their entire care records. There is good evidence that this will improve the safety of patients and reduce the administrative burden of paper record-keeping on clinicians, as well as enabling the other benefits of personal data transparency that have been discussed. Studies confirm that e-prescribing systems in hospitals reduce medication errors by as much as 50%, for example.

In November 2015, the British government announced that it would invest a minimum of £1 billion of public capital to support the adoption of digital record systems in England's hospitals by 2020.

In 2009, Barack Obama said that 'every citizen' would have access to an electronic patient record by 2014, and, following the investment of $31 billion by the federal administration to incentivise hospitals, more than 75% had achieved basic standards of digital record-keeping.

Another potential obstacle to these programmes is the commercial incentive to create proprietary data standards in order to limit portability. The creation of legal rights to data access and investment in shared digital records must be accompanied by effective policing of open data standards.

18

Surveillance, transparency and privacy

The spread of information technology has meant that ubiquitous mass surveillance is both possible and, to a very significant extent, practised in most parts of the world.

Surveillance is the ongoing collection and analysis of information about a particular target in order to identify risks. This term is frequently used to refer to surveillance of individuals, most often in relation to criminal or security investigations, or the tracking of communicable diseases through a population. Surveillance of organisations or processes tends to be referred to as monitoring. But the principle is the same. It is the ongoing collection of data in order to assess the risks/behaviours of a particular organisation or process.

We should distinguish between data collection and surveillance. Most government and commercial activity today results in the creation of electronic records about the individual. A bank cannot operate without recording our transactions. Amazon cannot sell us goods without recording our purchases, payments and deliveries. Government can only collect taxes by maintaining databases and records. Doctors are required to maintain medical records as part of treating patients.

The creation of vast amounts of data about us is not something that can be avoided. The question is what is going to be done with that data. Who gets to decide what is destroyed, what is kept and how it is used?

Surveillance is the area of most contention as it is not technically essential to the delivery of a service but has, in many cases, become the primary engine of efficiency and improvement in such services. Amazon does not have to use data about you to optimise its distribution chain or predict what to offer customers. But it represents, to a significant degree, its competitive advantage. Healthcare can be provided without using data about patients to calculate how many nurses are needed on each ward or to identify which treatments are making people better. But it is not possible to deliver high quality healthcare without doing these things.

Surveillance of population data is the way in which organisations work out how to deal with people, or customers, based on the information they hold about them. It is about determining the likelihood that the credit card order received by a company is fraudulent and should be rejected, or the likelihood that its product is causing harm to customers.

All surveillance is about ascertaining probabilities. Sometimes these probabilities are very high – there may be a huge amount of information about a robber on the run, for instance, and when someone meeting that description is caught there is very little doubt that he is the right man. But it is important not to consider some surveillance as being about 'facts' and some about 'suspicions'. All surveillance is about gathering data that points to some likelihood – that you are the person who robbed the bank three hours ago; that you are an associate of a known terrorist sympathiser; or that you are someone who might spend a large sum of money on a fancy watch.

To take one example, US drone strikes are either 'targeted' that is, intended to kill a specific individual who has been identified) or 'signature' (that is, designed to attack people fitting a sufficient number of criteria indicating that they are likely enemy combatants).[1] The first identify a specific individual, the second a class of people according to set criteria. In both cases, the processing of information involves taking what you know about someone and seeing whether he fits either into a category of one (i.e. what is known and believed about the target) or into a broader category (i.e. what is known about the features of enemy combatants). Both processes have an error

---

[1]   This example is taken from Bruce Schneier, *Data and Goliath,* W.W. Norton, 2015.

rate, and with both the aim is to achieve the most accurate way of identifying targets.

Thanks to Edward Snowden we now have a clear idea of just how deeply commercial and state surveillance systems are interwoven, with the information collected by internet services and mobile phone companies being co-opted as part of the information-gathering systems of the state. Surveillance is becoming ubiquitous. Commercial surveillance aims to categorise you according to the likelihood that you will be influenced by particular messages or purchase particular items. State surveillance aims to categorise you according to the risk you pose to the state and its ability to maintain order. Health service surveillance aims to categorise you according to health risks. There are few areas of life left that do not involve a significant degree of surveillance.

The history of the use of surveillance to oppress people through the twentieth century has led to many analyses of the dangers it holds. There is the risk of the 'chilling' effect that surveillance has on people's willingness to express themselves; the danger that society stagnates as the state becomes ruthlessly efficient at quelling any challenge to the status quo; and the simple danger that people are distressed at the invasion of their privacy. These issues are depicted most dramatically in George Orwell's *1984*.

US lawyer and author, Professor Daniel J. Solove, has distinguished between these dangers and a second set of concerns, which he argues are better captured in Kafka's *The Trial*. Here the protagonist is trapped in an interminable legal process but has no understanding of how or why he is being judged. Solove writes:

> In *The Trial*, the problem is not inhibited behavior, but rather a suffocating powerlessness and vulnerability created by the court system's use of personal data and its exclusion of the protagonist from having any knowledge or participation in the process. The harms consist of those created by bureaucracies –

indifference, errors, abuses, frustration, and lack of transparency and accountability.[2]

The distinction is a powerful one. Many people seem relatively uninhibited by the current level of ongoing surveillance that the internet allows. However, they may recognise the sense of powerlessness that occurs when information systems are used to categorise them and make decisions about their needs in ways that are opaque and at times frustrating or alarming.

The first and most obvious response to these problems is to strengthen individual control over how their data is used. In particular, Solove identifies the need to have much greater control over aggregation of data in which information from disparate sources is combined to create a more complete picture of an individual. As discussed in the last chapter, there is a great deal that can be done here, particularly in relation to commercial organisations where the individual's rights to know what algorithms are run on their data and the resulting categorisations could be greatly strengthened, even at the expense of commercial confidentiality.

However, control only gets us so far. There are two major limitations to what can be achieved through greater control and rights to opt out of surveillance. First, there are areas where opting out is never going to be an option. National security and communicable diseases are the two most obvious examples. This is true regardless of whether we feel national surveillance has overreached its legitimate boundaries and needs reining in or the opposite. Wherever the line is drawn, this is not an area where citizens can opt out. The same goes for any policing activities such as trying to identify tax cheats.

There is then a second reason why increasing personal control over data does not provide an answer to the dangers of surveillance. Control only lets me opt out of surveillance. But opting out of all surveillance harms me. The fact that Google can work out the information I am looking for with a remarkable degree of accuracy is an enormous benefit to me. The potential

---

[2]   Daniel J. Solove, '"I've got nothing to hide" and other misunderstandings of privacy', *San Diego Law Review* Vol 44 (2007), 745.

health benefits of ongoing surveillance of my state of health are significant. I want organisations to be able to surveil me so long as the process works to my advantage and does not enable them to manipulate me.

Greater control over my data is only of any real use if I can tell the difference between organisations that use my data in ways that are beneficial to me and those that do not. I need to be able to tell the difference between beneficial surveillance and harmful surveillance.

This is not something that I can ascertain from a description of how data is used, or from seeing how my personal data has been processed. It is something that I can only ascertain by seeing how my data has been processed in the context of how everyone else's has been treated. I need to understand how accurate the surveillance methods are and the degree to which I am being systematically disadvantaged rather than advantaged. This requires an understanding of the effect of a surveillance system across populations.

We are back at the problem of trying to determine whether allocation systems are operating fairly, whether systems for putting people into categories – such as 'compulsive gambler' or 'likely terrorist' – are accurate and fair.

Currently we have no way of knowing this. Bruce Schneier likens this situation to one in which users of electronic media are like 'feudal serfs' who have no real say over how information about them is used. 'We trust the feudal lords to treat us well and protect us from harm', he writes, adding: 'Given current laws, trust is our only option.'[3]

Trust does not feel like a good option. Transparency at a level that would give me reason to be trusting would be preferable. We have set out why we believe that sharing of underlying data with third parties competent to assess and make their own interpretation is the means by which this can be achieved.

In most areas of life, we are advocating this as a public process whereby secure sharing of data allows a public exchange of views as to the outcome of different types of rules, categorisations and

---

[3]   Schneier, *Data and Goliath*, p 59.

allocations. In other words, to assess the impact of surveillance systems.

But in areas where public debate of such questions is not possible, the same questions still need to be asked. For example, it would be helpful to have some idea of the error rate for 'signature' drone strikes. And it would good to have that information assessed by someone other than the organisations ordering the strikes. Transparency, we have argued, is a mechanism in which pluralistic society can police itself by allowing groups with differing interests make different assessments of the fairness of allocation systems. Is it no more than an extension of democracy and freedom of speech.

There are two related ideas here: first the idea that understanding the impact of a surveillance algorithm requires an ability to analyse the full population data set; and second the idea that rights to do this need to be vested in community organisations to allow a pluralistic debate about the merits of such systems.

Transparency requires both. But in areas where transparency is not appropriate, the first idea is still relevant where oversight takes place behind closed doors. National security is an area where transparency will always be limited. But this does not mean that the technical capacity of those tasked with overseeing national security agencies needs to be limited. Oversight of security arrangements would be greatly enhanced if those responsible had access to the data and the technical capacity to genuinely interrogate and test the narrative offered by those they oversee; to be able to form their own independent judgement as to the efficacy of security agencies. Doing this is expensive and difficult to implement. But it is preferable, we would suggest, to the alternative of impotent oversight.

Surveillance and monitoring

We are going to draw a distinction between surveillance and monitoring. We will use surveillance to refer to the use of information to identify individuals or groups of individuals and treat them differently. We want to use monitoring to refer to the use of data to assess the behaviour of organisations and officeholders whose actions affect allocations.

Both involve using detailed data about individuals. The difference is that the end product of surveillance is the identification of specific individuals in order to treat them in a different way to others. Credit scoring, for example, is surveillance. Most free online services are surveillance operations. Healthcare has some way to go, but the ambition of most healthcare organisations is to become effective surveillance systems, monitoring the health of their patients on an ongoing basis and determining the correct course of action accordingly.

Monitoring does not aim to identify individuals. It aims to uncover information about the system itself. It produces information about organisations, such as the degree to which organisations treat people differently and whether those differences are fair. It produces information about products – for example, whether they harm people or not – and about systems, such as whether markets look rigged. Monitoring is about looking for evidence of unfairness, inaccuracy and high rates of error in allocation including the surveillance that is now central to many allocation systems.

Good surveillance systems should include internal monitoring as a part of the overall programme. Figure 18.1 shows an idealised version of how a surveillance system operates.

We could start from either the 'assess' stage or the 'define' stage, but for convenience we will begin at the top.

- *Define target*: Outside of national security and criminal investigations, where the aim is sometimes to locate and track specific individuals, surveillance is, to use the terminology of drone strikes, most often looking for 'signatures'. The objective is to identify anyone (or more accurately any data record) that meets a specific definition. So, for example, you might be reviewing photographs from drones and trying to identify those that meet the following criteria:
  More than two people
  Travelling on foot within certain defined geographic areas
  Appear to be carrying guns
  No children in the group.

Figure 18.1: How a surveillance system operates

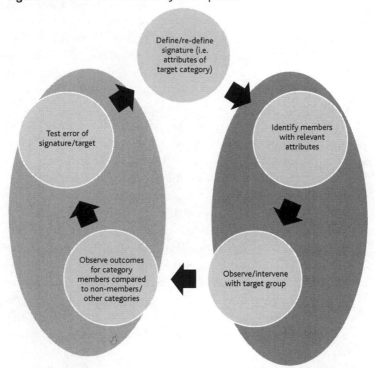

The photographs might be reviewed by a human or by a computer. The objective is to identify those that fall into a defined category which might be given the name 'enemy combatants'.

In health surveillance you may be looking for people at risk of a stroke by identifying records of individuals with, say, high blood pressure, a BMI (body mass index) over a certain level or past history of transient ischaemic attacks. In marketing, your target group might be women under 35 who watch pornography.

It is important to note that, in order to be implemented, targets have to be defined in terms of information that exists. If targets are defined in terms of attributes that are not recorded, proxies are used instead. So, if you want to target impulsive people, and have no direct measure of impulsiveness, some particular pattern of behaviour which is recorded – for example, late-night purchases online – is used as a proxy.

One aspect of surveillance that rightly causes concern is the tendency to start to treat the name of such categories as if they really were the thing being sought, rather than an imperfect attempt to identify them. Thus, a statement saying that a particular party was identified as 'enemy combatant' may be true insofar as they fitted the defined category But the degree to which someone was identified as fitting into the category of 'enemy combatants' is not the same as the degree to which somebody actually was an enemy combatant. That depends on the error rate in your surveillance system.

- *Surveil*: Run algorithms over the relevant data to categorise people (or more accurately records) as being within or not within the target group. It is important to note that surveillance systems can function without ever knowing the name of the people involved. The drone strike is not dependent on ever having worked out the names of the individual killed. Targeted advertising can place ads in front of someone based on their recent browsing history without having any information about who they are. Such systems have just as much potential for harm as a system that identifies targets.
- *Intervene*: For example, fire a missile at the target, invite the target to a doctor's appointment, refuse the target health insurance or place a particular advertisement on the web page they are viewing.
- *Measure*: Collect information post-intervention, such as rates of civilian casualties, rates of stroke, advertising response rates.
- *Assess*: Test the degree to which targeting is prone to error – for example, the degree to which you are killing civilians, reducing stroke rates or improving advertising response rates. Where possible and appropriate, randomisation can be used – intervening with one half of the target group and not with the other – to assess difference in impact. Assess the degree to which different target definitions would have improved accuracy. Review and redefine target definitions.

Most surveillance starts with the assessment stage, using existing data to create propensity models or risk models that seem most likely to work. But, in some cases, targets are defined using data outside of the surveillance system itself.

The two key assertions we want to make in relation to this model are:

1. *Monitoring*: All surveillance should involve a degree of independent monitoring. In some cases it is not possible, but we need to acknowledge in such circumstances that we are unable to assess the level of error in the system. Wherever there is sufficient public interest this should be done through data-sharing mechanisms that allow plural access to data from parties with conflicting interests. But, even in areas such as national security, independent monitoring of surveillance systems, even if not public, should still be conducted.

2. *'Opt-out from surveillance' and 'opt-out from monitoring' need to be treated differently*: People's rights to have their data excluded from surveillance are different to their rights to have data excluded from monitoring. As discussed in the previous chapter, the degree to which participation in surveillance is made a condition of the provision of a service should be reduced. But, in our view, the degree to which people's information should be available for monitoring purposes needs to be increased. Many business models only operate on the basis of surveillance and companies cannot be compelled to offer them on a different basis. However, if all such business models are subject to independent monitoring, we do believe that the viability of alternative business models will be greatly enhanced, thereby giving the public greater choice. For most activities in life, opting out of surveillance affects you alone and is nobody else's business. Opting out of monitoring affects the reliability of the whole system and the degree to which others can get justice.

Opting out from surveillance, monitoring and research

Monitoring and surveillance share a common feature – they involve the processing of data about individuals. For this reason, privacy advocates have often found themselves in opposition to transparency advocates because they regard the use of individual data for monitoring as an invasion of that individual's privacy.

At the heart of the case we are making is the belief that monitoring should not be regarded as an invasion of privacy. While we are wholly sympathetic to the idea that people might wish to limit the ways in which they are surveilled, we do not believe the same arguments apply to using information about people for monitoring purposes.

The strangest aspect of this debate is that the privacy argument is motivated often by fear of abusive surveillance. But by arguing for the right to opt out of monitoring, they make independent monitoring of the fairness of surveillance impossible. It plays directly into the hands of those who would misuse surveillance systems.

We have argued that, to the extent that my ability to assess the fairness of my treatment requires monitoring, there has to be a strong argument to prevent this information being accessed. The main argument here is that using individual data for monitoring means broader access to data that could potentially allow people to be identified. This must, therefore, increase the risk of an invasion of privacy.

This remains true to some degree even if solutions are developed that allow aggregate analysis of data by running queries against secure personal data stores. However, there are approaches to analysis of population data that can greatly reduce risks to theft or misappropriation of individual data. It is important to acknowledge that past claims that such risks can be avoided by 'de-identifying data' do not stand up to scrutiny.

However, our contention would be that it is possible to enable monitoring in a way that poses minimal risks to privacy, through a combination of controlling access to data, monitoring who is accessing it and building secure data systems, ideally created from the building blocks of personal data stores.[4] Given the

---

[4]   This is a rapidly developing area of research with a very extensive literature but a useful summary can be found here: Fung, BCM, et al, 'Privacy-Preserving data publishing: a survey of recent developments', *ACM Computing Surveys*, Vol. 42, No. 4, Article 14, Publication date: June 2010.

benefits to society of surveillance, and the risks of unaccountable surveillance, it seems disproportionate to claim that the risk to privacy from such activity outweighs the benefits of ensuring our institutions are fair and safe.

It is ironic that those who advocate data sharing to support transparency are often opposed by those who argue for greater privacy. Both positions are aiming to achieve a common goal, namely a reduction in our 'serfdom' to data-driven surveillance.

We would also agree with the sentiment that all monitoring of surveillance would ideally take place as a result of people volunteering the use of data for this purpose. It is conceivable that in future that is all that will be necessary. But while that is not the case, there are, we suggest, legitimate requirements that individuals can place on their fellow citizens to allow information to be used to establish the fairness of our institutions. We have gone further and argued that this activity is sufficiently beneficial and extensive that it should not occur only after a prima facie case has been made to the courts but on a more extensive and routine basis. But as to where that line should be drawn is a matter for society to determine democratically.

Using information for monitoring can be done without subjecting any individual to surveillance and in a way that adds insignificantly to the risk to their privacy. Indeed, we would suggest that by making the misuse of surveillance observable, the benefits in protecting privacy would far outweigh any increase in the risk of information theft.

While we can draw a clear distinction between surveillance (which involves using information to make decisions about the individual) and monitoring (which uses the same information to inform our understanding of the system), we have a much more difficult distinction to draw between monitoring and research.

In theory, the monitoring of surveillance is a form of audit – the use of data to establish that systems are safe and comply with the law. Audit is normally regarded as a use of data for which consent can be presumed, since there is an obligation on organisations to ensure they are acting safely and within the law. Our proposal that data sharing with independent third parties should be a necessary part of any monitoring arrangements adds a complexity to this, but one that is surmountable and of invaluable benefit.

However, as the complexity and completeness of data sets grow, drawing a distinction between monitoring and research becomes harder. In some cases, the distinction is easy. Any project that sets out to determine whether some new intervention or new categorisation would work is research. Research is not necessary to establishing the fairness of existing surveillance systems and, consequently, the use of data in research is something that should only occur when the individual has consented to it.

However, the process of monitoring surveillance systems that make use of rich data is likely to throw up new discoveries, even if inadvertently. To test the reliability of an approach to categorisation, it is necessary to compare it to alternatives and in the process to identify better approaches. There is therefore a need to constantly review the parameters under which monitoring takes place and to assess the appropriate protocols and those that are inappropriate. Furthermore, there will be circumstances in which the testing of a new approach to surveillance is seen as essential in assessing the fairness of the current system.

In a situation that will develop rapidly in coming years, it would be unwise to attempt to set out rules to govern how these judgements should be made in future. The only two principles that we can confidently articulate are that:

- The use of data in these ways should be transparent – that is, the activities made public and the results open to independent scrutiny by people with access to the same data.
- There should be an ongoing review process to reassess monitoring activities where people are *obliged* to make their data available and research activities where people are *invited* to do so.

A recent report on data sharing by the Nuffield Council on Bioethics, a British think tank, argued:

> Privacy is important to people for a number of reasons relating to their ability to maintain their

identity, relationships and well-being. Respecting people's privacy can be seen as an aspect of showing respect for them as persons. The public interest is an interest that people share as members of a society, e.g. the promotion of commonly valued conditions like security, physical and mental health and material prosperity. People are simultaneously both individuals and members of wider groups with shared values and interests: they thus have interests both in allowing other people to access data that relates to them and in guarding against this to preserve their privacy, just as they have interests both in access to data about others and in their privacy. Private and public interests are fundamentally entwined: there is both a private and public interest in maintaining acceptable levels of privacy, and a private and public interest in making responsible use of data compatible with this. Data initiatives therefore have to perform a 'double articulation' that seeks to reconcile the private and public interest in using data, and of the private and public interest in protecting privacy, rather than simply 'balancing' privacy interests against public interest.[5]

Getting the balance right between all of our interests in privacy and fair public institutions is something that will require an ongoing open and transparent public debate. This implies a new ongoing dialogue between citizen and state, and between citizens, about the reconciliation of the private and public benefit from data sharing and from the resultant transparency.

This conversation will not produce outcomes that satisfy all participants – hence the importance of continuous review of the moral justification for a data-sharing scheme by the community affected, whether through conventional democratic processes or using other methods. Most businesses and public sector organisations then have a further list of secondary uses that

---

[5]   *The Collection, Linking and Use of Data in Biomedical Research and Health Care: Ethical Issues*, Nuffield Council on Bioethics, 2015.

require your consent as part of the provision of that service. In the private sector you are normally required to consent, at least technically, to a lengthy legal agreement setting out how data will be used, although few bother to read it. In the public sector, there has been a history of assuming consent to many of these activities or arguing that consent is unnecessary if data is used anonymously. Neither approach is satisfactory.

Policy responses to this question are rarely sufficiently nuanced. Data protection laws give me little if any real control over the extent to which organisations can make processing of my data in a particular way a condition of the provision of service. I may have a right to opt out of direct marketing, but the relevance of that is reducing in a world where marketing is as much about changing the content on the page I am looking at as it is about placing advertisements in front of me.

In healthcare, a different set of rules is used to determine what you can and cannot opt out of. It is generally accepted that you cannot opt out of the use of data for direct provision of care because you cannot be safely treated without using this information. The term 'secondary uses' has been applied to any other use of the data with a question mark over whether such uses can be required. Health systems have often dodged this issue by using de-identified data and arguing that the patient no longer has a privacy interest in the use of this data.

But there are many secondary uses that are necessary to the provision of safe healthcare – for example, it is not possible to schedule operating theatre sessions or surgeon hours without reference to the medical needs of the patients scheduled for treatment. Managing theatre time in such a way as to ensure the right doctors and nurses are in the right building at the right time is a secondary use but also a necessary part of providing safe and effective care.

To be clear, it is possible to run a health system without using data for any secondary purposes. You can schedule theatre time, for example, by simply allowing surgeons to book it as and when they choose. However, it would be wasteful and less safe. The argument for required secondary use of individual data is where there are significant costs to everyone in not doing this and where doing it to the standard required to prevent those costs requires everyone to take part.

Auditing the quality of care is another purpose that medical codes of practices view as a legitimate use of patient data where doctors can assume consent. This area has become particularly contentious. However, this battle is in reality less about whether or not the patient has the right to opt out of such quality control processes so much as a dispute over who should have the right to conduct such audits with professionals in conflict with managers or external audit organisations.

Our criteria for determining what is a required use should be the same as a court would use – namely what is the risk that someone is going to suffer an unreasonable degree of unfairness as a result of the failure to use the information. Beyond that, there is a category of secondary uses which are not necessary but useful – such as carrying out research into new areas. But the line between what should be regarded as necessary and what is optional is far from clear. For example, using information to project future health requirements might be regarded as essential by some and useful by others.

One important dimension relevant to the question of opt-outs is the degree to which the use to which the data is being put requires everyone to take part. For example, the question of whether or not patient data should be used for scheduling operating theatre time makes sense as a collective decision. Allowing people to individually opt out of the use of their data for scheduling carries a significant risk of rendering the entire exercise useless as it only takes one or two patients unaccounted for to throw the whole schedule. In some cases, audit will suffer significantly if the record is incomplete since small numbers of missing records from an audit can have significant effects on the results. However, there are also examples of audit where incomplete records would be less important.

In contrast, research into new treatments does not require complete data from a particular patient group and can be left entirely to individual choice. Unfairness as a result of slowness to discover new treatments is not unreasonable since it affects us all in a way that we cannot predict.

If I withhold my data from research, I may be acting as a free-rider but I am not hindering you from achieving your objective. If I withhold my data from the administrative and audit tasks, I may risk undermining the system for others. In healthcare, the distinction between primary and secondary purposes is perhaps not as useful as the distinction between necessary purposes (including some necessary collective secondary purposes) and those secondary purposes for which it would be unreasonable to require people's participation.

We do not want to argue for any particular line to be drawn between necessary secondary uses and voluntary secondary uses. Our argument is purely that, from the point of view of transparency, necessary secondary uses will include activities to ensure the quality of services and the accuracy of surveillance systems. The significant public interest in ensuring that such systems can be trusted requires that there be rights vested in appropriate community organisations to access the data used and provide independent narratives and assessments.

Finally, we need to recognise that the 'administration' of consent and opt-outs is a significant technical problem. One of the major challenges in trying to reach the above arrangement is balancing broad and specific consents. Specific consent – in which every use of data requires someone to positively say yes – carries very high transaction and data acquisition costs. These costs are a significant obstacle to research.

Broad consents – in which say I could agree to lower risk data about me being used by accredited universities for research – greatly reduce transaction costs with a consequent public benefit. However, such broad consents need to be devised in ways that do not expose the citizen to finding they have agreed to something they did not intend. The Human Genome Project developed a sophisticated system that involves allowing both specific and broad consents, including different categories of broad consent

The National Information Board (NIB), a body set up by the Department of Health in England in 2014, to advise on data and technology strategy (and chaired by co-author Tim Kelsey) has recommended that the healthcare system should move towards a system of consent in which an individual is given the right to set preferences for sharing of their medical records. They might choose to allow for their data to be shared with NHS organisations, or with public health or life sciences researchers; they might specify which parts of their records they are happy to be shared. This implies they also have real-time online access to their clinical records, as discussed above. An individual should be able to access this preference tool whenever they wish and alter their selection at any time. The tool should also describe which data have been shared and for what purposes. The NIB proposals were accepted as government policy in 2014,[6] and are to be implemented before 2020, with first technical trials due to commence by 2016.

But we would expect that the parameters used to define broad consents will shift over time and respond to new unforeseen developments. We would hope that data organisations acting on behalf of individuals would not only be continually reviewing the way in which data was used for surveillance, not only continually assessing the fairness of systems but also continually reshaping the way in which consents are framed in order to provide the most appropriate levels of control.

INFORMED CONSENT FOR DATA SHARING TO EMPOWER TRANSPARENCY: THE STORY OF CARE.DATA

In 2013, NHS England launched a programme to link data between GPs (general practitioners) and hospitals. Since the late 1980s similar data on hospitals had been available to researchers – it was this data that helped the research unit at Imperial College to identify hospitals with outlying statistical outcomes. Similar analytic resources in primary care services were called for.

It was hoped that this would lead to better information to regulate the quality of healthcare, better information for patients to make choices about their own care and faster scientific discovery of better, more efficient ways to deliver care. The care.data programme was to set a new standard in healthcare for data sharing. One of the authors, Tim

---

[6]   *Personalised Health and Care 2020*, National Information Board, November 2014.

Kelsey, was the National Health Service (NHS) director responsible for the project.

The proposal was simple: that data would be extracted from GP practices with certain personal identifiers but not others – for example, the patient's NHS number but not their name or address – and made available to the Health and Social Care Information Centre (HSCIC), a public body that is allowed, by law, to manage sensitive personal data. The HSCIC would then link the data, at an individual level, to hospital records so that for the first time one could track patient outcomes across the pathway of their treatment.

Linked records already existed. The Clinical Practice Research Datalink is a national database of linked records created for research purposes. Around 13% of general practices in England contributed patient-level data to this resource. In addition, some parts of the local NHS had created linked-record databases covering particular geographic areas. The key difference with care.data was that it would allow comprehensive national comparison of patterns of care.

The value of care.data was widely recognised. Without information about the patient's whole course of treatment and the ability to compare that information with the same data about other patients, healthcare providers themselves could not properly assess what was or wasn't working in the provision of care. The same dilemma was faced by researchers investigating different treatments, commissioners planning how to spend budgets, and regulators trying to assess quality standards. They could only get comparative information about small pieces of each patient's treatment and this gave only a partial picture.

All the identifiers would be removed as soon as the data had been linked. The proposal was that this de-identified data would only be released to 'authorised' organisations – for example, to the clinical commissioning groups responsible for paying for routine hospital services; to national bodies such as NHS England, which commissions primary care; as well as public health and life sciences researchers. There would be full transparency concerning how the data was used, so that the public could see the benefits of their data sharing.

Because of concerns about privacy, it was decided people would be given a right to 'opt out' of the initiative.

On 19 January 2014, the *Guardian* published a front-page story with the following headline: 'NHS patient data to be made available for sale to drug and insurance firms'. The article followed an interview with an official from the HSCIC in which he reportedly confirmed that de-identified individual-level data could be accessed by pharmaceutical and insurance companies. The important nuance – that under HSCIC rules this data could not be used for purely commercial purposes but only for health and care benefit – was lost in the subsequent media storm. In addition, the official acknowledged that there was a 'small, theoretical' risk that the data being supplied to these companies could be re-identified. 'You may be able to identify people if you had a lot of data', he said. 'It depends on how people will use the data once they have it.'

In early February 2014, the HSCIC confirmed that its predecessor, the NHS Information Centre, had released de-identified individual-level data to actuarial bodies and to other parties, at least one of which was passing it on to other organisations. There was no evidence of any attempt to re-identify individuals or of any inappropriate uses of the data, but it announced an inquiry to be chaired by Sir Nick Partridge, a non-executive director, into historic data releases and proposed an overhaul of the process.

At this point, NHS England decided to postpone the planned data extraction. There were three interrelated problems: uncertainty as to what was legally permissible; a long-standing lack of transparency about the way that patient information was used; and an approach to de-identification that was no longer tenable and which had enabled data to be used in ways that the public might expect to be informed about.

In the early months of 2014, the government – whose commitment to care.data remained firm despite the media furore – made a legislative amendment to the Care Bill which was passing through parliament to outlaw any use of patient data for analysis for 'solely commercial purposes', explicitly ruling out insurance purposes, as well as determining that only health and care purposes were permitted. It also proposed the following measures: the establishment of a body with statutory authority to oversee the granting of access to de-identified individual-level data; that any abuse of this data would result in potentially permanent removal of access rights; and a review of care.data by the National Data Guardian before any data extraction proceeded.

In the months following its postponement, care.data was overhauled and new proposals for patient communications were drawn up. In addition, the HSCIC has instituted new processes which provide complete transparency of all permitted data uses.

In the space of a year, a new framework for data sharing has been constructed in England's healthcare, something which may provide a model for public services in general:

- All personal data must be treated as identifiable – because the theoretical risk that it can be hacked even on the most secure digital database is not disprovable – and for this reason citizens should have a right to opt out of its use for analytic purposes.
- There should be statutory safeguards that prevent data being used for purposes that are not socially or morally justifiable.
- Citizens must have complete transparency of uses of their personal data and the benefits that accrue.
- Citizens should expect to be individually informed of their rights to opt out.

These principles are important not only to ensure the best framing for a data-sharing scheme but also to avoid perverse behaviours which can cause individuals harm. For example, a legitimate scheme run by a group of charities in Oxford to share health and social care data to help improve the efficiency of services caused some mothers to stop disclosing postnatal depression – and even seeking help for the condition – because of fears that social workers would take their children away.

In the context of successful delivery of Transparency 2.0, care.data suggests that the only viable policy response to the challenges of privacy and consent is a combination of legislative safeguards for the purposes of personal data sharing, complete transparency of those uses and their benefits to citizens, authentic participation in design of the programme, and continuous evaluation of its justification.

Part Three
Transparency 3.0

This part looks at the scale of data that technology is creating and the need to increasingly rely on machine-driven systems to interpret information. We set out some views as to how a more complete form of data sharing is required in order to be able to enjoy the benefits of these technologies without fear of surrendering to unaccountable forces that may harm us.

19

Artificial intelligence and allocation systems

Frank Rosenblatt may be the most important person that the majority of people have never heard of. In 1957, with a grant from the US Office of Naval Research, Rosenblatt invented the Perceptron, a machine that was capable of learning. This was an analogue computer – a mechanical device which looked a little like a telephone exchange overrun with wires. It had an array of 400 photocells which Rosenblatt connected to the mechanical 'neurons'. It was first tasked with learning how to distinguish between different letters of the alphabet – and even when its 'intelligence' was degraded by pulling out some of the wires, it could still tell the difference between basic letters.

Rosenblatt gave a press conference in 1958 and the *New York Times* reported the Perceptron to be 'the embryo of an electronic computer that [the Navy] expects will be able to walk, talk, see, write, reproduce itself and be conscious of its existence'.[1] Some of Rosenblatt's colleagues in the early community of scientists researching artificial intelligence (AI) objected to these claims.

Rosenblatt was an eclectic character. He built an observatory in his garden and used it to look for extraterrestrial intelligence. He was intrigued by the fact that artificially intelligent machines can inherit knowledge – whereas humans have to learn everything from birth, an AI computer can import all the learning of its predecessor – and in the 1960s he conducted a series of

---

[1] 'NEW NAVY DEVICE LEARNS BY DOING; Psychologist Shows Embryo of Computer Designed to Read and Grow Wiser', *New York Times*, July 8 1958

experiments to see if extracting brain cells from trained mice and injecting them into untrained mice would cause them to be trained. It did not.

Rosenblatt died in 1971, aged 43, in an accident. Artificial intelligence had achieved little by that time and scepticism about its potential grew in subsequent years. Some considered his entire enterprise to have been misconceived. Today, his reputation is being restored. The consensus is that the Perceptron was, as Rosenblatt claimed, a machine capable of learning and confidence in the potential of AI is high, as the internet has allowed the creation of data sets of sufficient size for machines to demonstrate their ability to learn very quickly given enough data.

Google Translate is perhaps the best known example. Enter a word or phrase in most common languages and it will give you an equivalent word or phrase in almost any other language. The remarkable thing is that no one told the computer how to do this. Previous attempts to build translation engines had attempted to do just that. They began with the model of the dictionary and tried to get people to expand on the idea by identifying the correct translations of ever more complex phrases and sentences, taking into account all the different contexts in which a phrase might appear. But the task proved too hard for the same reason that it is hard to give a computer a rule that lets it see the difference between 'time flies like an arrow' and 'fruit flies like a banana'. The sheer scale of trying to write a translation engine, plus the fact that language is constantly adapting and changing, made the project unfeasible.

Then Google tried something different and found that the whole problem could be solved without asking translators to lift a finger. It simply pointed its computers at all instances it could find of texts, from the Bible to European legislation, that were published in multiple languages. It told the machines to look for associations – look for any pattern where a word or phrase in one language is associated with a word or phrase in another. The result is Google Translate.

One of the remarkable things about it is that, rather like the rules of human grammar, no one can tell you precisely what data or rules it has used to identify the fact that 'tongue in mouth' is rendered in Italian as 'lingua in bocca' where as 'tongue in cheek' translates as 'ironia'. The machine just worked it out from experience – in a way reminiscent of the way that humans learn that 'tongue in cheek' is not to be understood literally.

Deep neural networks are capable of far more than learning to distinguish letters. They have advanced skills of image and speech perception and of recognising movements, as well as intelligent analysis of large, complex data sets and learning, through trial and error, to make judgements of probable accuracy and, in the case of medicine, to recommend appropriate courses of treatment. In some contexts, these are becoming rather everyday applications: you can download free speech-recognition synthesisers on the web which allow you to speak English as you Skype a friend and for this to be rendered, in your own voice, in Mandarin. New-generation video games which can recognise movement are another example.

Michael Osborne is associate professor in machine learning at Oxford University. He designs 'intelligent algorithms capable of making sense of complex data'.[2] He has been working with Carl Benedikt Frey, an economist and co-director of the Oxford Martin Programme on Technology and Employment, to try to understand the limits of what sort of jobs robots could be designed to do.

Working with the innovation charity NESTA, their report *Creativity vs Robots* assessed the extent to which different jobs were likely to be taken by robots.[3] At the top of the list, to no great surprise, were routine tasks such as assembling products or handling call centres. The ability of computerised robots to use sensors to carry out actions requiring fine motor skills or to understand common language is developing rapidly enough that tasks such as manufacturing jewellery or growing crops will quite likely be given to robots. Similarly, the advent of driverless cars has the potential to make transport and logistics areas that no longer require people.

---

[2] http://hamba.oxford-man.ox.ac.uk/people/michael-osborne

[3] Hasan Bakhshi, Carl Benedikt Frey and Michael Osborne, *Creativity vs Robots, the Creative Economy and the Future of Employment*, NESTA, April 2015.

Perhaps more surprising are the jobs further down the list. Today we highly value tasks that require large amounts of knowledge and the ability to quickly retrieve that knowledge and apply it in real life – professionals such as lawyers, doctors and bankers command some of the highest salaries in the world. The researchers conclude, however, that these jobs are the next most likely to be taken over by robots. When it comes to storing and retrieving information, machines already outclass people by a large margin. Until recently they have lacked the ability to apply any judgement to that information to determine when a particular interpretation is most likely to apply. Machine learning is changing that. Machines are getting better at categorising objects in the real world than we are. For example, Watson, the IBM computer that won the quiz show 'Jeopardy' in 2011, has proved itself far more reliable than doctors in reviewing scans and assessing whether a patient has a tumour or not.

Among the professional jobs Osborne and Frey think likely to be computerised, tax accountancy is rated as one of the highest with a 77% probability. Jobs in banking, insurance and financial intermediation are rated between 40% and 50%. In healthcare, it is the highly paid doctors who are most at risk of being replaced with a machine (41%) while low-paid nurses are among the least likely. Lawyers (22%) are easier to replace with machines than nursery school teachers (7%).

Knowledge-based jobs such as finance, accountancy, medicine, marketing and the law are the most at risk. Professionals who today command some of the highest salaries will become replaceable, while jobs that enjoy less status, a lower salary and are regarded as less demanding will be the ones where people can add most value – for example, nurses, teachers and carers – along with creative activities in the arts, design and communication.

Our interest lies in the fact that many of these knowledge-based jobs perform crucial roles in allocation decisions. These are the people who currently exercise discretion in determining what category I am put in with significant consequences for my life. These are the people whose human judgements currently inform whether I should be prosecuted, whether my children should be taken from me or whether it is worth trying to save my life (along with a host of less dramatic decisions).

The Centre for the Study of Existential Risk (CSER) is a new institute at Cambridge University which has been set up by a number of leading AI researchers and ethicists concerned about the lack of international policy development in the field. In January 2014, the CSER was one of the organisers of a conference in San Juan which brought together experts from all over the world and concluded with the drafting of an open letter that called for the robust and beneficial development of AI and for more urgent research into its safety and societal benefit, with a particular emphasis on development of appropriate public governance arrangements for the integration of machine learning into health, education and other core public services. Who, these experts ask, will ensure that the 'black box' algorithms of artificial intelligence are held to account for their decisions?

Ruled by robots

The natural instinct of many confronted with this scenario is to insist that no robot should be making decisions about them. It is a point of view that seems like common sense and which appeals to lawmakers. For example, UK data protection laws currently grant me the right to object to any decision about me being taken by a computer. This is intended to provide 'safeguards against the risk that a potentially damaging decision is taken without human intervention'.[4]

We do not believe that this approach is sustainable, any more than the medieval concept of a right to trial by your peers could be sustained in the modern world. It relates to an idea of legitimacy that has already been shown to be fallacious, however instinctively appealing it might be.

This debate is rooted in one of the longest running arguments in medicine – one that was effectively kicked off in 1954 by a US psychologist, Paul Meehl, but which began much earlier with the publication in 1928 of a report by the Illinois State Board of Parole. The paper compared two different methods

---

[4]   Information Commissioners Office Guide to Data Protection, https://ico. org.uk/for-organisations/guide-to-data-protection/principle-6-rights/ automated-decision-taking/

for assessing the risk of releasing prisoners under parole. One method, the one standardly used, was to ask a psychiatrist to assess the prisoner and make a risk assessment. The second used an actuarial model that combined a range of data about the prisoner such as their age, their criminal record and the length of their sentence to predict the likelihood of reoffending. The results showed that the actuarial method was far more accurate than the psychiatric approach.

Fascinated by this, Meehl started to collect similar studies – for example, a 1943 study showing that a simple two-factor model was better at predicting student grades than the assessment of college tutors using far richer information. In 1954 he published *Statistical vs Clinical Risk Prediction*, which summarized the 20 studies then available comparing human judgement with statistical methods. The answer was clear-cut: the statistics won.

Since then much more research in this area has been published, but as the evidence accumulates it only confirms what Meehl first identified – that human decision making is often far worse than mechanised decision making.

This astonishingly important observation still fails to have the impact it should. Like Copernicus observing that the earth actually moves around the sun, it will take some time for humans to fully absorb the implications for our understanding of the relationship between human intelligence and the universe. It is deeply unsettling and has prompted some people to try to simply evade the issue.

The most common response is to suggest that we don't really have to choose. If machines are good at prediction, let's get them to make predictions! Then we'll look at them, take them into account in our decisions and use them to improve the accuracy of our judgements. We don't have to choose between man and machines. We can have the best of both worlds, the argument goes.

One can almost hear Meehl biting his knuckles as he tries to point out that this utterly misses the point. In 1986 he wrote:

> Let me state as loudly and as clearly as I can manage
> ... [we] did not artificially concoct a controversy ...
> between two methods that complement each other

and work together harmoniously. I think this is a ridiculous position when the context is the pragmatic context of decision making. You have two quite different procedures for combining a finite set of information to arrive at a predictive decision. ... [These two procedures] disagree a sizeable fraction of the time. ... The plain fact is that [a decision maker] cannot act in accordance with both of [two] incompatible predictions. Nobody disputes that it is possible to improve clinicians' practices by informing them of their track records actuarially. Nobody has ever disputed that the actuary would be well advised to listen to clinicians in setting up the set of variables.

His point is that at the end of the day a decision must be made and it is either the human or the machine that makes it – and any way you structure it, for a wide range of problems, machines are more reliable.

The second point is that the appropriate test of an allocation system is its fairness – and its fairness is a function of its rate of error. If computers are prone to lower rates of error than humans, then that is the fair way to determine allocations.

This feels highly counterintuitive because we sometimes regard human judgements as in some way more real than a machine-driven judgement. In the example of the drone strike, to say that a group of people were 'identified as enemy combatants' may feel more true if it describes a process in which a human looked at a picture and made the call than if a computer had done so automatically – *even if we know that the computer is less prone to make mistakes than the human.*

Preferring human judgement over AI because of such instincts has the potential to reduce the fairness of allocation systems. The right response to anxieties about computer-driven allocation systems is transparency. It is entirely appropriate that humans determine whether or not they think a computer-driven allocation system is fair. But if, on the basis of good evidence, such a system is demonstrably fairer, we should submit to it while continuing to monitor its performance.

Our difficulty in coming to terms with this is partly, as Meehl observes, our reluctance to accept that our normal method of making decisions, even if we describe it as intuition or a gut feeling, is in reality no more than a synthesis of available evidence to form a statistical prediction. The degree to which this is true is becoming ever more evident as neurologists unpick the most fundamental mechanism by which the brain establishes the identity of perceived objects. Research by Stanislas Dehaene at the Collège de France and others has shown that when humans are asked to perform a task as simple as identifying whether one Arabic numeral is higher or lower than another they have a rate of error and that this rate of error behaves statistically according to the problem at hand. In other words, if we are asked the question 'is four larger than five?', a mechanical calculator will always give the right answer and will do so because it is programmed with the logic that allows this. In contrast, a human assesses the probability that it is so and says yes if the probability exceeds a threshold. The brain stores the information necessary to know that one plus one is two not as a logical fact but through learned statistical relationships.

The other common objection to reliance on machine-driven decision making is the 'broken leg' problem. I may have a remarkably accurate algorithm for predicting whether people will go to the cinema on a particular evening using lots of data which confidently predicts that Mr Smith will go to the cinema tonight. But that is because the algorithm does not know that Mr Smith has broken his leg. A human would not make the same mistake.

The challenge is the idea that there is always the risk of extraneous circumstances that might not be captured by the machine and which a machine could not know were relevant because they were outside its experience. Only humans have human experience.

The broken leg scenario is the reason that laws have been introduced to 'protect' people from machine-made decisions. But it is not a protection from harm. As Meehl rightly insists, you either have humans making decisions or machines. If you let humans override the machines because of the broken leg issue, we have no way of distinguishing between 'broken legs' – things that we all agree should cause the decision to be overridden – and any other piece of information that the human decides should override the machine. In other words, in many circumstances, the cost of preventing erroneous 'broken leg' decisions is a reduction in the overall accuracy of predictions. Far from protecting people, laws allowing humans to override machine-driven decision making will, on the evidence, result in higher rates of harm. The main benefit will be the avoidance of the anguish caused by exceptional situations in which a machine makes a plainly unjustifiable decision. It is not unreasonable to say that such events are so unacceptable that it is better to live with more harm than to live with even the occasional instance of this nature.

This is the Gary Reinhardt situation we began the debate with – the moment when an individual case exposes consequences from an allocation system that had not been envisaged. When this happens it is right to review the rules. But the review can never be of an individual case, it must look to change the rules wholesale for all subsequent cases. It is often the case that such reviews cannot be completed in time to save the individual whose case has exposed the problem. That is the tragedy. But it is a tragedy that occurs daily in our courts, our hospitals and in every institution that makes decisions of great significance for our lives.

The preference for human decision making is also influenced, as discussed previously, by the fallacy of perfect implementation. Here, the sort of transparency we are advocating will go some way to addressing this by making the levels of errors in our allocation systems more visible. Also, comparison between computer-driven allocation systems and human-driven systems will make it easier for us to understand that error is an inevitable aspect of all such systems.

In the end, as always with technology, it is simple economics that will push these debates to one side. The sheer economic efficiency of computer-driven decision making is such that it will become ubiquitous. And while laws may insist that such decision-making processes must be overseen by humans, there is no way to stop this collapsing into an entirely formal exercise in which the organisations employing humans to do such reviews effectively limit the discretion to override.

Indeed, in many areas of economic activity there will be a strong push to stop people trying to override such decisions. Notably, in medicine, computer-assisted diagnosis instead of speeding up diagnostics has slowed the process down because the information generated is then reviewed by doctors, which can increase the both the cost and the chance of error.

Again, as discussed previously, the cost of making fair allocation systems is a major barrier to fairness in most areas of life. We simply don't have the time and money to exhaustively investigate the accuracy of every individual allocation of diagnoses, parking penalties, university places, jobs and so forth. The use of computerised decision-making systems opens up the potential to create far fairer allocation systems.

It will also force us to increasingly recognise the degree to which we like imperfect allocation systems because they make life more tolerable. For example, we have the technology necessary to make speeding an offence that is almost always caught. But it is quite likely we will choose to continue to live in a world in which speeding tickets are issued by highly fallible systems somewhat randomly to those who speed. Imperfection in allocations makes the world bearable.

In short, computerised allocation systems will be resisted in part because of their increased accuracy and the dehumanising impact that this has. However, we would predict that there are many areas of life where accuracy will outweigh this concern – for example, if more accurate diagnosis results in a significant increase in your chance of living. For that reason, it would be wise to start to prepare now for the eventuality of machine-driven decision making becoming widespread.

The issue for the authors is that the whole argument in favour of machine-driven systems is that they are more cost effective and have a lower rate of error than human systems. But such a defence is only tolerable if it is wholly transparent and open to challenge. It would certainly not be reasonable, to our minds, to allow the use of AI systems in allocation decisions of public interest, on the basis of some form of regulatory standard that requires the user of such systems to meet certain processes or to publish certain information about their activities. This approach, as we have tried to demonstrate throughout this book, is inadequate to the task of policing largely human-driven allocation systems. We have advocated that population-level data sharing has to form the basis of transparency for a fair society. The belief that regulatory standards and inspection would be capable of containing the potential errors, biases and abuses of AI systems risks, in our view, causing significant harm to large numbers of people.

There are a number of reasons for this. First, regulatory approaches are better suited to process regulation than outcome regulation (for the reasons set out earlier – primarily the inherent complexity of outcomes and the monoptic nature of regulation). AI systems are by their nature less transparent and less open to examination of the process. At the extreme it is possible that the most accurate AI systems would work with data at a scale and speed that made the process by which a categorisation was determined as inscrutable as trying to unpick why a psychiatrist has a gut feeling that a prisoner will not reoffend.

Second, consider the speed with which organisations adapt to regulation by devising ways of operating that meet the regulatory standard but defeat the object. We should expect AI-assisted systems to be several orders of magnitude quicker at doing the same thing.

This does not mean that we abandon such regulatory initiatives. But we should be aware of their limitations and demand true transparency, driven by data sharing, to allow a plurality of analyses of the effect of such systems regarding their outcomes, in terms of both distributions of categorisation and impact.

Speaking personally, both authors are excited rather than scared by the potential for AI systems to take information about our lives and tell us things that we did not know, whether that is diagnosing an illness or informing us that we would be better employed in a different occupation. But only in a world in which there is sufficient transparency to know that this is not putting us at the mercy of those systems. To feel comfortable in this brave new world there are two things that we want to insist on. The first is having access to and appropriate control over *all* the data that goes into such an algorithm. The second is that the population-level data – by which we mean all the inputs, the resulting categorisations and as much information as possible about the impact of applying this categorisation in real decision making – is being looked at by multiple organisations with conflicting interests as to how the data should be interpreted.

A sense of urgency

If all this sounds futuristic, it is not. These applications are already being created. Diagnostic engines that use AI and run on large data sets of symptoms are already being built and marketed. Other applications are in the pipeline: the first autonomous, or driverless, cars are already being tested (with human co-drivers) on the streets of at least two British cities – Leicester and Milton Keynes – and so far the algorithms that control them are suggesting they are safer than we are. One Japanese car manufacturer is already developing a prototype for mass production.

AI-driven decision systems strip away areas of moral ambiguity of personal conscience and force us to make uncomfortable choices – to confront the tragic choices of life. For example, AI cars will have to be programmed to behave in a particular way if someone steps out in front of the car and there is not time to stop. Should it, for example, run down the person in front of it or should it swerve even if that means hitting a tree and potentially killing the passengers? Today the decisions made in those vital few seconds are something that only the driver involved in an accident ever truly knows. With AI, we all know and it gets to be decided in advance, according to what we collectively decide are the right rules. Researchers have found that, on the whole, in these situations, people do support cars that sacrifice the driver if it reduces the overall number of deaths.

But how will car manufacturers respond? They will be aware that car buyers are influenced by the statistics about how many drivers die in accidents with their cars. How will we know if a car that seems to have fewer driver deaths has achieved this through better safety systems or by tweaking the AI systems to be a tad less self-sacrificing than other cars in ways that are hard to detect? The statistics needed to tell the difference are exactly the sort of complex outcome that a regulatory approach will fail to deal with adequately unless it is accompanied by multiple access to the necessary data – that is, by plural access among organisations with competing interests.

Governments are competing to attract the global car industry. The UK is a major centre of automotive manufacturing within the EU but the only G7 country aside from Canada that has no significant domestic car manufacturer. Referring to the need to put in place legal and regulatory arrangements to allow for driverless cars, UK policy documents state: 'We believe the UK is … uniquely positioned to become a premium location globally for the development of these technologies.'[5]

Testing cars on public roads is now legal in the UK and in parts of the US. The UK Department for Transport is reviewing the existing legislation to see how it would need to change to allow wider use. It recognises the need for 'greater certainty around criminal and civil liability in the event of an automated vehicle being in a collision. Under the current legal framework these issues would be dealt with on a case by case basis by the Courts. We will aim to provide additional clarity and certainty in legislation, to provide a sound basis upon which to allocate criminal and civil liability'.

The policy goes on to state the need to establish standards of what makes a 'safe' vehicle. It also states that regulations will require all cars to carry 'some form of' data recorder that could be interrogated by the relevant authorities in the event of an accident.

This is precisely the situation the industry would like to get to and which a government keen to bid for inward investment will accede to – but which is inadequate. We are dealing with a world where we are trying to assess complex outcomes, which can only be understood through the construction of competing narratives. We are dealing with a world where there are clear industry incentives to be selective in disclosure and to manage information flows to our disadvantage.

---

[5]   *The Pathway to Driverless Cars*, Department for Transport (UK), February 2015.

The requirement for data recorders is modelled on the idea of aeroplane safety and it is an idea that has worked well in aviation. It is certainly a good idea to introduce it in automated cars as well. But an initial assessment of the complexity and consequences of car transport compared to air transport would suggest this is insufficient. There are somewhere in the region of 10,000 commercial passenger aircraft in operation globally and fewer than 500 deaths a year from air crashes. When a plane crashes, what matters is understanding the specifics of that event.

In contrast there are over 1 billion cars and over 1 million deaths a year on the world's roads.[6] In this situation, it is the patterns that will be more informative than the specifics. What is needed is not a data recorder to be investigated after a crash has occurred, but an ongoing data-sharing arrangement that gives independent plural access to the same data flows that are running through the companies that are manufacturing, selling and maintaining automated cars.

In these circumstances, the opening up of raw data will be the necessary ask in return for the legal protections required to make the operation of driverless cars possible. This is the quid pro quo that should accompany the introduction of AI into every area of life that it touches.

If the moral dilemmas of self-driving cars are complex, the equivalent dilemmas in medicine will become ever more so. Our ability to determine more precisely the trade-offs we make in terms of cost of treatment, accuracy of diagnosis, likelihood of death or disability and the consequences of the patient's own past and likely future actions is something that will make the idea of allowing nature to take its course an ever-diminishing consideration.

Transparency through data sharing may strike many involved in the relevant industries – cars, healthcare, finance – as problematic because of the threat to intellectual property. Data-sharing transparency in relation to AI requires that both the data inputs and the outcomes of any particular algorithm be available to others. With that information, it is possible to reverse-engineer an algorithm that captures much if not most of the learning and

---

[6] World Health Organization, *Global Status Report on Road Safety 2013*.

ingenuity that went into the original. So why would anyone create such an algorithm if they have to give it away?

Will it be possible to patent particular approaches to AI? To some degree, particular techniques will be protectable. We could also allow the patenting of a particular outcome – that is, a patent over an AI approach that causes driverless cars to behave in a way we regard as morally acceptable. But, as with pharmaceuticals, this risks creating monopolies and would require a radical transformation of the car market. We manage to work with the problem in medicine because most medicines are bought by governments and governments can negotiate with monopolists. Individual car buyers cannot. Will we require the government to negotiate car prices with Ford?

The industry would prefer to be able to duck the issue in the market, put out driverless cars and rely on old-fashioned information systems to regulate the market. This would put most of the high value cards in their hands. However, they too have a problem. If knowledge exists it cannot be wished away. The fact that they have the information that enables them to see the extent to which cars may be harming or protecting people makes them potentially liable under the law. If the car is driverless, all the lawsuits for reckless driving no longer go to the driver but land on the doormat of the car manufacturer.

The introduction of AI will almost certainly produce lower levels of risk, but the aggregate level may be more unpredictable and its distribution wholly so. Rather than being randomly distributed across drivers it could end up all falling on one insurance company that happened to cover the wrong piece of software. The insurance risk could end up being assumed by manufacturers or through broader insurance pools. But here again, for this to work, a high level of transparency around the error rates of the different AI systems will be needed.

The role of the data organisation in relation to AI

We have argued that if pluralistic democratic societies wish to make use of data-driven information systems, we will need a mechanism by which competing independent organisations – organisations that can come into existence independently of the state – manage data on behalf of citizens. Furthermore they must be forced to share information about their operations to make them open to challenge by their competitors as well as empowered with rights to access data about relevant populations.

The requirement that such organisations be transparent limits the degree to which they could build a business model around intellectual property. However, if our assessment of the likely growth of automatic decision making is correct, the value of such services to individuals is likely to grow considerably and could create a situation in which people would happily pay for these services.

In this scenario their importance would be such that we would want to see universal access through state intervention to guarantee everyone the possibility of engaging with the digital world. It would become, like water and electricity, a utility where basic levels of access were supported. In this scenario, information flows as easily as water around markets and allocation decision makers, with the system policed through the difficulty of organisations concealing how they are acting.

In such a world, the more traditional forms of regulation and oversight would still be necessary – not least as many outcomes are simply not visible, or at least not within a useful timeframe – with the result that we have to rely on regulation of other aspects of organisations. But to the degree that this approach is possible, we would be putting ourselves at considerable risk by not adopting it.

However, where we are today is a long way from such a scenario. So, to end, we would like to take a step back and address the more practical question of what organisations can do now to create a more transparent and fair world.

20

What happens next?

In 2014, Sir Tim Berners-Lee, inventor of the World Wide Web, called for an international magna carta for the internet to be developed, to protect everyone's right to a perpetually open, free and universal web.

> The internet has thrived by the collective empowerment of capable, public-spirited people: initially from the technical community and academia, and more recently, also the private sector in general, civil society and governments. We need a system of internet governance that allows each community to bring its particular strengths to the common table, but allows none of them to elevate its own interests above the public good.[1]

We believe that the same principles should apply to transparency. We have argued that to achieve this it is necessary to share individual data with citizens and to enable multiple qualifying organisations to access data across populations.

A democratic society requires that individuals and organisations compete for influence, question each other's opinions and are able to do so from positions of sufficiently equal authority. We have argued that democratic plural access to population data sets for monitoring purposes is a necessary precondition if we wish to

---

[1] Tim Berners-Lee, 'We need a magna carta for the internet', *The World Post*, June 6, 2014, http://www.huffingtonpost.com/tim-bernerslee/internet-magna-carta_b_5274261.html

make proper use of big data and artificial intelligence. We have argued that individuals must have custody of the data about them and that, while they may be required to share that data in order to receive certain services, those services should then be subject to independent monitoring. We have maintained that the only time monopoly rights can exist over data about people is when the individuals are controlling information about themselves.

These arrangements are necessary in order to:

• Prevent the misuse of data assets to take advantage of people. While regulation may be of some help, a more efficient approach would be to enable competing interests to police each other through a process of scientific transparency, each one empowered to continually challenge the ways in which data is being used.
• Allow a pluralistic democratic debate about the fairness of institutional arrangements in society, based on competing narratives about their impact in improving both the fairness and efficiency of allocation systems.
• Create the conditions under which citizens can safely make use of big data technology to help them make decisions – be it deciding which treatment to opt for, what mortgage to take out or whether to accept an online date.

The potential for these technologies to greatly reduce the cost of decision making has enormous implications. First, as we have indicated, it makes significantly fairer social institutions possible through a better understanding of how our social arrangements affect our lives.

Equally importantly, reducing the cost of decision making – if we know that it is operating fairly – can create important savings in the provision of education, health and community safety services. These activities currently take in the region of one-fifth of national income in developed countries, which spend a rapidly increasing proportion of their resources in processing information and working out what needs to be done. The prize for achieving significant increases in productivity in these areas is immense. The prize is nothing less than a means by which we can ensure access to high quality health, education and safety for all. It is the route to abundance for many of the things we value most highly.

Agriculture used to take over 99% of human activity globally and as a result of productivity gains in food production now accounts for less than 2%. Industrial manufacturing took over 50% of human activity at its peak in the 1950s but is now falling due to the productivity gains of automation. Services are increasingly taking up the bulk of human time, but the most crucial of these services are only increasing in cost. The ability to make education and healthcare globally available depends on the effective use of automation in these services, including the use of artificial intelligence (AI). But delivering these benefits fairly requires transparency and data sharing. The economic gains that could be achieved through lowering the cost of health and education are huge.

There is a double efficiency here. AI is both the only means by which we are likely to be able to make sense of data on the scale that is now being produced at a reasonable cost. Making sense of data at this level is in turn the key to transforming the productivity of data-driven services.

The technologies required to operate societies built on shared data will themselves be a significant industry in the future. Countries that move first towards genuine data-sharing platforms will be at the forefront of this new 'knowledge economy'.

While these broad principles may, on some level, make sense – and the social and economic opportunities they support may be credible – the challenge of trying to move towards this objective is daunting. It is understandable, therefore, that many governments will decide to label it 'too difficult' and continue with an approach built around regulation, access to information (ATI) and forced disclosure. In this final chapter we set out some practical steps for implementing Transparency 3.0 and harnessing the opportunities of the modern information revolution.

These are just suggestions. They are intended to promote debate. Everyone concerned at the dangers posed by control of information can help to make the case for real transparency as an agent of social and economic improvement. But there will be a long and deep political dialogue over the coming decades to determine in detail the rights that different interested parties have to access the vast data assets that are rapidly coming into existence.

Government has a role to play in encouraging this debate and being open in the way it engages in it. But it needs to recognise that for many it is governmental access to data that is the most troubling area of all. Governments need to come forward with ideas as to how they can genuinely surrender control over their own data assets.

If we look at the forces currently lining up to try to change the current distribution of power over information, the key players are:

- *Government*: Government is motivated by the need to reduce the cost of the provision of public services as well as a desire to reduce risk in important areas such as financial markets. It is also motivated by the desire to encourage the development of new industries.

- *Community interest organisations*: Campaigners representing specific groups that believe they are not being treated fairly have a strong incentive to try to access the information that can demonstrate this, whether they be people required to take medical tests to claim benefits, people being passed over for promotion or people being refused medical treatment or financial products. The work of US legal academics has led the way in establishing this as a basis to demanding access to data. There now needs to be a push to establish community rights to access information on a sustainable basis.

- *Companies and entrepreneurs*: A fair arrangement around control of information will require businesses to operate to different rules than many of those that currently dominate the information landscape. It is very hard right now for companies to pursue business opportunities based on transparency since the moment you have access to a flow of data, the most immediate opportunity is to adopt the standard techniques of surveillance capitalism. Investors will expect businesses to follow this route. However, businesses that establish themselves on the basis of data portability and transparency today may prove the long-term winners.

- *Citizens*: Individuals will need to acquire – and be supported to acquire – the skills to become effective participants in the information revolution. Ensuring equity of access to data and the life management tools it will underpin will be key to personal wellbeing and prosperity.

Of these different forces, we would estimate that it is governments that are likely to make the most impact in the short term, followed by companies and then, in time, community interest organisations. But that is nothing more than a guess and may prove to be very wide of the mark.

Below we have set out a range of suggestions as to what different organisations might do to promote the transparency agenda, develop public and professional trust in data sharing, and clearly set out the social and economic benefits.

What can governments do?

i. Initiate independent public consultation and debate concerning the appropriate extent of community rights to access population data

This should look at what a person can and cannot prevent their data being used for. It should examine the appropriate limits to commercial property rights both in data assets and in algorithms derived from those assets. This public dialogue requires innovation in the design of conventional consultations: it needs to prioritise deliberative engagement with the largest possible community of advocates and actively empower more disadvantaged populations. It will need to be refreshed and tested on a regular basis.

ii. Legislate to confirm the framework for data sharing and the obligations of data organisations and the rights of citizens

It should be explicit that all bodies handling personal data – whether public sector or non-governmental – must provide transparency to the individual citizen concerning all uses of that data. It should ensure appropriate criminal sanctions for illicit data sharing – for example, introducing custodial sentences for any attempt to re-identify a person from data without consent. At the moment, under much data protection legislation, such an offence would normally incur only a financial penalty.

iii. Incentivise adoption of transparency in publicly funded services

Government has financial and other contractual levers to promote transparency. It should make it a precondition of public investment in IT systems that data is recorded according to public standards, that it is wholly accessible and extractable and that it supports sharing with individuals. It should use regulatory levers to apply the same standards to relevant industries.

iv. Set new standards of transparency for regulation

That is, require regulators to put in place information systems that are designed to support an assessment of the real-world impact of regulation. This implies creating an information universe in which data is captured not simply to prove compliance with regulatory standards but also to provide insight into broader unregulated real-world social outcomes.

Require public data assets including market data sets collected by regulators to be under the legal control of judicial entities that are wholly independent of the executive branch or regulatory branches of government. The data sets might be collected by such organisations and might even be held by them, although it might be more appropriate for these to be held independently. Whatever the solution, an independent judicial authority should have the legal oversight of such arrangements to ensure that data is held securely and shared appropriately, to guarantee sufficient transparency to be assured that it is being used fairly. This is a natural extension of the role of independent information commissioners that already exist in many regimes that have implemented ATI laws, but one that requires much wider specific technical skills.

v. Support development of independent data organisations

If transparency is to work in the way we suggest it needs to, it will depend on the creation of independent data organisations that can hold citizens' data, aggregate it, analyse it and compare it with population data sets. Key to any successful strategy is establishing the rules by which such organisations might work and encouraging their development. There are a number of ways in which government can create the conditions under which a more naturally pluralistic and self-sustaining form of transparent and open society can operate. Indeed just as the early American republic allowed newspapers free postage on the grounds that they were good for democracy, we would advocate mechanisms whereby government, without taking sides or artificially creating data organisations, could nonetheless smooth the path towards the development of such organisations.

There are numerous start-up businesses that see their role as a potential infomediary and many corporations, universities and not-for-profit organisations that are attempting to do the same. So far they are operating in a world where their control over the data they receive from the public is often unclear and many lack appropriate legitimacy in seeking access to public data sets. Government should establish systems of independent accreditation (see role of judiciary, below) to ensure effective oversight and identification of data organisations that citizens can be encouraged to trust.

Government should be willing to set aside tax-funded resources to stimulate the development of these organisations and data stores. It might explore models in which organisations which are appointed to manage data on behalf of citizens receive a per capita or per use subsidy. In the long run such services will be a form of public utility, with a requirement for universal provision.

vi. Create flagship programmes in core public services to stimulate engagement and investment in independent data organisations

Bring political capital to bear in promoting transparency in partnership with independent data organisations. Initiate a small number of 'test beds' in public sector activity (for example, health, education or municipal services) which are characterised by one or more of the following:

- Public concern at standards, and therefore prospects of public support for new initiatives.
- High levels of inefficiency, waste or corruption, and therefore prospects of a good economic return through better data sharing.
- The existence of at least one civil society organisation that you trust and can work with.
- Enough of a data infrastructure, or a willingness to invest in creating a data infrastructure (either directly in the case of public services, or indirectly by requiring it of industry through regulation).

vii. Develop capabilities in central government to support implementation

Countries which are making the political commitment to transparency generally have the senior responsible official reporting direct to the president or prime minister, or a senior cabinet minister. It is critical that the administrative responsibility for open government and transparency is not set far apart from the source of ultimate political authority in a country.

viii. Support construction of expert networks

These networks can provide a route through which the government, its funded public authorities and independent data organisations – as awell as society more widely – an access specialist skills in making data sharing work.

As Professor Beth Noveck of GovLab at New York University has observed, the capabilities required for the successful implementation of transparency – from technical architecture to consumer interface – are often rare and highly specialised.

Global or supranational expert networks should be encouraged by governments to enable easier access to these capabilities.[2]

ix. Take part in multinational and global initiatives

Join the Open Government Partnership (OGP), as a minimum, but also develop careful approaches to transnational issues like surveillance. It is important for governments that are positive about the opportunities for transparency to improve social and economic outcomes to work with states that are not. This is because successful domestic implementation will, in part, depend upon trading partners and members of international alliances adopting common data standards, regulatory legislation and consistently open political behaviours.

What can citizens and NGOs interested in promoting transparency do?

i. Develop legal and technical ways to create trusted data organisations

We have suggested some principles that data organisations would need to work to in order to allow for a transparent and fair society. Sir Tim Berners-Lee has suggested the concept of the 'beneficent app', proposing that the right unit to focus on is not the organisation but the application. If the application can be shown to meet certain criteria it can be safely allowed to access data. To the extent that this application involves any aspect of surveillance, one important standard would be transparency about the inputs and outputs of such systems.

The Respect Network, for example, is one of a number of attempts to create information services that give individuals more complete control over how their data is accessed by third parties. These services provide a solution to some of the issues of individual control. They do not provide a mechanism for

---

[2] Beth Simone Noveck, *Smart Citizens, Smarter State: The Technologies of Expertise and the Future of Governing*, Harvard University Press, 2015.

transparency around the accuracy and bias in surveillance systems. But they could put pressure on current commercial models.

ii. Form alliances

There are many areas where there is a community of interest between academic researchers, technical developers and organisations representing groups with grievances. Often they are coming at the same problem from very different directions. By forming alliances they can bring together the skills to make the political argument and, if necessary, the legal argument for access to data; to create technical solutions for how data will be handled; and to apply the expertise to intelligently reinterpret data.

iii. Develop open standards

Engage in development of common data standards to support citizens in accessing their own data and to maximise intelligence of population-based data. This may, in the short term, imply a loss of competitive advantage but in the longer term offers much more valuable opportunities to design new personalised information services for population cohorts and individual people.

iv. Engage with the professions

Rapid portability of data is challenging for professions such as medicine and teaching because it alters the traditional information relationship with the patient or student. Some public service professionals express fear of inappropriate use of such data (as well as concern at its use to monitor their work by authorities whose expertise and legitimacy they question). Such concerns are valid but they are countered by a strong interest in improving the quality of services and in conducting research that can support this. There is, furthermore, a growing recognition that holding teachers and doctors to 'account' for the quality of their services is increasingly outdated as the delivery of social outcomes depends not on the actions of the professionals but on the joint actions of the professional and the individual patient or pupil. There is great scope for alliances between professionals and citizens to work collaboratively on developing transparency systems that will provide information on how best to develop in ways that support rather than undermine professional esteem.

v. Use your power as a consumer

This is harder than it sounds as, on the whole, you will face a choice between products that give you no control over your information or products that prevent any access to data about you. The latter protect your privacy but make surveillance – both good and bad – impossible. Nonetheless, by buying these privacy protecting products or using privacy protecting browsers you will be supporting the development of alternative approaches to information rights and helping to force a change in the way your ability to control your information environment is currently being eroded by private companies. More importantly, get yourself a data store and start to demand your data from everyone you do business with. Consider the business model of the data store and the degree to which it incentivises them to act in your interest. Some work on a commission basis which can create tensions. Others, such as Personal.com, have moved to a fee basis.

The digital you and the open society

We already live in a world where 'digital personification' is of enormous significance to our lives and yet something over which we have little or no control or understanding. In future decades it will become increasingly true to say that we are our data. In medical terms, for example, we will be understood more in terms of data held about us than from a physical examination of our person.

The effective management and analysis of the digital me will determine, to large degree, whether I live a long, productive life or not – or rather help me improve my odds of doing so. For this we need a datastore and a trusted data organisation that can tell us what it means and what we can do about it – one that is subject to transparency and cannot hide what it does with our data from others who have the expertise to identify categorisations that are inaccurate, unfair or harmful.

This is not about wearing a personal fitness tracker – it is about monitoring ourselves and our families: it is a constant process of evaluation and mitigation. It is impossible to know quite how a properly transparent society will operate, but it is unlikely that people will want to have to police the way in which information is used about them. While it is essential that individuals have the right to know in precise detail how information about them has been processed, it is unlikely that anyone will ever want to spend too much time investigating. It is more likely that AI-driven algorithms will work out what we are and are not happy with. And we will trust those algorithms because the organisations that operate them are constrained by transparency.

Without wanting to suggest this is the right solution, let us cite one possible model to illustrate the idea. A society might operate a market in which the state-funded or subsidised data stores for every citizen and for every company competed to collect that funding in part by adopting different approaches to monitoring and surveillance. Because every organisation was required to submit to monitoring not just by regulators but also by competitors (under regulated conditions), I could take sufficient comfort from the fact that those using my data were not doing so in a way that harmed or unfairly exploited me.

Such institutional arrangements will not, however, reduce the need for greatly enhanced digital literacy. We will become increasingly aware of the extent to which life consists of a series of interactions with social institutions that categorise us and process us. If that description sounds negative, it is a description of how we are educated, healed, employed and, indeed, presented with the astonishing array of opportunities that the modern world can in theory provide.

The difference between oppression and freedom is the extent to which this is done well and done fairly – and this can be reduced to the degree it is done in a way that is transparent and open to challenge.

Karl Popper's definition of the open society as one in which authority was always open to challenge is an idea that we need to hold close to our hearts, as information technology becomes perhaps the most important aspect of power in our societies. An open society is not one in which there are certain select interests with the ability to challenge authority. It is one in which it is possible for the challenge to come from anyone.

Popper's analysis identified that there have been many bogus attempts to pit objective scientific truth as the enemy of the open society, on the grounds that certain social arrangements can be proven to be preferable and beyond debate. These efforts have suggested a conflict between 'science' and 'democracy'.

In reality, the attitudes of science and those of an open society are the same. In science, no truth is ever beyond question or incapable of being overturned by new learning or insight. There are routes through which anyone can, in theory, challenge the most deeply held truths in our scientific understanding. Science has developed a mechanism to ensure that every claim to truth is permanently on trial.

Democratic institutions such as freedom of speech, free elections and freedom of association are designed to make social institutions similarly open to challenge by the widest number of people. They have worked well in destroying attempts to claim authority grounded in social position or divine anointment. The growth of data and information technology has shifted the ground on which these institutions are based. They have given significant power to those organisations that hold and can manipulate information. We now face a choice between simply submitting to these authorities or demanding transparency in a form that will lay open to challenge every claim that a particular arrangement is the best that can be achieved; that will make institutional claims to be acting in my best interests something that I can place my trust in.

Index

A

absolute error 93–4
academic organisations 275
  see also research
access to information (ATI) 103–4
  and forms of power 30
  and shaping of information
    115–20
access to information (ATI)
    legislation 10, 20–1, 28, 103,
    151–72
  government exemptions 34–5
  impact on access to personal data
    162–3
  impact on corruption 108, 155–8
  impact on privacy 161–2
  media and public interest 158–9,
    165–72
  reviews of 107
access to own data 281–96
accountability 48, 64
  impact of ATI legislation 158
  release of data responsibilities 279
accuracy
  of assessments (categorisation)
    89–93
  of record keeping 213
'adjudications' 75–6
adverse incidents (healthcare) 265–8
Afridi, Farzana and Iversen, Vegard
    175, 180
agency 75–6
aggregate data 217–21, 300
agri-businesses 159–61
AI *see* artificial intelligence (AI)
Akerlof, George 22–4
Albania 136
Alfter, Brigitte 159–61
algorithms 118–19
  surveillance 302

see also artificial intelligence (AI)
'allocation outcomes' 80–4
allocation systems 76–9, 85–97
  by AI 324–32
  categorisations of people 300–2,
    324–5
  models of 75–9
    information flows 78
  transparency in 76–9
    evidencing of unfairness 79–84,
      276–7
    open data programmes 198–200
    use of population-based data
      85–97
  vs. commercial data sharing
    organisations 275–6
'allocative decisions' 57–61, 70
Amazon 290
Anderson, David 10, 12
anonymisation of data 44, 306–9
antidepressant drug trials 238
apps, for self-care 295–6
Areopagitica (Milton 1644) 18–19
Arrow, Kenneth 86
Article-19 group 201
artificial intelligence (AI) 321–5
  in allocation systems 324–5,
    325–32
  moral and ethical considerations
    332–5
  role of data organisation 335–6
Asian Development Bank 62–3
ATI *see* access to information (ATI);
    access to information (ATI)
    legislation
audit use 105, 308–9, 312
  see also public reporting; social
    audit

Australia, MY Health Record
    programme 295–6
averages 217–18
Ayres, Ian 82–4

B
Banerjee, A. and Duflo, E. 251
Bangladesh 233
Bank of England, transparency
    policies 35–6
BBC, and staff emails 170
BBC news 169
Ben-Shahar, Omri and Schneider,
    Carl 47
benchmarking tools, NHS 182–3
'beneficent app' (Berners-Lee) 345
Bentham, Jeremy 19–21, 46
Berners-Lee, Sir Tim 337, 345
Bernstein, Ethan 36–7
bias in allocation systems 88–9
bioethics 309–10
Birmingham News 159–60
births records 205–6
Blair, Tony
    on education 253–4
    on the FOIA 17–18, 35
    on healthcare performance data
        267–8
blame culture, media and FOI
    requests 38
blogging 114
BlueButton (US) 295
Boyle, Robert 25–6
BP
    Deepwater Horizon oil rig
        explosion 264
    sponsorship of Tate gallery 168
breast screening 33–4
bribery and backhanders, extractive
    industries 188–92
broadband access 293–4
'broken leg' problem 328–9
Brooke, Heather 153
Brown, Graham 222
budget accountability, standard
    setting initiatives 200–1
budget allocation systems *see*
    allocation systems
budget projections 216
Burn, Sir John 285–6

Bush, President George W. 211–12
business lending 95–6
Butler Review (2004) 211

C
Calderon, Ania 139–40
Cameron, David 137
Campaign for Freedom of
    Information (UK) 154
Canada
    'deliberative privacy' policies 34
    'duty to document' policies 212
    records of HIV-contaminated
        blood transfusions 211
cancer treatments, personalised
    protocols 282–3
'capability' 104
car hire industry 81–4, 89
car manufacturers
    driverless cars 332–5
    EPA emissions scandal 235–6
Care.Data study 314–17
categorisation 57–8, 89–93
    and accuracy 89–93
Centre for the Study of Existential
    Risk (CSER) 325
change and change theories 103–9
Chavan, Madhav 249–52
child criminals 171
choice-making 32–3, 105
    and regulatory standards 229–31
    see also decision-making
citizen.me 275
citizen's rights 105
    see also human rights
civic feedback platforms
    Tanzania 272
    UK 261
    US 257–61
civil society organisations (CSOs)
    20, 48, 107–9, 120, 134, 140,
    182–5
    description and role 277
    funding of 273–4, 276–7
    future roles 340, 345–7
    international initiatives 188–94
    modes of action 105
    motivations 272–3
    release of information 271, 274

role of independent review panels
274
UK fiscal analysis 198
see also data organisations
Clare's Law 169
clientelism 102
Clinton, Hillary 133–4, 212
Coalition for Clean Parliament
(CCP) (Romania) 206–8
Cochrane Reviews 33–4
Cochran, Loren 151–2
coding of information 200
cognitive bias 39
Cohen, Mark 83–4
Collective Impact 179
Combined Online Information
System (COINS) 216
commercial confidentiality 6, 44–5,
50, 127
overriding of 71
patenting AI 335
commercial organisations
data sharing enterprises 275–6
negative impacts of reporting
requirements 41–3
'not-for-profit' entities 276
see also commercial confidentiality
commercial surveillance 299
communication methods and
transparency 211–14
comparator groups 230
compliance and conformity 40–3
costs of transparency 50
gaming and cheating behaviours
233–6
conflicts of interest, in regulation
design/publication 228, 237–9
'conflicts of interpretation' 78
conformity to public opinion 50
consent systems 285–6, 313–14
Care.Data study 314–17
see also opting out and
withholding data
consumer associations 276
consumer choice 32–3, 105
in a digital age 347
and regulatory standards 229–31
consumer reports 229
control of information 289–93,
299–302
see also editorial control of data

corruption 66–7, 70, 74, 87,
99–103
disclosure methods 158
elections in Croatia 131–5
evidence for ATI impacts 108,
155–8
case studies 165–72
evidence from social audits 175–6
government policies 102
and Open Data programmes
197–201
perceived levels of 156–7
creativity 36
credit applications 81–4, 89, 95–6
credit scoring 303
Croatia, war veterans fraud 131–5
CSOs *see* civil society organisations
(CSOs)
Cunningham, Duke 197

D

Daily Mirror newspaper 169
Daily Telegraph 152–3
data anonymity 44
and de-identification 306–9
data assets
ending monopoly control 119–20
impact of ATI 159–61
'data blocking' 289–90
data collection, vs. surveillance 297
data control (personal level) 289–93
see also editorial control of data
data organisations 275–7
categories of 275–7
funding 273–4
future of 343, 345–6
independent reviews of 274
rules for 273–4
structure of 275–7
data portability 289–93
obstacles to 296
data portals 212, 218–19
data preparation costs 31
data processing
and decision making 115
growth of 114–15
data protection laws 289, 311
data reliability 209–17
improvement mechanisms 255–7
data sharing

benefits and drawbacks 2–3, 50–1, 119–20

description and aims 28

and forms of power 30

key recommendations for 273–4

methods of improving reliability 256–7, 257–64

model (transparency 3.0) 120–8

moral justifications for 310–11

new framework proposals for 317

population vs. individual level 247

and privacy 240–1

rationale for use 2–3, 114–20

and regulation 239–46

see also surveillance

data standards 25

data types 216

death penalty 92–3

death rates 178–9, 266–8, 269

deaths records 206

deceit behaviours 233–6

decision-making

and consumer choice 32–3

and data processing 66, 114–20

for allocation purposes 57–61, 70, 73–84

methods of challenging 58

machine vs. human 325–32

'non-judgemental' vs. 'fairness' 56–7

role of executive bodies 34–7, 85–8

and short-termism 41

use of performance indicators 41–2

definitions of transparency 61–7

potential consequences 67–72

'deliberative privilege' policies 34–7, 223

threats to 50

democratic accountability 106–7

Denmark, 'deliberative privacy' policies 34

'deservedness' in allocation systems 56–7

destruction of documents 211–12, 213

Detroit, misuse of public funds 151–2

diabetes drug trials 237–8

diagnosis 90–1

business models for 275–6

digital health records 294–6

digital inclusion 293–4

digital personification 347–9

digital technology strategies 140–1

'Direct Transparency' 122–3

disaster scenarios, citizen feedback platforms 14–15, 263–4

'disclosure'

description and aims 28

and forms of power 30

selective / edited 69

undermining of 68

'disguising' data 215

dishonesty 40–3

DNA technologies 92–3, 281–6

Dr Foster publications 1–2, 268

reception of 269–71

review panels 274

shared terms and conditions 271

domestic abuse disclosures 169

driverless cars 332–5

driving test fraud 171

drone strikes 298–9, 302

drug trials 27, 45, 237–9

dual control over data 291–3

Dying to Know (Nuffield Trust and RAND 2000) 266–7

E

e-prescribing 296

'earmarking' 99–101

East Devon Alliance (EDA) 222–4

economic implications *see* financial costs of transparency

economics-based transparency 21–5

vs. political traditions 24–5

editorial control of data 209–24

methods 210–17

possible countermeasures 213–17

education systems and transparency

impact of publishing standards 177–8

India 249–52

Mexico 145–50

Tanzania 183–5

Uganda 175–6

UK 253–5

'efficiency' 69–70

EITI *see* Extractive Industries
Transparency Initiative
Elkins, Caroline 11–12, 14, 88
email communications 212, 213
'ends justifying the means' 96–7
error (statistics) 93–4
ethics review panels 274
EU Common Agricultural Policy
43–4
European Central Bank 41
European Medicines Agency 240
'exclusions' from data disclosure
requirements 213
executive decision-making, impact
of transparency 34–7
expenses scandal (UK) 152–5
expert networks 344–5
expertise within society 20
Extractive Industries Transparency
Initiative (EITI) 188–92, 209

F
'fairness' 61–72
descriptions 55–61, 74–5
and transparency 61–7, 67–72,
74–5
Falconer, Lord 18, 223
false generalisations 218
false negatives / positives 94–6
farming subsidies 43–4, 159–61
financial costs of transparency 31–4,
50
'fit for work' programmes (UK
welfare payments) 220–1
FixMyStreet 261
flood alert systems 141
food labelling
financial implications of 31
and GMO products 45
forced disclosure 24, 195–6, 230–1
Ford, launch of the Pinto car 241–6
formats, for record-keeping 213,
214
forms of transparency (overview) 28
Fox, Jonathan 179–83
Francis, Robert 270
'free-market' perspectives 22–4
Freedom of Information (FOI)
legislation 10, 113
government exemptions 34–5

impact in the UK 108, 157–8
introduction 17–18
request types 37
and the media 37–8
see also access to information
(ATI) legislation
Freeman, Paul 223
Frey, Carl Benedikt 323–4
Friends and Family Test 261
Fundar 99–101, 192–3, 216–17
funding of data sharing
organisations 273–4, 276–7
funding of research, pharmaceutical
industries 27
Fung, Archon *et al.* 47, 229
future of transparency
citizen and NGO actions 345–7
government actions 341–5

G
G20 Anti-corruption Transparency
initiative 134
'gaming' behaviours 40–3, 233–6
Garrido, Perez 192–3
GCSEs and modular exams 254–5
genetically modified organisms
(GMOs) 45
genomics 45, 281–6
Genomics England 283–4, 313
GlaxoSmithKline (GSK) 237–8
GoCompare.com 290
Goldacre, Ben 118, 237–9, 240
Good Hospital Guide 268
Google 114, 117–18, 283
Google Translate 322–3
government
future steps to promote
transparency 341–5
impact of FOI legislation 46,
157–8
impact of transparency on
decision-making 34–7, 157–8
leaked information 225–6
opening up access to data assets
119–20
'editing' of data 210–17, 220–1
spending and funding allocations
99–101
funding of CSOs 276–7
use of regulation 225–46
granular data 216, 217–21, 256

see also data sharing; raw data sharing
granularity 217
Grayling, Chris 37–8, 159, 165
Greece, budget crisis 198–9
Griffiths-Jones, Eric 11, 15
Guardian newspaper 159, 161, 165–72, 316

H
Haiti, disaster relief and citizen feedback 263–4
HakiElimu organisation (Tanzania) 183–5, 269
Han, Dong-Pyou 27
Hanslope Park (Milton Keynes) 9–12
Hayes, Jeremy 153–4
Hazell, Robert 34–5, 46, 157–8, 211
Heald, David 36–7, 45–6
health screening programmes 33–4
health surveillance 299, 304–5
  opting out of 311–14
healthcare
  adverse events studies 265–8
  commercial diagnostics 275–6
  and data sharing 4–5
    concerns about 27–8
    rights to access 21
  heart surgery outcomes 178–9, 267–8
  hospital star ratings 270–1
  linked records initiative (Care. Data) 314–17
  patient-reported data 262
  personalised treatment protocols 281–6
  'postcode lottery' of 266–8
  treatment allocations and fairness 55–61, 79–81, 285
  use of 'data blocking' 289–90
  use of population data and diagnosis 90–1
  and wearable monitoring technologies 262
  weekend mortality rates 269
  see also National Health Service
heart surgery outcomes 178–9
Hendy, Peter 172

Heywood, Stephen 261–2
Hofbauer, Helena 99–101, 156
Holmstrom, Bengt 41
honesty 40–3, 73–4
Hood, Christopher 16, 62–3
hospital performance ratings 266–9, 270–1
human error 86–7
Human Genome Project 283–4, 313
human rights 20–1
  detentions and 'disappearances' 201–5
  unwanted outcomes 96–7
  vs. 'privacy' policies 201–6
Hunt, Jeremy 182–3
Hunt, Liz 56
hygiene standards 229
hypothesis testing 106

I
Icahn Institute for Genomics and Multiscale Biology (US) 281–2
IMCO (Mexico) 141–3, 269
  education website 145–50
independent review panels 274, 310–11
India
  fund diversifications 199–200
  child literacy data 249–52
  electoral roll registrations 162–3
  MKSS (Association for the Empowerment of Workers) 173–4, 214
  on social audit (MNREGA) 174–5
individual agency 75–6
individual-level data
  access to own records 281–96
  described 247
  models of sharing 123–5
  storage systems 286–9
  who has rights over 289–93
  see also personal information
Indonesia 162
  on social audit 175
'infomediaries' 290–1
information
  limitations of 99–109
  quantity vs. quality 67–9

types 28
'information overload' 32–3
informed consent for data sharing,
   case study 314–17
input information transparency
   76–9
Institute of Fiscal Studies (IFS) 198
institutions and fairness 85–8,
   99–103
   need for population based
   transparency 88–97
insurance industry access to data
   316–17
International Budget Partnership
   200, 216
International Consortium of
   Investigative Journalists (ICIJ)
   159–61
International Criminal Court 204
international transparency initiatives
   187–93
Iraq war, review into intelligence
   failings 211
Irvine, Sir Donald 268
ITV News 170

J

Japan, illness mapping 283
Jarman, Sir Brian 265–8
Johnson, Stephen 258–61
jury trials 85, 90, 92–3

K

Kant, Immanuel 15–16
Karr, Jonathan 281–2
Kay, John 41
Kelsey, Tim 2, 134, 314–15
Kenya
   1950s Mau Mau detentions
   10–12, 14, 88
   2008 elections and citizen
   feedback 14–15, 263
Keogh, Sir Bruce 178–9
Kilpatrick, Kwame 151–2, 211–12
Klitgaard, Robert 101, 210
Kodokushi (lonely death) 283
Krafchik, Warren 137–8, 200

L

Lagunes, Alejandra 139
Lane Fox, Martha 294
law courts and information access
   68, 85, 90, 92–3
   see also access to information
   (ATI) legislation
league tables
   in education 253–5
   statistical importance of
   differences 39–40
   see also hospital performance
   ratings
'leaks' of information 152, 154, 158,
   225–6
legislation
   on access to information 10, 20–1,
   28, 103, 151–72
   on personal control of own data
   292–3
Lessig, Lawrence 47
'leverage' 104
life expectancy 110
linked data sets 292–3, 315
liver transplants 55–61
loans and credit arrangements 81–4,
   89, 95–6
Locke, John 19–21

M

McGee, Rosemary and Gaventa,
   John 48, 103
machine learning 281–2, 324–5
   vs. human decision-making
   325–32
   see also artificial intelligence (AI)
Magna Carta 22
Makamba, January 272
Manchester Evening News 166, 171
MapLight.org 198
market perspectives on transparency
   22–4
marketing practices, use of
   categorisation 91
'markets' 75–6
mathematical algorithms 118–19
Maude, Francis 134
Mayorwatch 172
media

FOI requests 37–8, 152–5,
158–60, 165–72
generating pressure for change 148
information handling activities
31–2, 116
in opposition to transparency
initiatives 272
press freedoms 115
release of information agreements
271, 274
'stings' 222
medical screening programmes 33–4
medicine 33–4, 118
biomolecular diagnostics 284–5
DNA sequencing 281–3
drug trials 27, 45, 237–9
new personalised treatment
protocols 281–6
treatment allocations 55–61,
79–81, 285
wearable sensors 287
see also healthcare
Meehl, Paul 325–8
meetings, record-keeping 211–13
Meier, Patrick 264
Mexico
chairmanship of OGP 139
deaths in childbirth 139–40, 206
mining and oil industries 192–3
OGP commitments 138
'pork barrel' budgeting 99–101
public birth records 206
tracing the 'disappeared' 201–5
Microsoft healthvault 275
Mid Staffordshire NHS Foundation
Trust 233, 270
Midata programme 290
Milburn, Alan 267–8, 269–70
Milton, John 18–19
minority quota systems 97
minutes of meetings 211–13
MKSS (Mazdoor Kisan Shakti
Sangathan) 173–4
MNREGA (National Rural
Employment Guarantee Act -
India) 174–5, 180
Moberg, Jonas 192
mobile phone communications
211–12, 213
SMS platforms 263, 272, 278–9
models for transparency 120–8

molecular diagnostics 284
monitoring, and surveillance 302–6
MPs expenses scandal (UK) 152–5,
212
Mumbai, child literacy levels
249–52
Mungiu-Pippidi, Alina 108, 156–7,
208
Mydex 288
MyNHS 182–3

N

narrative creation 106–9, 215–17
national digital strategies 140–1
National Health Service
categorisation of CLABS
infections 235
consent and Care.Data study
314–17
data access programme 294–6
Dr Foster publications 1–2, 268,
269–71
Friends and Family Test 261
performance and accountability
266–71
on replacing performance targets
182–3
Stafford Hospital failures of care
233
see also healthcare; medicine
National Information Board (NIB)
313–14
national security 300, 302
Nature journal 26–7
negative effects of transparency
34–45, 49–51
New Labour
on education 253–4
on healthcare performance data
267–8
on transparency 17–18
Newton, Sir Isaac 25–6
NGOs (non–governmental
organisations) 273, 276–7
see also civil society organisations
(CSOs)
NHTSA (National Highways and
Transportation Safety Agency)
241–6

NIB *see* National Information
Board (NIB)
Nigeria, oil revenue
misappropriation 187–8, 189–92
Nissan Motor Acceptance
Company (NMAC) 81–4
Nissen, Steve 238
'no-ambush rule' 274
Norway, tax record publications 205
'not-for-profit' enterprises 276
Noveck, Professor Beth 47–8, 136,
344–5
Nozick, Robert 96
Nuffield Trust
adverse incidents (NHS) 266–7
on bioethics 309–10
star ratings system 270

O

Obama, President Barack 133–4,
135–6, 212
on patient records access 296
OECD, on EITI quality of audit
information 190
Office for Budget Responsibilities
198, 216
OGP *see* Open Government
Partnership (OGP)
oil revenue misappropriations
187–8, 189–92
O'Neill, Onara 46
open budgeting 198
open data 195
recording of information 200–1
Open Data programmes 195–7
and corruption 197–201
and privacy 201–8
Open Government Partnership
(OGP) 113–14
current commitments 135–6
future importance of 345
inaugural meeting 132–3
steering committee 134
Tanzania 271–2
UK representations 134
open platforms 257–64
Open Public Services Network 2
Open Society and its Enemies (Popper
1947) 5
Open311 smartphone app 260–1

'openness' and personal
accountability theories 16–18
OpenPDS (open personal data
store) 288
opinion polls 40
opting out and withholding data
306–14
'oral cultures' and record-keeping
211–12
organ transplants 55–61
organisations *see* commercial
organisations; data organisations
Osborne, Michael 323–4
outcome transparency 37, 77–9
democratisation of narrative
power 109–11
ways of evidencing 79–84
outcomes of regulation 231–6

P

paroxetine (antidepressant) 238
'participation' 105, 107
Partridge, Sir Nick 316
Pasquale, Frank 118
patenting of AI 335
patient-reported data 262
'Patients Know Best' initiative 288
'Patients Like Me' initiative 261–2,
275, 288
pay disclosures 39
Peisakhin, Leonid 162–3
Pena Nieto, Enrique 138–9
'Perfect implementation fallacy'
86–7
performance indicators
and complex social outcomes
270–1
manipulation of 41–2
outcomes vs. processes 42
replacement initiatives (NHS)
182–3
to 'shape' narratives 226–46
see also outcome transparency
personal data stores 286–9
personal information
access through ATI mechanisms
162–3
access to own data 256, 281–96
consent systems 285–6, 313–14
protection from disclosure 43–4

rights over data 289–93
storage systems 286–9
see also individual-level data
Personal.com 288
personalised treatment protocols 281–6
pharmaceutical industry
drug trials 27, 45, 237–9
potential threats 118
police, underreporting concerns 234
political corruption, and Open Data programmes 197–201, 206–8
political donations and finance 197–8, 235
political opposition 105, 108
political theories of transparency 16–21
'information as a right' 18–21
'openness' and trust 16–18
vs. economic traditions 24–5
Popper, Karl 5, 348–9
population data sharing 80, 85–97
benefits of 88–96
described 247
models of 123–5
terms and conditions for 271–4
uses of 96–7
see also data sharing
'pork barrel' budgeting 99–101
postcode lottery (healthcare 266–8
power
forms of (Toffler) 29–30
and transparency 15, 29–30
unintended consequences 37–40, 50
Pratham organisation 249–52
Prison Service funerals 170
Pritchett, Lant 251–2
privacy
and creativity 36
and data sharing 240–1
impact of ATI 161–2
negative effects of transparency 43–4, 50
loss of data anonymity 44
loss of 114–20
opting out from surveillance 306–14
vs. Open Data programmes 201–6

see also 'deliberative privilege' policies
private communications 211–12, 213
Pro-Vida 100–1, 156, 216
process transparency 37, 77–9
ways of evidencing 79–84
profiling from data 292
proxy data 220
public data types, and privacy 205–6
public expenditure, tracking of 99–103, 105, 107–8
public interest 158–60, 165–72
public reporting 176–9
public services
future of the professions 346–7
new flagship programmes 343–4
publication of service standards 177–9
league tables 39–40
and outcomes impacts 38–9
regulatory performance management data 32
see also named services
'publicity' (Bentham) 19–20
'publishing' of information 4
see also data sharing
Pulitzer Prize nominees (2005–14) 159–61
Pulitzer, Joseph 13

Q

quota systems 97

R

Rakar, Marko 131–5
random error 94
raw data sharing 123–5, 137
and source data 257
vs. ATI/FOI requests 209–10, 213–17
see also data sharing; granular data
Rawls, John 96–7
record-keeping, methods of obscuring 211–14
regulation
essential role of 228–9
management of data sharing 239–46
minimal compliance 233–6

outcomes 231–6
potential solutions 240
unintended consequences 232–3
within AI technologies 331–5
regulatory failures 225–46
distorting effect of regulatory
processes on outcomes 227–8,
231–6
enforcing standards but failing the
public 227, 229–31
significant conflicts of interest
228, 237–9
see also social audit
Reinbach, Gary 55–61, 329
release of information 271, 274
research
consent systems 313–14
opting out of surveillance and
monitoring 306–14
producing change 105
'The Resilience Project' (Mount
Sinai US) 281–2
Respect Network 345–6
retrospective transparency 36–7
review systems (data sharing) 274,
310–11
'right to information' (RTI)
and transparency 70–1
see also 'access to information'
(ATI) legislation
rights over data 289–93
'rights-based' transparency 18–21
risk factors of transparency
(summary) 49–51
risk registers (DoH) 35
road traffic deaths
car safety regulations 241–6
post-9/11 232–3
Roberts, Professor Alasdair 18,
211–12
robots 323–4
computerisation of jobs 323–5
Romania 206–8
Rose-Ackerman, Professor Susan
209–10
Rosenblatt, Frank 321–2
rosiglitazone (diabetes) 237–8
Rousseau, Jean-Jaques 16–18
Ruelas, Ana Cristina 201–5
rules and fairness 65–7, 74–5, 85–7
rules for data sharing 273–4

S
The Sacramento Bee's 160
The Sceptical Chymist (Boyle 1661)
25–6
Schadt, Eric 281–2
Schneier, Bruce 289
Schonhardt-Bailey, Professor Cheryl
36
school league tables 239–40, 253–5
Schwartz, Gary 245–6
science-based transparency
traditions 25–9
and fairness 71–2
scientific method 25–9
screening programmes 33–4
'scrutiny' of information 63–4
Seattle Times 161
'self' and digital personification
347–9
self-drive cars 332–5
shared access to data *see* data sharing
'short-termism', in public
companies 41
Short, Clare 191
Sidmouth 222–4
Singh, Shekar 173–4
skew of errors 94–6
smartphone apps, for civic feedback
259–61
Smith, Jacqui 153–4
SMS (Short Message Service)
platforms 263, 272, 278–9
Snowden, Edward 299
social audit 173–6, 179–85
effectiveness of 179–83
evidence from developing
countries 174–6, 183–5
social media 263–4
'social outcomes' 80–4, 87
'sofa culture' 211
Solove, Professor Daniel 299–300
Soon-Shiong, Patrick 282–3
South Korea, illness mapping 283
specificity of information 230
Spence, Michael 22–4
Spitz, Malte 289
Stafford Hospital failures of care
233, 270
standards
budgetary transparency 200, 216
in future regulation 342

public sector publications 177–9
  see also regulation; regulatory
  failures
statistical significance 230
Stiglitz, Joseph 22–4
The Sun newspaper 168
Sunday Times newspaper 268
Sunlight Foundation (US) 197–8
Sunstein, Cass 136
surveillance 116–17, 297–317
  characteristics of good systems
  303–6
  definitions 297–8
  forms of 299
  and monitoring 302–6
  opting out and withholding data
  306–14
  problems of 299–300
  reasons for 300–2
survey data 257
Swartz, Aaron 215
systematic error 94

T

Tanzania 136
  commitment to transparency
  271–2
  HakiElimu organisation 183–5
  Maji Matone water project 181,
  263
  malaria treatment stock-outs
  277–9
tax records 205, 300
Taylor, Roger 2
texts *see* SMS (Short Message
  Service) platforms
Thatcher, Margaret 253
theories of transparency 16–30
  economic 21–5
  political 16–21
  scientific 25–9
  see also Three Degrees of
  Transparency model
theory of change and information
  103
  components required 103–9
Three Degrees of Transparency
  model 120–8
Transparency (1.0) 122–3,
  131–246

Transparency (2.0) 123–5,
  247–317
Transparency (3.0) 126–8, 319–49
311-feedback service (US) 257–61
The Times newspaper 172
timing of data releases / disclosures
  63, 213
Tinker, Dr Jack 268
Toffler, Alvin 29–30
torture disclosures 96–7
Tragic Choices (Calabresi and Bobbit
  1978) 73–4
transparency
  benefits (summary) 29–30
  definitions 62–7, 75, 116–17
  and 'fairness' 55–72, 74–5
  downsides and critiques 49–51
  financial costs of 31–4, 50
  ineffectiveness of 45–8
  negative effects of 34–45, 49–51
  funding of 277
  institutional arrangements for 117,
  120
  international initiatives 187–93
  key forms (summary) 28
  real-time vs. retrospective 36–7
  loss of 114–20
  manipulation and editing data
  210–17
  methods to improve data reliability
  255–64
  models for 120–8
  monitoring and surveillance
  297–317
  theories 16–30
  see also data sharing
Transparency (1.0) level 122–3,
  131–246
  difficulties and political challenges
  131–43
  lure of ineffective policies
  143–50
  editorial control of data 209–24
  international initiatives 187–93
  legislation for 151–72
  current efforts 131–50
  open data and forced disclosure
  195–208
  regulation challenges 225–46
  social audit and public reporting
  173–85